The Emerging Catholic Church

To: Fr. Tom Worth

With all good wishes,

Tom

1/18/12

The Emerging Catholic Church

A Community's Search for Itself

TOM ROBERTS

ORBIS BOOKS

Maryknoll, New York 10545

Manufactured in the United States of America.
Manuscript editing and typesetting by Joan Weber Laflamme.

Library of Congress Cataloging-in-Publication Data

Roberts, Tom.
    The emerging Catholic Church : a community's search for itself / Tom Roberts.
        p. cm.
    Includes bibliographical references (p.   ) and index.
    ISBN 978–1–57075–946–8 (pbk.)
  1. Catholic Church—History—21st century. I. Title.

    BX1390.R58 2011
    282.09'051—dc23

                            2011017951

To my wife, Sara
Your love and friendship are extraordinary graces

In memoriam
Joe Feuerherd
1962–2011

Contents

Acknowledgments

The series In Search of the Emerging Church, which first appeared in the pages of the *National Catholic Reporter* and on its website, ncronline.org, was not a scientific study. It was, instead, an array of stories demonstrating that the church has been changing steadily, inevitably, and in some ways dramatically during the past half century. The final product depended heavily on the willingness of scores of people to convey their thoughts on the church, on their hopes for the institution, on how their faith survives the turmoil of the current moment. To all of you I am greatly indebted. Some of your stories made it onto the page. I tried to choose the widest range of representative stories possible, realizing they barely scratch the surface of the reality of this church. For those who opened their homes and the assembled groups who spent hours over meals discussing the state of things, my sincerest gratitude. The stories of your experience with the church, often as part of the mission of a diocese, provided a valuable window into the working of the institution and those moments of grace that yet occur amid scandals and challenges.

At about the halfway point in reporting the series, I received a note from Robert Ellsberg of Orbis Books suggesting that the series might grow into a book. I am grateful for the nudge in that direction. I've since become the beneficiary of his encouragement, patience, and direction.

National Catholic Reporter is a small enterprise with a thin line of editors and reporters as the foundation for an operation with an outsized ambition. I also know that thin line as a wonderful group of colleagues and friends whose generous spirit allowed me the time and opportunity to do the reporting for the In Search of the Emerging Church series.

Special thanks go to managing editor Dennis Coday for turning the series into an attractive web presence and to special sections editor Teresa Malcolm, whose unfailing attention to detail saved this writer from himself countless times.

Thanks also for assistance, encouragement, insightful tips, and conversation to Rich Heffern and Josh McElwee.

Pat Marrin, editor of *Celebration*, NCR's invaluable worship resource, knows how and when to offer encouragement, wisdom, and the occasional in-house retreat. His insights and enthusiasm helped keep me and the emerging church project on course.

To Arthur Jones, whose counsel I have valued since I arrived at *NCR* in 1994, heartfelt thanks for creating, those years ago, the position of editor at large. The church may someday even thank you for your prescient insights at the start of the reporting on the sex abuse crisis. If only someone had listened.

I am indebted to the work of colleague John L. Allen Jr. who, with the late Peter Hebblethwaite, provides the most thorough record of John Paul II's papacy to be found anywhere. Allen's obituary of John Paul remains, in my estimation, the most balanced, insightful, and concise assessment of that papacy in print.

Joe Feuerherd had been publisher only a few months when I suggested the In Search of the Emerging Church series; it took him about two seconds to respond, "Do it!" He provided the resources, the time, and the consistent encouragement to back up that initial enthusiasm. Not a small commitment in this era of shrinking journalistic enterprise. Joe understood *NCR* to the very core of its mission. In the too-brief time he had as publisher and editor-in-chief, wielding the admonition "Report! Report! Report!" as the antidote to the paper's sagging fortunes, he reestablished *NCR* as a strong and essential player in the ongoing drama of Catholicism in the twenty-first century. He died at age forty-eight on May 26, 2011.

More than seventeen years ago Tom Fox called me when I was working in Manhattan and asked if I'd consider coming to the Midwest. I'm forever grateful that I got over my initial resistance to moving west of the Hudson. I found that the heartland, indeed, has a heart, and my family and I found in the Kansas City area an unusually savvy and active Catholic community, smart and committed people who lived the faith deeply and welcomed us warmly. And I stepped into a long association with the treasure called *National Catholic Reporter*. More than that, I found in Tom Fox a colleague who became a friend, someone so devoted to the *NCR* project and the larger journalistic enterprise that he was willing to put his job on the line long ago for the sake of a story that he knew had to be told. That kind of integrity is the foundation on which *NCR* is built.

My thanks to Sr. Charlene Smith, FSPA, a contemporary and biographer of Sr. Thea Bowman, for her work, for providing a video of Thea's appearance before the bishops—a great aid to this writer's memory—and for taking the time to read the relevant chapter and offer valuable suggestions.

Thanks to friend Fr. Dirk Dunfee, SJ, for reading initial chapters and making suggestions that aided clarity and forced me to think deeper about some issues. I am grateful to Frances Pierce, more of an editor that she would admit, who read portions and made suggestions that also influenced other segments.

As one convinced that getting at the truth of the sex abuse crisis is the only path to health in the church, I have great regard for the years of courageous work of Barbara Blain and David Clohessy of the Survivors' Network of those Abused by Priests (SNAP) and Fr. Thomas Doyle, OP. Against great odds they dared to name the sin and seek accountability at a time when few would hear them. An invaluable source of information for this writer and for journalists everywhere is bishopaccountability.org. Terry McKiernan and Anne Barrett Doyle have developed an archive of original documentation comprising the first and most important step toward shattering the secrecy that has allowed the scandal to persist.

Using a journalistic model to which I have become accustomed over the years, I have attempted to keep notes to a minimum, relying on them when I considered it necessary to recognize a writer's contribution properly or to identify sources more precisely. Much of the material that I present from the series remains unchanged in the book, or only slightly altered to accommodate needs of clarity and timeliness. Some of it has been rearranged to fit the flow of narrative.

I have taken liberty in book form with interpretive and conclusive elements that I am restrained from employing in the normal course of news coverage. One of the values I tried to bring to the book is a greater coherence and flow to the uneven and staccato presentation of news that occurs as we attempt to keep informed "on the run." I realize that these are but one person's interpretations and conclusions from a small corner of the church. My hope is that the effort will contribute something substantive to the discussion.

Finally, thanks to my family for their forbearance with endless discussions of religion news and church politics. Dearest Sara, whom most know as Sally, has listened kindly and patiently over the years as themes and ideas get worked out aloud. Every bishop should know her look that gently asks, when the ecclesiastical chatter begins to grind to fine points: Why should anyone consider that important? At the Roberts household the dinner table was a place of discussion, storytelling, and debate. Rebecca, Daniel, William, and James, you probably have little understanding of how profoundly your ideas, questions, and challenges contributed to my work along the way. You continue to inspire me in ways you can't imagine as you go on with your own lives and families. Blessings on you all.

Introduction

In the spring of 2009 I began traveling to different parts of the country to report on the state of the church on the ground for a series titled In Search of the Emerging Church. Along the way I realized that most of my career as a religion writer and editor has, in one form or another, been a search for the emerging church, in particular the emerging Catholic community. It is a search bracketed at one end by the Second Vatican Council of the mid 1960s and at the other by the yet unknown.

The idea for the In Search of the Emerging Church series was sparked by data that had been accumulating for decades, ongoing information developed by the Center for Applied Research in the Apostolate (CARA) at Georgetown University, and a five-year study funded by a Lilly Endowment titled Emerging Models of Lay Leadership.

The big picture, simply put, and as we all now understand it, is that the church during the past half century has changed forever and irrevocably. Dr. Marti Jewell, who oversaw the lay leadership project through its initial stages, put it bluntly to a gathering of lay and ordained ministers: "There's no going back."

This book is not confined to the boundaries of the series. I have drawn on earlier reporting in a number of instances, particularly in the first half of the book, because I think the broader frame provides the space for a deeper look at themes and issues affecting the church today. What this book aspires to show is that U.S. Catholics of the late twentieth and early twenty-first centuries are living through a time of tension set up by myriad forces, not least among them the dramatic reforms of Vatican II; deep shifts in demographics in the church and wider culture; the new cosmology and its effect on belief and church structure as articulated by a range of Catholic thinkers; the rise of women as a voice in the church; and the growing inadequacy of a hierarchical culture owing more to royal constructs of the period of kings and princes than it does to the teachings of the Suffering Servant. Of that last point it can be said that the sex abuse crisis is but the ugliest symptom of its failings, a symptom that has horribly distorted and distracted the Catholic community.

The sex abuse crisis will be given considerable treatment because of its lasting effects—both for good and ill—on the church. It is a deep malady within the body of the church and it has resisted treatment because its symptoms were first ignored and later misdiagnosed. The scandal has caused enormous upheaval and the diversion of untold amounts of human energy and financial resources from the life of the church. Its cost financially in the United States is said to be more than $2.5 billion and counting. Its cost in credibility and trust, in the morale of the community, both its lay and ordained members, is incalculable.

A link exists between the sex abuse crisis and the crisis of authority within the church. While in recent years the use of authoritarian methods has been on the rise, the exercise of what many term an authentic authority, an authority that doesn't have to be self-announced in endless proclamations, has been sadly missing. Popes, bishops, and heads of dicasteries have shown that they do, indeed, have the power to isolate and publicly rebuke individuals and institutions and declare them outside the fold. Many of those same leaders, however, have shown little inclination toward pastoral skills that accomplish leadership by listening, persuasion, generating consensus, and acknowledging at times uncertainty over questions for which no easy answers exist.

The sex abuse crisis notwithstanding, considerable signs exist that out of all of the tensions tugging at the twenty-first-century church—tensions that I believe are an inevitable result of the significant changes initiated in the 1960s—a stronger and more capable community is emerging. It will be a community far more dependent on lay abilities and leadership and far less on a Catholic identity that springs from the needs of a clerical culture. That notion may run against the common wisdom of the day, which sees the hierarchical attempts to regain authority and to exercise greater control by way of excommunications and turning back the reforms of Vatican II as harbingers of the future. I see them as a futile grasp at retaining the past, unsustainable given the facts on the ground and the theology that has undergirded the understanding of the church for the past half century.

While I don't hold much hope for a "can't we just all get along" solution to the current deep divisions, I also think that the differences need not split us apart. I think they can be reduced to the level of healthy tensions on which a community builds a future. The theology, the thought necessary for moving forward, is already out of the tube, as the expression goes, and for all the determination on the part of some, it will not go back into the tube. The thought—the new language, the new ideas, the horizontal approach of Vatican II, and the determination expressed in the documents for greater collegiality and dialogue—will not disappear.

We live in the tension between those who most benefit from an old order, from the knowable if unsustainable practice of hierarchy as it has existed, and those who envision a church in which the leadership is less prone to royal bearing and distance from the everyday lives of its people. It was the latter model, the case can be convincingly made, that was envisioned by Vatican II, though it was taught badly, and church leaders at the time used a pre-conciliar ecclesiology (it is so and you must go along because the pope and the bishops said so) in attempting to impose a new post-conciliar collegiality. We see now that the strategy either didn't work very well or perhaps was simply destined to be swallowed by the kind of conflict that would have resulted with any such significant change.

My vantage points for viewing events in the church have been fairly unusual. I had the privilege of working at two news outlets— *RNS (Religious News Service)*[1] and *NCR (National Catholic Reporter)*—that are dedicated to religion reporting and really have no comparable counterparts. Founded at different times but with similar motivation, each sought to bring the best aspects of U.S.-style journalism to the reporting of religion, an arena not accustomed to such scrutiny. In the case of *RNS*, the thought was that straight, unadorned reporting on the whole panoply of religious experience and expression would ring in a new era of interfaith and interdenominational understanding.

NCR grew from a conviction of a group of creative souls in Kansas City, Missouri, about the people's right to know. If there is a founding document for the enterprise, it is the long speech by Jesuit theologian John Courtney Murray, one of the fashioners of Vatican II's approach to the modern world, to Catholic journalists in Rome in 1963, the year before the paper published its first issue. Murray probably never intended it as such, but his talk was a perfectly crafted mission statement for anyone contemplating the launch of an independent newspaper focused on the church. "The societal character of the church creates a public right to information about all that concerns the church," he wrote, "about her teaching, about her discipline and law, about her policies ... about the total action of the church in history in this present moment of history. What is the church doing here and now today? The people of God need to know all this. The subject of this right to know is, first of all, the people as a people. And this right derives to you and me through our membership in the people of God."

Further, he said, "the need to know of a free people, in a free and open society, is in principle unlimited." It was startlingly new language being applied to an institution that historically had shown little interest in the sort of free public flow of information that Murray envisioned.

RNS was modeled loosely on the Associated Press and the old United Press International wire services, and it maintained a gray neutrality that gained it wide trust and acceptance in the general press. It did little interpretive or deep investigative reporting. It covered Catholics and Baptists, Episcopalians and Mormons, Muslims and Jews with the same sober equanimity. There were no judgments. Creationists received the same consideration as evolutionists, biblical literalists the same as the Jesus Seminar. News was news, and there was no smirking or dismissing. All God's children brought something to the table, and all deserved a civil hearing. Directing the news coverage there was a great hands-on education for this 1950s-era Catholic who had been told in childhood never to go inside the Methodist church across the street from my hometown parish.

NCR, on the other hand, was anything but gray or neutral. From its inception it was bound to cause a stir simply by virtue of its mission. The editors, who distributed copies of Murray's talk to promote their new venture, announced in its first issue their intent to "report the life of the church in the world . . . to press for as much information as can be had about events and their meaning; and, just as importantly, constantly assessing the overall situation of the Church, the quality of Catholic life and of particular aspects of Catholic life." *NCR* called itself "a religious paper with worldly interests" and spoke in the initial issue of "professional skepticism." It declared its "orientation" as being "toward reporting the news, toward enterprise and relevance, toward dialogue with practically everybody." The founders declared that they were "committed to the Church, and secure enough in our commitment to keep wondering what the Church is and will become." It was a manifesto of seekers and questioners caught up in all the talk at the time of renewal and change. But they were giving birth to this new species of communication within an institution that remained deeply uncomfortable with the notion of open discussion and with being questioned.

In 2007, on returning from a three-month sabbatical, I wrote a paragraph that summarizes my feelings for the paper: "In my time away from the office, I acquired a deeper appreciation for this little publication, for its independence and gumption; for its love of the deepest and most essential elements of the faith and tradition; for its willingness to turn over pages to thinkers whose words are not the somnolent recitations of dogma and rules that constitute so much of today's 'religious' discourse; for its dogged pursuit of stories that might shake loose our presumptions about issues of peace and justice."

That's the journalistic context out of which and through which I worked on the ongoing story about the Catholic community.

In 1978, then ten years into a career in daily journalism and on a path as an investigative/political reporter, my head began to be turned by the big, broad religion story. I saw it at the time as an entrée into some of the most important questions and issues of the era. I was inspired by a growing sense of lay involvement across denominational lines, fed by the enthusiasm that had erupted in so many Catholic circles the decade before as a result of Vatican II. I wanted to know more about the increasing numbers of people who were applying their faith beyond the church walls to the issues and challenges of the day—to cultural questions, to foreign policy questions, to conditions beyond our shores.

The discovery that religion reporting and writing could mean more than the tepid "church news" that too often passed at the time as a newspaper's acknowledgment of the religious community opened up new worlds of journalistic inquiry. Religion reporting fed both a personal fascination with big questions and a relentless curiosity about the smaller details of individual lives that so often make a difference. I now often use the expression *religion story* as a kind of shorthand to refer to the expansive universe of stories that originate in one of the multitude of religious traditions or that are affected by religions and their adherents.

This is not a memoir. It is not intended as a detailed account of a career, but there is about it a very personal view of events. Journalism was my window into the religion story, particularly that of the Catholic community. It remained my window through ten years in New York as news editor for *RNS* and in now more than seventeen years in various capacities at *NCR*. What I bring to this effort is the peculiar view of a journalist. I think that the discipline and how it applies to the subject at hand is worth a more detailed treatment. It is, perhaps, appropriate here to say that most of us get our news, including religion news, episodically, a bit here and a bit there depending on what stories our eyes happen to fall upon on a page or a screen. Some of us, however, make our living keeping tabs on a particular small corner of the human experience in all of its detail. That's been the case for me regarding the Catholic community for more than a quarter century.

The hope, then, is that such observation over that long a period would eventually spawn a more coherent narrative than one might be able to construct from random doses of the headlines. If there is a value in sticking around so long in quest of a story, it is that one becomes familiar with some of the connective tissue, the soft and subtle stuff, that quietly and unobtrusively binds the episodes but that would take too much time and space in the normal course of the craft to be included in the usual treatment.

Happenings large and small in the church are rarely discrete, disconnected moments. They almost always are part of a larger, if sometimes disguised, context. I'll attempt in this book to detail some of those connections, fully realizing that an organism as complex and immense as the Catholic Church would frustrate a comprehensive portrayal by any individual, especially one practicing a craft that has been said to produce "the first draft of history." I am well aware of the implied lack of completeness and need for constant revision in that description. I am further aware that this is a "U.S.-centric" view of the church, and while there can be severe limitations to any broader assessments one might make from that point of view, it can also hold valuable, if limited, lessons for the wider church as it searches for itself at the start of the twenty-first century. John L. Allen Jr.'s *The Future Church: How Ten Trends Are Revolutionizing the Catholic Church,* a reporting tour de force on the global church and the new and seismic forces that are changing it, takes as its starting point the fact that a church once dominated by Europe and North America "today finds two thirds of its members living in Africa, Asia and Latin America," the "global South." If demographics are destiny, the global South, in terms of the numbers of new Catholics, new priests, new sisters, and perhaps even challenging new ideas about models of church, certainly is a sign of the future.

At the same time, numbers never tell the entire story. If the church insists in the global South on using the same leadership template—clericalism, secrecy, power, and privilege without accountability—that has been used in the global North, the church of the South can already see its future. Beyond the enthusiasm of the early generations, it can predict the trend toward diminishment and scandal. What the global North might teach, as it confronts a period of diminishment, is the need for a humbler, more inquisitive institution for the future.

Further, the church in the United States deserves special scrutiny because it exists in the wealthiest, most powerful and arguably most militarized democracy in history. How it navigates the ethical thickets that arise out of that combination and whether it can retain its spiritual and religious integrity amid such wealth and power should remain important questions to Catholics in other cultures aspiring to similar national values.

I don't think the way ahead is an either/or situation. I once attended a 1960s-era workshop by the Jewish actor and singer Theodore Bikel, who admonished his audience of young seekers not to abandon "what is in grandfather's attic." The wise and obvious point being that a healthy life doesn't abandon its history at the discovery of some new insight or purpose. At the same time, grandfather's understanding of the universe, of science, of God would be inadequate for today.

So it is, I think, with the healthy community. The reporting I've done in recent months has reinforced the conviction that ideologically driven analyses almost always fall short of the mark. While acknowledging ideological currents and how they might shape the meta-narrative of a given era, in the individual lives that project the church into its surrounding culture, the story is almost invariably more complex than an ideology. The people of God are, simply put, more intriguing and complicated than any interest group's talking points. The neat and orderly lines of narrative are few in the Catholic story. It can be messy.

The image that has occurred to me repeatedly in approaching this story is one of shadow and light, not in the sense of competing polarities, but more signifying a range of darkness to brilliance that entertains both ambiguity and paradox. Darkness, which can portend and hide evil, can also be the saint's solace. Brilliance can mark clarity and virtue, but it can also symbolize fleeting glory or the momentary light that can accompany horrible destruction. Most of us, I think, live somewhere along the spectrum, in and out of shadow, seeking hope and faith, trying to act out of love. I think we want a community that expresses our sacramental belief that God infuses every detail, even the most mundane. I think we want leaders who are aligned more with the "horizontal" language of Vatican II than with the legalistic approach to belief, leaders who are convinced that mercy and compassion are principal elements of the very transcendence that we all also seek.

Chapter 1

TRUE TRUTHS

On a bright June day in 1989, Sr. Thea Bowman took the stage in a gymnasium at Seton Hall University in South Orange, New Jersey. She was resplendent in turquoise and gold African cloth that lent her a certain regal air. She was there to preach to the assembled bishops of the United States, sitting behind neatly arranged rows of tables on the gym floor, rank after rank of mostly white, elderly, gray-haired men in identical black suits and Roman collars, pectoral-cross chains glinting across their chests.

The morning had been given over to celebrating African American Catholics and the recently completed *National Black Catholic Pastoral,* a plan that would be formally adopted by the U.S. bishops the following November. I was one of a handful of press people from organizations that felt duty bound to cover the bishops' meetings, even a spring meeting with a limited agenda. Few of us, if any, anticipated the unusual twist this gathering would take when Sr. Thea headed for center stage. An electrifying video had preceded her appearance, a presentation alive with African American song and dance and worship. Black church leaders— Archbishop Eugene Marino, Bishop Wilton Gregory and Bishop James P. Lyke among them—were in attendance, and some were on stage with Sr. Thea. Black Catholic pride was thick in the air.

An unusual choice for keynote speaker at a national gathering of bishops, Sr. Thea sat in her wheel chair before the assembly three ways marginalized: she was a woman, she was African American, and she was dying of cancer. Yet there was a radiance about her as she took the stage. This preacher, singer, evangelizer, linguist, and academic, who moved easily from the eloquence of the highly educated to the rhythms and cadences of the street, seemed

1

unfazed that she was about to address an audience whose members were more accustomed to being front and center than in the pews.

Always a bit of a free spirit, a surprise waiting to happen, Sr. Thea rarely allowed considerations of career or status to get in the way of proclaiming what she called "true truths." She gave the impression that on this day—a few weeks beyond her most recent radiation therapy and facing another regimen of chemotherapy— she was not about to waste the opportunity on polite conversation.

"What does it mean to be black in the church and society?" she began in a strong voice. "I want to tell you about the church." From her wheel chair she launched into a searing rendition of the sung lament, "Sometimes I feel like a motherless child . . . a long way from home."[1]

"Can you hear me, church, will you help me, church?" she pleaded. "I'm a long way from home, a long way from home."

She had nurtured a deepening connection to Africa during the latter years of her ministry, and she brought a full sense of that association to this meeting: "Our history includes the services of Simon of Cyrene, the search of the Ethiopian eunuch, the contributions of black Egypt in art and mathematics and monasticism and politics, the art and architecture of Zimbabwe, the scholarship of Timbuktu, the dignity and serenity of textile and gold and religion in Ghana, the pervasive spirituality and vitality of Nigeria, the political and social systems of Zaire."

Much of her life as the first black member of the Franciscan Sisters of Perpetual Adoration had been about bridging borders among cultures, faiths, racial groups and within the church. In the 1980s, speaking to representatives of religious communities, black and white, who had gathered in Mississippi, she was well ahead of others in understanding a reality that would only begin to become generally understood in the West decades later. Black Catholics, she told the group, "are at the cutting edge of Catholicism: you know, the majority of the people in the world are *not* white Europeans!"[2]

In her quest to bridge cultures, however, she was not advocating dissolving differences: "When I say, 'we're all alike,' I'm copping out. If I say 'we're all alike,' I'm saying, 'I don't need you. You know what I know, and I know what you know, and I don't need you.' But we're different. We don't look alike, we don't walk alike, we don't talk alike, we don't play alike; we don't see life alike, we come from a different history, a different past, a different experience." Instead of denying differences, she said, "Come to each other in our diversity, carrying one another, giving and receiving."[3]

Thea came before the bishops as an African American Catholic to represent that community's hopes and history, its struggles and promise. It is probably unfair to ask the woman and her speech to carry any more of a burden. In a broader sense, however, in articulating the particulars of African Americans' efforts to integrate into the church and to be included in church decision-making processes as "fully functioning" adult Catholics, she was speaking for other large constituencies within the church. It is among the reasons her words, even today, strike rich and sympathetic chords across gender and ethnic lines.

She anticipated the tensions that would grow throughout the church, not only within the black Catholic community, over the next two decades when she said: "I travel all over the country, and I see it: black people within the church, black priests, sometimes even black bishops, who are invisible. And when I say that, I mean they are not consulted. They are not included. Sometimes decisions are made that affect the black community for generations, and they are made in rooms by white people behind closed doors."

This day, no one would be invisible.

"Some of us are poor. Some of us have not had the advantages of education. But how can people still have a voice and a role in the work of the church? Isn't that what the church is calling us all to?"

Even the educated and experienced who were willing to work, religious and lay, she said, were often excluded from planning and decision making. "Now, I know you are bishops and I'm not talking about somebody coming into your diocese and trying to tell you what to do. I'm talking about the normal, church-authorized consultative processes that attempt to enable the people of God to be about the work of the Catholic Church. If you know what I'm talking about, say Amen."

And they did.

"See," she smiled, "y'all are always talking about what you got to do to be a multi-cultural church. It means sometimes we do things your way and sometimes we do things mine."

"What does it mean to be black and Catholic?" she asked again. "It means that I come to my church fully functioning. That doesn't frighten you, does it? I come to my church fully functioning. I bring myself, my black self, all that I am, all that I have, all that I hope to become, I bring my whole history, my traditions, my experience, my culture, my African-American song and dance and gesture and movement and teaching and preaching and healing and responsibility as gift to the church."

She said she brought a spirituality that is "contemplative and biblical and holistic, bringing to religion a totality of mind and imagination, of memory, of feeling and passion and emotion and intensity, of faith that is embodied, incarnate praise, a spirituality that knows how to find joy even in the time of sorrow, that steps out in faith, that leans on the Lord, a spirituality that is communal, that tries to walk and talk and work and pray and play together—even with the bishops."

The words seemed to pour out in such a breathless stream at times that it was easy to get the impression that she wanted to use every precious second, that she wanted to leave nothing unsaid that was important to her. What black Catholics could also teach the bishops, she said, was about solidarity. She spoke with gratitude of the ground that had been covered and with hope of the contemporary call "to walk together in a new way toward the land of promise and to celebrate who we are and whose we are. If we as church walk together, don't let nobody separate you. That's one thing black folk can teach you. Don't let folk divide you, or put the lay folk over there and the clergy in another room, put the women over here and the men over here.

"The church teaches us that the church is a family. It is a family of families and the family got to stay together. We know that if we do stay together, if we walk and talk and work and play and stand together in Jesus' name, we'll be who we are, truly Catholic; and we shall overcome—overcome the poverty, overcome the loneliness, overcome the alienation, and build together a holy city, a new Jerusalem, a city set apart where they'll know we are his because we love one another."

She was near the end, more exhausted and sore than anyone in the audience could have guessed. The bishops were spellbound, malleable to her leading. With the suggestion of overcoming, she led the bishops, asking them to rise, in the singing of "We Shall Overcome," the civil rights anthem. The members of the U.S. hierarchy held hands, as she suggested, and they sang and swayed to the slow rhythm of the song. After a verse, she instructed them to cross their arms in front of them, which required them to come closer together. She explained that civil rights leaders, especially religious leaders, would go in front of a march like that, closing ranks, to keep the dogs, the horses, and the streams from fire hoses from harming those behind them. And the bishops complied and sang, "We shall live in love; we shall live in love today."

The bishops' applause was extensive, the room charged with emotion. The bishops presented Thea with a huge spray of red roses, and she told them that in the names of their mothers and sisters, their aunts and nieces and "all the women" who had helped bring them to the episcopacy, she would accept the flowers. More than a few bishops were by this point in tears.

Then she left the stage, wheeled off along a back wall to return to her room. What happened next was spontaneous and remarkable. The bishops left their seats and formed a line along the wall and waited for her to come by. Most of them stopped her to talk, many knelt at her wheel chair, and they touched and hugged her. It was a long while before she returned to her room.

Those of us left on the margins of the scene stood and marveled at the sight, this moment that transcended ideology, theology, liturgical norms, and all the strains that arose around women's issues in the church.

The bishops, we all knew, would return to being bishops, caught up in the demands of administration, of the clergy culture, of the new emphasis on loyalty to Rome and protecting their flanks from conservatives (who increasingly had access to Vatican officials) and from liberals (who pestered them with accusations that they were abandoning the vision of Vatican II). Some may even have had a sense of foreboding about the sex abuse scandal that had begun breaking out all around them and the problems that lurked in sealed personnel files in their chanceries. This morning, though, it was as if none of that mattered for a precious hour or two. Something deeply human and compelling had just occurred, and the bishops were stirred to abandon normal decorum and protocol. Few who were there would have argued with the view that we had been witnesses to a rare show of the power and presence of God in that room that morning.

When someone asked if she would answer some questions from the few members of the press who had attended the session, she agreed, requesting only that no one touch her because she was hurting. The cancer had metastasized to her bones, and she ached following the speech and the long line of bishops' greetings. She was gracious during the brief interview, which she conducted lying on a bed in a dorm room, expressing deep concern for the state of the black family and especially African American men who disproportionally filled the country's prisons and death rows.

The bishops' meeting was one of Thea's final major appearances. She died the following March.

Thea was proof that the church had already changed on the ground and that the international gathering of bishops that had occurred over a four-year period in Rome in the 1960s, and that had become known in shorthand as Vatican II, had altered expectations in ways that would have been unimaginable to most Catholics in the early 1900s. She did not come from any of the Western European Catholic traditions, did not even come from a Catholic background. She had converted as a youngster and brought, beyond her black self and all of her African heritage, her own peculiarly American and Protestant view of the church to her ministry, which in many ways had culminated in this powerful moment before the bishops.

She was a living symbol of the emerging church—the one emerging in the upper-case Catholic Church, as well as that in the broader Christian community—long before that term came into popular use. She represented far more of what was to come in the twenty-first century than she did of the century that was about to end. She was a post-slavery black woman, a representative of the browning of not only the culture but also the church. She was part of the long push toward a more global and inclusive community.

If the day was a marker of sorts for how far along some paths the church had come, it was also a day that secretly held within it the rumblings of issues—of gender and power, sex and abuse, control and accountability—that would, at various points in the not too distant future, convulse and divide the Catholic community.

In more mundane business that day, the bishops gave final approval to a controversial document that had been nine years in the making about the relationship between bishops and theologians. One of the final steps to approving it was to placate Vatican concerns that the document equated theologians and bishops, one irritant among others that had required extensive meetings between U.S. theologians representing the bishops and officials of the Vatican Congregation for the Doctrine of the Faith. The document was an indication of the kind of centralization and gathering of control that was underway in Rome.

It was a quietly played counterpoint to Thea's song of celebration and liberation.

Though not invited around an altar to concelebrate, Thea had been invited to take a place of prominence among the bishops, an invitation that would have been unheard of earlier in the century. In a telling bit of intra-episcopal politics, one bishop went to the microphone after Thea's appearance to note that the powerful words that had so moved the assembly had been delivered by a woman. Some of the bishops, particularly those overseeing the process of developing a pastoral on women, had already felt the sting of the Vatican's displeasure with the idea.

The pastoral letter eventually was abandoned, a victim of differences among bishops, constant interference from Rome, and the objections of women who wondered, among other things, why the bishops would not consider doing a pastoral about men. The demise of the letter might well have served as a harbinger of changes that would unfold in the conference as a result of the influence of Pope John Paul II's episcopal appointments, bishops who would display a stiffening resistance to exploring issues having to do with sexuality, ordination, and expanding leadership roles for laity, especially women.

One can only presume—given her wide contacts within the church, not only among the people in the pews, but also among bishops and other leaders and thinkers—that Sr. Thea understood the forces that had gathered on the Catholic horizon and that were already descending and would eventually cause deep divisions within the community. Such an understanding would explain the sense of urgency she displayed in appealing for a collegial approach to church governance, a greater participation by lay people, attention to those on the margins, and a broader embrace of traditions outside the normal scope of the North American brand of Catholicism. Her exhortation was at heart a plea for a change in the church's hierarchical culture, not, as she noted, a change that would sweep away the authority or office of bishops, but one that would see the bishops accepting the laity in more responsible roles.

Her appearance, though, was a rare moment. The prospects that a gathering of U.S. bishops would register such an overwhelmingly positive reaction to someone such as Thea Bowman and the admonitions she delivered at Seton Hall would diminish quickly over the next decade. The bishops wouldn't invite such an open critique of their governance again until they were forced by public outrage over the sex abuse crisis to endure several critical talks by lay people during their 2002 spring meeting in Dallas.

Any discussion of what is emerging in the church has to take some note of the enormous role John Paul II's papacy would play in unleashing forces that would shape the church into the future. The year that Thea delivered her speech was close to the halfway point in his twenty-five-year reign, and the church at the grassroots level was beginning to feel the effects of his governance style and episcopal appointments. It is well beyond my competence and far beyond the scope of this book to do a comprehensive assessment of the John Paul papacy. My personal assessment falls somewhere between the abundant hagiography that sometimes paints a kind of comic-book "super pope" and those who would generally dismiss his papacy as destructive of the church. The full story is still unraveling.

John Paul was, indeed, a towering figure in an international arena overpopulated by the ordinary; a man who was able to project his own deep faith and spirituality onto a world starving for transcendence and meaning; a savvy politician who never had to pay his way with the coin of the political realm, compromise. The temptation to depict him as super human is understandable. If he had accomplished nothing more than standing up to Polish and Soviet communists, openly defying them in speeches on their turf and stirring a people to a bloodless overthrow of brutal governments at the end of an unimaginably bloody century, that would have been enough to assure him a sizeable place in history. He was a central force "in the collapse of European communism," wrote colleague and Vatican expert John L. Allen Jr. "He did it not by fueling an arms race or by threatening Armageddon, but through moral leadership and the social idea of Solidarity."[4]

There was, of course, much more. He was "a stunningly successful historical actor," Allen wrote in his obituary of John Paul. "Through his constant travels, John Paul carried a media spotlight to corners of the globe that would otherwise never have commanded public attention. He urged people to think of this as one planet, to recognize a common humanity beneath and beyond differences of language and race and class."[5]

He had been a youthful actor and playwright, and as a global figure he bore a sense of drama's power onto the largest stage one might tread. He was a bold and charismatic figure. He loved the lights and huge events. His timing was impeccable, his body language, until Parkinson's Disease began robbing him of control, was confident and often challenging. He truly brought the Vatican out from behind the walls, taking 104 trips to 129 countries covering some 690,000 miles, and he taught in ways no other pope had taught before. His preaching devices, though perhaps staid by standards of the quick-cut world of late-twentieth-century media, were innovative for a pope. He was energized by crowds, and hundreds of thousands regularly packed into the staging areas for his events. Those crowds included young people, who thronged to enormous youth rallies. He was the most traveled, most viewed, most cheered pope in history. Even critics who didn't agree with his teaching, with his stern positions on sexual matters and certain issues involving lay people and women, often viewed favorably the idea that someone of his stature spoke moral certainty across political, religious, and national barriers.

In interreligious matters he created some of the late-twentieth-century's iconic moments. He was the first pope to visit a synagogue, the first to visit a mosque, the first to kneel with the archbishop of Canterbury in prayer at Westminster Cathedral, and the first to invite leaders of the world's religions to pray together for services he hosted three times in Assisi. No matter what academic or historic arguments might occur regarding Jewish-Catholic relations, we will always have the images of John Paul at Yad Vashem, the Holocaust memorial in Jerusalem, as well as the photos of the pope placing a prayer in the Western Wall. We will always have his words to describe the relationship between Christians and Jews: "Brothers in Abraham."

We also will have the shocking images of a fallen pope, shot by a gunman in St. Peter's Square, who later visits his attacker's prison cell to offer forgiveness.

This pope, who once commented to someone that he had the "antibodies" to communism in his blood, could also be strongly critical of Western democracies and their extreme individualism, unbridled capitalism, and lack of concern for the common good. He was a strong and persistent opponent of international violence, including the U.S. invasions of Iraq.

Allen refers to such events as John Paul II's *ad extra* activities, matters that involved issues and people beyond the boundaries of the institutional church. He was a master of the *ad extra*, at setting the tone, the agenda, the staging, and at taking advantage of the moment. Even in his extended infirm state, John Paul II continued to use the big stage to send messages of substance to the world, becoming an endearing figure who bore his suffering publicly. In so doing, he conveyed more eloquently than any words could have that humans possess an inherent dignity that transcends youth, good looks, marketing ploys, strength, vigor, and disabilities. His life in the public sphere heroically backed up his preaching.

The longest papacy of the twentieth century will resound down the ages as one that forever changed the job description of that office and its relationship to the world.

All of that travel, all of that *ad extra* activity, had its downside. John Paul left the running of the church to subordinates, and they could make a hash of things. Church governance was shortchanged. Some elements of John Paul's personality, personal history, and governing style would deeply affect the church's internal workings and direction, and often in a negative way.

Allen captured some of the tension of John Paul's tenure in the lead paragraph of the pope's obituary: "He was a magnificent pope who presided over a controversial pontificate, at times daring and defensive, inspiring and insular. John Paul II, 263rd successor of St. Peter, leaves behind the irony of a world more united because of his life and legacy and a church more divided."[6]

John Paul wasn't good at the *ad intra* part of the job. Commentators across the board agree that his management style inside the church left much to be desired. Even Allen, whose hallmark as a journalist is a generosity of spirit and magnanimity toward those he covers, had to conclude of John Paul's episcopal appointments that they "tended to be gray men, noted more for doctrinal reliability than vision or pastoral competence."[7]

If John Paul was a champion of human rights and ecumenical outreach and understanding on the world stage, inside the church he could be brittle and unyielding, a practitioner of "a form of absolutism that some critics could not help comparing with the Soviet system he helped bring down."[8] He disciplined scores of theologians, took hold of the Jesuit order and forced it to change leadership, reined in liberation theologians, put the brakes on liturgical reform, and redrew the line between ordained and laity. He came to the job with a self-imposed mandate to restore order, square the lines, and redefine boundaries. His bishops would toe the line. Loyalty was key; leadership was defined as following every detail of his program.

The late Peter Hebblethwaite, one of the most distinguished bylines in the *NCR* files, was early to question whether John Paul's authoritarian approach even worked within the church. It was a prescient question and one that remains relevant today. Hebblethwaite noted that John Paul, during his trip to the United States in 1979, informed the bishops that there would be no variance from the Vatican position on a list of moral issues, including contraception.

The following year the U.S. bishops showed up for a synod in Rome bearing polling evidence that U.S. Catholics rejected the ban on artificial contraception. "There was a genuine misunderstanding here," wrote Hebblethwaite. "What, to the Anglo-Saxon mind, could be more sensible than to give evidence based on question-naires and polls?" But to John Paul's "heroic view" such evidence was "useless," merely an indicator of "how far the rot has set in, and the urgency of decisive counteraction."

The same sort of "misunderstanding" occurred about the same time between the pope and African prelates, who had been told that the pope would make no concessions on the matter of "cus-tomary marriage." Six months later, however, the African bishops were in Rome for a synod and "insisted on discussing this taboo topic as though he [the pope] had never spoken."

Hebblethwaite calls those two examples instances of "inopera-tive authority."[9] One could add to the list of examples of "inop-erative authority" John Paul's repeated declarations, including the 1994 document *Ordinatio Sacerdotalis*, that the discussion of women's ordination was forever closed. No one was even to speak about it. Six years after his death and a hundred or more ordina-tions (which began, we are told, with duly ordained male bishops, as required by canon law) of Catholic women, the debate has hardly been abandoned. Hebblethwaite was among the earliest, if not the first, to write of the growing difficulty in the post–Vatican II era, of asserting authority within the church.

It isn't that John Paul and his bishops spared the rod. Quite the contrary. He and the bishops he appointed were rather quick to censure and silence, even excommunicate. The tactic worked, at least to the extent that thinkers and leaders throughout the insti-tution became fearful of a run-in with the Congregation for the Doctrine of the Faith. Theology departments and theologians became more cautious, and some theologians headed for secular institutions where a rebuke from Rome would not jeopardize their jobs or their work.

The question that lingers, however, was whether the exercise of authority had its intended effect. Did it persuade people to accept the viewpoint of the pope or bishop? Or did it merely harden di-visions? As we will see further along, the use of authority may it-self have pointed out a crisis of authority within the church. John Paul was, in Allen's description, "the apostle of unity *ad extra* and the bruiser *ad intra*."

In one area of concern within the institution, the priest sex abuse crisis, the bruiser looked the other way. That glaring inconsistency was confounding to many over the years. John Paul may have been quick to pull the trigger on the intellectual dissenter, but when the least and most vulnerable in the community were in greatest need of a pastor of biblical proportions, a true hero to intervene, he was nowhere to be found. It took nearly the entirety of John Paul's reign for him to acknowledge that a problem existed, and then it was in the most cursory and legalistic manner. He never once met with victims of priests' sexual crimes. In the case of one of the most egregious offenders, Fr. Marcial Maciel Degollado, founder of the once powerful, secretive order the Legionaries of Christ, he not only ignored the pleas of victims but repeatedly celebrated the predator.

The two spheres of *ad intra* and *ad extra,* of course, never operate in complete isolation from one another. John Paul's attitude toward, say, Jews or his opposition to U.S. war making or his stinging critique of U.S.-style capitalism had an effect on dialogue and teaching within the church. Priests and others could be emboldened by his uncompromising stands, for instance, in areas of social justice.

In the same way, his unyielding positions on women in the church, homosexuality, abortion, birth control, and divorce, his refusal to entertain any discussion of altering requirements for ordination, as well as his determination to reverse what many considered hard-won reforms helped shape the wider world's attitude toward the church.

By 1989, the year Thea spoke before the bishops, John Paul and members of his curia were deep into the intra-church project of rolling back the reforms of the Second Vatican Council and reshaping the episcopacy around the globe.

Some will object to such a characterization of his approach to the reforms of Vatican II, claiming that he was refining or redirecting the renewal or merely correcting course on a misguided interpretation of the council. There is some truth to such assertions. A certain amount of chaos naturally followed a council that, in ways different from any council before it, endeavored to bring about nothing less than "a new Pentecost."

The ongoing dispute over what the council meant and how the debate affects church life will be taken up in more detail later in the book. It is sufficient here to say that reported evidence as well as the case compiled by a growing list of scholars and historians show that, "ad intra," either John Paul, or those he appointed to influential positions, worked methodically and deliberately to roll back or modify Vatican II reforms. The aim was to restore previous practice or to blunt innovation, as far as possible, in such areas as liturgy, the role of laity, and the role of national conferences, and to curtail theological inquiry and speculation, particularly in the fields of liberation theology, Christology, and relationships with other faiths.

Some argue, and in instances rather persuasively, that John Paul was simply reacting to reforms that overreached and to interpretations of the council that misinterpreted the degree of change envisioned by the council fathers. Those who think the council was less about change than about reinforcing existing teaching and practice often cast the dispute in the continuity *vs.* discontinuity framework. In that paradigm the argument holds that by nature the church would not suddenly change course, severing itself from past understandings of itself. Vatican II, in that construct, becomes merely an attempt to restate, in language and form more accessible to modern sensibilities, ancient truths and practices.

That dispute has certainly shaped, or warped, depending on one's point of view, the post-conciliar church in the sense that so much energy has been expended in defending one or another competing claim. Whatever one's perspective, however, John Paul II's initiatives over a quarter century as head of the church, his politics within the church, and the issues that he chose to highlight left the Catholic community indisputably more divided than it was when he was elected.

If John XXIII and Paul VI were the two popes who oversaw the council, John Paul II becomes, by virtue of John Paul I's brief reign, the first significant post-conciliar pope. It is a not unimportant set of circumstances if any stock is placed in the presumption, broadly held, that Pope John Paul I, who was elected August 28, 1978, and died thirty-three days later, on September 28, would have staked his papacy to a much different view of the council than that of his successor.

Hebblethwaite, in *The Year of Three Popes,* characterized Albino Luciani, Pope John Paul I, as a direct intellectual descendant of John XXIII. Luciani, he wrote, was a man open to new ideas "or to rediscovered old ones," a trait that he said "could be seen in the way he trusted his pastoral council and senate of priests" when he was bishop of the Diocese of Vittoria Veneto.[10] The members of the council and senate were elected, and Bishop Luciani "accepted their decisions even when they went against him." In one instance he disagreed with a decision to close a junior seminary but went along with it anyway. "And I haven't regretted it," he said. He also sent his seminarians to state schools "and welcomed the adult vocations that started to flow in Vittoria Veneto as 'a sign of the times.'" He disliked "ecclesiastical display" and "encouraged parish priests to sell precious vessels and other church valuables for the benefit of the poor."[11]

In a conversation with the esteemed Vaticanologist Giancarlo Zizola, Luciani articulated his positive outlook amid the era of confusion following Vatican II. "The remedy is to proclaim the truth but in a positive way, stressing the essential, expressing it in a way that will make sense for contemporary people, and remaining in touch with modern culture. There is usually a grain of truth and goodness even in false opinions."[12] Hebblethwaite notes that in that exchange Luciani "was echoing, and no doubt knew it, the words of Pope John in his opening speech to the council when he rounded on the 'prophets of doom' and insisted on a positive, non-judgmental approach to the modern world."[13]

I make the point only to call attention to the essential humanity of the Catholic enterprise even as it mediates the divine. In that essential humanity our steps are necessarily hesitant, flawed, ambiguous, driven by layers of motives and insights, even if, at the same time, they appear determined and certain. One pope approaches converting the world with open arms, persuasion, and a presumption of good will. Another sees the mission in terms of rebuke, of drawing clear lines between those who are in and those who are out. One is a shepherd who thinks the extended hand is the best evangelism. The other is a shepherd who sees wolves, beyond reform, lurking in the shadows.

For most of the five-plus decades since the council, the debate over what it means has been largely cast in a right-left, liberal-conservative frame. There is a great deal on the record to justify such a characterization, just as the record will also show that the debate leads, almost without fail, to a kind of stalemate. For starters, there is no measure for declaring victory and no referee who can make the call. The process of the council rolls out, we are all keenly aware at this point, over time, and the post–Vatican II era will only end when Vatican III is convened, should that ever occur.

Further, change keeps occurring on the ground because of shifts and changes in demographics, in the makeup of priesthood and religious life, in the ecclesiology of other denominations, and in the practices of ordinary Catholics. The sober fact is that the reality of the church in the United States in the present is wildly different from that of the mid-1960s. It is clear that simply to keep the church running, theology and ecclesiology often have to catch up to a real need that has developed within the community. The theology and ecclesiology most frequently employed—the source of the permission to do things differently even as segments of the church resist the changes—come directly from the council. The stalemate over the council's meaning often marches in lock step with the changes that have to occur if the church is to keep functioning.

It is a testament, perhaps, to the significance of the Vatican II event and its potential implications that, in an information age where history is compressed into seconds and consumed on the run, the mining of the council's deeper meaning continues. The left-right, liberal-conservative framework, however, may have outlived its usefulness. Everyone is weary of the arguments and the inconclusiveness of the debate. What effect sheer weariness will have on the debate is open, itself, to question. We obviously can possess our points of view with a tightfisted rigidity that doesn't yield to argument over interpretations of the council. Perhaps, however, trying to discern which camp owns the patent on the purest strict constructionist understanding of the Vatican II documents is searching for answers in the wrong place.

What we may be living through, then, is a period in which the liberal-conservative construct ultimately fails as an explanation and yields to what Jesuit Fr. Mark S. Massa sees as a time of tension between those who understand that the church has changed over time and will continue to change and those who believe the church is timeless and cannot change. "Whatever the intentions of the bishops of the Second Vatican Council—and the debate over those intentions is a heated one—historical events have a life, and a logic, of their own, and even ecumenical councils cannot control them," he writes. In the same way, believers are not exempt from the "messiness of history."[14]

In Massa's view one gets a truncated idea of the council and its effects if it is perceived as a discrete event that occurred over a four-year period (1962–65) without reference to the forces of history that led to it or the unintended consequences that followed it. Such a view would be like saying the Protestant Reformation was the result solely of Luther's posting (if such an act actually occurred) of his 95 theses at Castle Church in Wittenberg.

The reality is that fifty years before Thea Bowman took the stage, a mere blink in church time, it would have been impossible to imagine such an address being delivered to the bishops. The bishops' conference as it was constituted in 1989 didn't exist fifty years before; black Catholics, in many parts of the country, would have been hidden away in their own churches or consigned to the back pews of the church.

"Change happens," writes Massa, "whatever the intentions of historical actors, even infallible ones."[15]

Chapter 2

THE SHRINKING, EXPANDING, CHANGING CHURCH

In the spring of 2009 the church in Cleveland was in turmoil. Bishop Richard Lennon had recently mandated that twenty-nine of the diocese's 224 parishes would close, another forty-one would merge, creating in all eighteen new parishes and a net loss of fifty-two parishes.

During a week that spring I spent hours talking to pastors, parishioners, and lay pastoral leaders throughout the diocese. A large segment of the black Catholic community was especially upset because it was losing not only its parishes but also longstanding ministries that served the community. A mix of loss, anger, and frustration hung over the Catholic community.

It would be difficult to overstate the spiritual, emotional, historic, and sometimes ethnic connections that people have with their parishes. Those connections are why people camped for years in empty church buildings in Boston hoping to change the mind of the archbishop who had ordered them closed. Members of one parish in Cleveland eventually decided that the bishop could take their building, but that they would keep the community intact. Hundreds of the parishioners and their pastor moved to an industrial site and continued to meet and worship as a parish. Other Catholics in Cleveland and Boston backed up their protests with costly and futile legal appeals to the Vatican judicial system.

Change is unsettling in any circumstance, but the disorientation arguably is uniquely profound when wrenching change occurs in the realm that nourishes and claims our faith. Even though some Catholics now move easily from one parish to another looking for a place that best matches their preferences, we still hold a certain notion of timelessness about our churches, those places where week after week, and in life's most significant moments, we intersect with the divine. In Cleveland that sentiment mixed with a strong reaction against the decrees of a new bishop who set aside a reorganization process that was under way and imposed his own plan. "Gone are the days when parishes could have two or three or four priests or more. The church is being strained in its resources. We had to face reality and do something," said Bishop Lennon. Indeed, the number of active diocesan priests had dropped in Cleveland from 427 in 1990 to 257 in April 2009. At the time, 42 percent of the diocese's parishes were operating in the red. So parishes were ordered closed, victims of some of the same economic realities and social forces that claimed local businesses.

The situation in Cleveland was but one more indication of the seismic shifts in demographics, structure, and ministry rattling the Catholic Church in the United States at the start of the twenty-first century. Population shifts, priest shortages, and financial troubles caused by a combination of sex abuse pay outs, financial mismanagement, and the exodus of factories and businesses from the old rust-belt cities for cheaper labor in the South and the developing world had forced the church itself to downsize. From North Philadelphia and Camden, New Jersey, to Boston and areas of New York, from Cleveland to Detroit to Chicago, the church is abandoning the institutions that once defined it. It is the bricks-and-mortar side of the Catholic identity crisis. Taking a view from any of these dioceses one could understandably become convinced that the church is on a dangerous and even irreversible downward slide.[1]

The spot where one stands amid the immensity of the church, however, has everything to do with shaping one's impressions. If it is the incredibly shrinking church in the Northeast and upper Midwest, that is one viewpoint, but in the Southwest and West, as well as areas of the Southeast, the church is booming. Individual parishes are serving thousands of families, and dioceses can't build churches fast enough. I recall a story told by an involved Catholic in South Carolina who arranged a meeting between some concerned parishioners and an official of the diocese in the mid-1990s. Churches were packed to capacity, and there was no room for all the Catholics who needed a place, for the snowbirds from the North who had decided to retire to South Carolina and for the immigrants from Latin America and Mexico who had followed the trail of work to the state. The official shook his head and said he was sorry, the diocese couldn't build more churches because there were no more priests. "But we have more Catholics!" the people responded.

Allowing for a certain apocryphal component to that story, it nevertheless represents a central tension of the day. It also points up the difficulty one encounters in applying statistics to the national situation. While the steady decline in the number of priests and a shifting population combine to create a troubling situation (a common cry might be, "Don't close our church. Get us a priest!"), the problem is exacerbated by the fact that priests and people are not evenly distributed throughout the country. A few dioceses are still "priest rich" while others, especially in expanding areas and locales with a heavy influx of immigrants, are desperately trying to come up with both more priests and models of parish life that will best use the resources at hand.

The priest shortage may eventually force church leadership to a deeper examination of old presumptions about parish structures, how those local communities should operate, and what might be expected of a dwindling ordained priesthood in the twenty-first century.

It would be a mistake, however, to see either the despair of the rust belt or the new energy of the Southwest as holding the key to where the church is headed in the future. Each brings its own set of circumstances, including problems, to the table, and those problems quickly beg larger, systemic solutions.

One thing is certain: the days of the iconic, muscular, grand 1950s-era church of the Northeast, its rectories spilling over with priests and its convents full of women in habits, is a thing of the past. Something new is in the works.

"Emerging church" is a convenient tag, but it suffers from the limits inherent in any headline.

People are likely to infer that a new entity is emerging all of a piece when that is hardly the case. Something far more complex is going on, an emergence that is as rich in tradition as it is in new possibilities. Exactly what shape the new reality will ultimately take, or when, is impossible to predict, but it is clear that on the ground and in our era, the reality is being shaped in many ways at that point where need intersects with theology and ecclesiology.

The need is evident on several levels. One level is amply documented in the rich store of demographic and other sociological data that has been gathered by Catholic scholars in recent decades. Theology and ecclesiology enter the picture when local churches discover the need to span the gaps created by the historic demographic shifts under way among both the church's membership and its vowed and ordained leadership.

Demographic data and a theology of growing lay involvement were central to the discussion that took place during a 2008 conference in Florida, the culminating event of a four-year study titled "Emerging Models of Pastoral Leadership."[2] The study and the gathering of twelve hundred mostly lay ministers constituted a rare, national conversation about the future of the church. The promise and tensions that surfaced during the study were set up by two keynote talks, one by Bishop Blase Cupich, episcopal adviser to the project, and another by Marti Jewell, then director of the project. Cupich grounded the efficacy of the study in the theology and tradition affirmed during the Second Vatican Council. He said lay people who are increasingly involved in ministry are answering the call to holiness that is part of their baptismal heritage. The new involvement was not merely a response to need resulting from a clergy shortage, he said. "Lay and ordained all have a stake in the future of our church."

That may be so, but the numbers are driving much of the change. It is almost certain that if the rectories and convents were still full, we wouldn't be having the same compelling discussion about lay ministry. Jewell, who describes herself as a practical theologian, immediately cut to the bottom line. "For those of you who like to flip to the last page of a book and read the end of the story right away, I'll tell you what the research concluded," she said. "Parish life as we have known it has changed. In the Southern tier, California, and on the Atlantic seaboard, mega-parishes are growing, serving as many as 10,000 families in a single parish." Often, parishes in small towns either share a pastor or are led by lay people. And contrary to common perceptions, immigrant worker populations can now be found everywhere, with some rural parishes serving large populations of people from other countries.

As these new challenges and populations surface, the priesthood is not only shrinking, but it is also aging. Of the 27,182 diocesan priests officially recorded, fewer than twenty thousand are available to serve the eighteen thousand parishes. The rest are either infirm or too old to take on pastoral responsibilities. But even those who are available aren't all in areas where they're needed and, further, about 70 percent of that available clerical workforce is over the age of fifty-five.[3]

The number of priests who are members of religious orders has dropped as well, from 22,707 in 1965 to 12,811 in 2010. Although religious priests have done parish work in the past, many orders are moving away from such responsibilities because they are strapped for personnel to run their core ministries, such as schools and universities. The downward trend includes religious brothers, who have fallen from 12,271 in 1965 to 4,690 today; and religious sisters, from 179,954 to 57,544 during the same period.

Total priestly ordinations per year have fallen in that time from 994 to 459, and the number of graduate level seminarians plunged from 8,325 to 3,483 in 2010 (which is actually 311 more than in 1995, when only 3,172 were enrolled in graduate-level studies).

The number of parishes in that period grew from 17,637 to a high of 19,331 in 1995. Since then, the number has dropped, through consolidations and closings, to 17,958. At the same time, the number of U.S. parishes without a resident priest has grown from 549 to 3,353, while the number of parishes for which a bishop has entrusted pastoral care to a deacon, religious sister, brother, or other lay person has grown from 93 in 1985, the first year such figures were kept, to 469 today.

Other figures that indicate an incredibly shrinking church are the drop in Catholic elementary schools from 8,414 in 1975 to 5,889 today; the elementary school population has dropped from 2.5 million to 1.5 million. Catholic secondary schools numbered 1,624 in 1975, and that number has dropped to 1,205 today. The number of secondary students in that time has gone from 884,181 to 611,723.

In subsequent interviews and talks Jewell, who has since become assistant professor of theology at the School of Ministry at the University of Dallas, repeated that the church has changed and was continuing to change in dramatic ways. "There's no going back," she said. Researchers were discovering a growing need for collaboration between priests and lay ministers as the priest work force grew smaller and older. Nearly half of the parishes in the United States now share a pastor with another parish or mission. Jewell described a church at once in great stress and on the verge of new possibilities.

"The church is grieving," she said, in a May 2009 interview at her offices at the Washington Theological Center. "There's no way around that." Change is occurring everywhere, she said, and in every sector of the church people are going through one or another combination of Kübler-Ross's stages of grieving—denial, anger, bargaining, depression, acceptance. After years of research that compiled not only mountains of data but also books of detailed stories from around the country, she is convinced the change "is inevitable and unstoppable." The data concludes, in short, that the clergy shortage crisis is real and ongoing and that the number of trained lay ministers available and in use is increasing.

If "priest shortage" has become one of the accepted realities of twenty-first-century Catholicism in the United States, the initial predictions that the church was in for a long and sustained decline in clergy numbers delivered an unwelcome jolt to the system.

The first to pick up on this leading indicator of change in the church were researchers Richard Schoenherr of the University of Wisconsin in Madison and Lawrence A. Young of Brigham Young University in Provo, Utah. The two sociologists began studying the trajectory of the priest shortage in the United States in the mid-1980s, and in 1993 they published *Full Pews and Empty Altars: Demographics of the Priest Shortage in United States Dioceses.* The rigorously documented study projected a 40 percent reduction in the number of active diocesan priests in the United States, from thirty-five thousand in 1966 to twenty-one thousand in 2005.

The actual figures have adhered over the years rather closely to Schoenherr and Young's projections, and the drop in priests is arguably the single most significant bit of empirical data affecting the shape the church will take in the future. Without priests, the reasoning goes, it is not possible to conduct a canonically correct eucharistic service, and without the Eucharist, Eucharist communities—Catholic parishes—cease to be.

The study was initially funded by a Lilly Endowment grant and by the U.S. bishops. The bishops' interest in the distressing data would wane over the years. So would their financial support. They stopped funding the project in 1990, following a third interim report. In a preview of the kind of attitude the bishops would exhibit in the future toward sociological data, three members of the hierarchy, in a letter to their peers, downplayed the significance of the findings.

Cardinal Roger Mahony of Los Angeles was particularly aggrieved and lashed out in a personal attack against Schoenherr, who earlier had left the active priesthood to marry. "I reject that pessimistic assessment and feel that the Catholic Church in our country has been done a great disservice by the Schoenherr report," Mahony said. He accused Schoenherr of pushing a "personal agenda" of opposing mandatory celibacy for priests. He also said that the study "presumes that the only factors at work are sociology and statistical research. That is nonsense. We are disciples of Jesus Christ. We live by God's grace, and our future is shaped by God's design for his church—not by sociologists."

If that were truly the case, God might have been suggesting a future with ominous implications for ordained clergy. In the span of time covered by Schoenherr's projections, the number of diocesan priests fell to 28,702 (in 2005). By 2010 that number had dropped to 27,182. According to the *Official Catholic Directory*, approximately eighty-five hundred of that total were either sick, retired, or absent. That means slightly fewer than twenty thousand U.S. priests are available for duty, according to Mary Gautier, senior research associate for CARA, a highly regarded, if unassuming, enterprise that generates mountains of essential data about the Catholic Church in the United States.

The church has tried to fill the growing gap by importing more and more foreign priests each year. Exactly how many foreign priests have taken up pastoral duties in dioceses is unknown, but the best estimates place the number at slightly more than six thousand in 2009. While immigrant priests were the norm in the infancy of the U.S. church, founding parishes and accompanying the various waves of European immigration, foreign priests today are brought in to plug gaps in the ecclesial infrastructure that threaten the stability of the institutional edifice. The longstanding model of the parish "plant," with a pastor and several associates and religious sisters to staff the school, has proven unsustainable, but exactly what will replace that model is yet unknown. In Cleveland, for instance, Bishop Lennon clearly had no intention of entrusting the running of parishes to lay pastoral associates. He said that his strategy was to match the number of parishes to the number of priests available. Of course, that strategy leads to the obvious question of what happens if the number of priests keeps declining. Will he keep shaving the number of parishes, creating huge communities just so each has its own ordained minister in charge?

In answer to a question in late 2010, a spokesperson at the United States Conference of Catholic Bishops told me that no one in the organization was studying the phenomenon of the influx of foreign priests or exactly how many are working in the United States and where. CARA was working on such a study at the time, but the work was not expected to be completed for another year. The only figures available were generated by the Office of Child and Youth Protection, an outgrowth of the bishops' Charter on the Protection of Children and Youth, adopted in Dallas in 2002. The office compiled information on the number of international priests in 2009 as part of its mandate to monitor the practices dioceses have in place for protecting children.

Mary Jane Doerr, associate director of the office, said that the number of 6,146 tallied from the totals submitted by U.S. dioceses might not be precisely accurate because some priests may have been counted twice as a result of having moved from one diocese to another. However, she said she thought six thousand would be a solid number. While that's the best figure available, it still resides in the realm of estimate. For example, no one knows for certain how many of the foreign priests have been incardinated, that is, transferred permanently to U.S. dioceses, and how many remain extern priests, that is, here temporarily with the intention of returning to a home diocese. Nor is anyone certain how many religious order priests, if any, are included in the total or how many of the incardinated foreign priests are counted among active and available diocesan priests.

Taking into account such qualifications, the office does provide rough estimates on the number of foreign priests per diocese, and the diocese with the highest number in 2009 was New York, with

379. It was followed by Sacramento, California with 166; the Archdiocese of Military Services, with 147; and San Antonio, Texas, with 144.

The countries sending the most priests to the United States, according to the lists provided by the Office of Child and Youth Protection, are India, 797; the Philippines, 682; Ireland, 658; and Nigeria, 562.

Someone has likened statistics to a bikini, what's revealed is suggestive, and what's hidden is vital. So it seems, at times, with church statistics. The late Dean Hoge, one of the giants of Catholic sociology, who, with longtime colleague William D'Antonio, produced groundbreaking studies at what was then the Life Cycle Institute at the Catholic University of America, showed that what is perceived as a priest shortage in the United States would be a wealth of clergy in many other parts of the world.[4] Speaking in 2006 of trends that have not appreciably changed since, he said that while membership in the Catholic Church in the United States had grown by 23 percent since 1985, largely due to immigration, the number of priests had fallen by 16 percent. In Europe, membership growth was flat and the number of priests had dropped by 12 percent. The number of Catholics in Europe may have dropped even further in more recent years based on reports of large exoduses in Ireland, Germany and Belgium, which were particularly hard hit by the sex abuse crisis.

At the same time the numbers were exploding in Africa, Asia, and Central America. In Africa, for instance, the number of Catholics jumped by 89 percent between 1985 and 2002, and the number of priests increased by 44 percent. In Asia membership increased 54 percent during that period, and the number of priests increased by 65 percent. In South America the figures were 27 percent and 24 percent, respectively, and in Central America, 26 percent and 44 percent.

Yet, while the church in the United States perceives it has a priest shortage, the figures show that we actually have far more priests than the countries that have begun sending us clerics. Throughout Africa, for instance, the ratio is one priest for every 4,875 Catholics. Throughout Asia the ratio is one to 2,300; in Central America it is one to 6,894; in South America the ratio is one to 7,138.

In the United States the ratio is one priest to every 1,375 Catholics. As we've seen, and the reality surely applies worldwide, doing simple ratios for large land masses gives only a gross outline of the problem. Much depends on how priests and people are distributed.

A great deal also depends on one's experience. Hoge said that *priest shortage* can be defined in three ways. The first is statistical, and such a measure, "objective and simple, leads us to conclude that the United States faces no priest shortage relative to other parts of the world."

The second definition has to do with "the *feeling* of lay Catholics in one nation or another that a priest shortage exists. For anyone to feel there is a shortage, he or she would have had to experience a situation in which more priests were available, either in their own nation at an earlier time or in another nation." That, of course, describes the case in the United States, where, Hoge points out, "there was no discussion of a 'priest shortage' until the 1980s," when changes under way "began to produce a perception of shortage."

The third definition "derives from opportunities lost," or "not having enough priests to do what is needed." Countries in Africa or India, where millions are either joining or poised to join the church, could use far more priests than they currently have. So why should they send their priests to the United States? Isn't that depriving poor but growing churches of essential leadership? The answer, said Hoge, has to do with the expectations of such churches and with money. First, Catholics in many areas of the developing world have never known Catholicism with the kind of priest-rich parish structure that the United States has experienced, "and furthermore, in many of those countries there is not enough money to sustain a large cadre of priests. . . . Poor nations cannot support a large priesthood."

Hoge draws another correlation that may be instructive: areas of the world with the highest gross national product per capita (the United States, Canada, Europe, Oceania, Australia) are all losing priests, while some of the poorest countries are ordaining large numbers. "In sum: the wealthy nations have the money, and the poor nations have the people and the seminarians."

The definition which most influences attitudes is the second one, how people feel about conditions in the church, and one need only consider the reactions bishops have faced to closing parishes because of the priest shortage to understand how deeply Catholics feel about regular access to priests and sacraments. "The laity want more sacraments, more presence of priests and more priestly services such as weddings and baptisms," Hoge writes, while "the priests desire to pastor one parish and not more than one; and the bishops want enough capable priests to staff the parishes for which they are responsible. It is a lose-lose situation."

Mark Gray, director of Catholic polls for CARA, points out: "Many compare the church today in the United States with the way it functioned in the 1950s and 1960s, when, indeed, there were large numbers of priests. Yet these two decades are really the exception rather than the rule, and in no other span in church history in the United States has this country experienced such an abundance of clergy. If you start from the highest point, you will always notice the steepest decline."[5]

Nine Alternatives

Hoge advances nine possible alternatives to the status quo, ranging from "large departures from present-day disciplines" to much smaller initiatives, several of which have already taken hold.

The most obvious step is to try harder to recruit more seminarians. However, he notes, the Catholic Church is already trying harder than any other denomination to recruit seminarians, and while there are tiny increases here and there, the efforts are nowhere close to producing the tripling of ordinations that would be necessary to reverse current trends. "Recruitment should continue, but taken alone it is not a solution."

Another obvious step would be making celibacy optional for diocesan priests, a move that is favored by a majority of U.S. Catholics (71 percent in 2006) but that the hierarchy won't consider. It is unlikely, given the makeup of the U.S. hierarchy at the moment, that any U.S. bishop would advance the cause, and far more unlikely that anyone in the Vatican would entertain such a proposal.

Hoge notes, "There is no occupation in America except Catholic priest or sister that demands a lifelong promise." Protestant denominations don't require such a promise because they have "a lower theology of ordination" that doesn't involve ontological differences or sacramental significance. Still, he wonders if "an honorable discharge" for priests could be considered, even though it would require "an adjustment in the theology of priesthood." The adjustment, he said, would be "less drastic than some other options."

One of those other options is to ordain women, a prospect that Hoge said was also favored by a majority of lay Catholics in earlier studies. In reality, however, polls of lay Catholics have no effect on the hierarchy. If the prospects for optional celibacy for men are dim, the chance of the church endorsing women's ordination might exist, at this point in church history, in some parallel universe, but here on earth women priests exist only outside the Catholic Church's formal institutional structure.

Bringing in foreign priests seems to be one of the top options in use today. The numbers have been increasing each year, though as Hoge points out it is a solution that carries with it a number of problems. "From the point of view of American priests and laity, the most serious of these are: inadequate English skills, cultural misunderstandings, and a too-conservative ecclesiology. From the point of view of the foreign-born priests themselves, the main problems are inadequate orientation to American culture and the ways of the American church, lack of appreciation and respect by American priests, and unfair treatment by diocesan leaders in placements and appointments." It is only fair to mention that in my travels in 2009 and 2010, it was clear that some dioceses were learning from their experiences with foreign priests and employing sophisticated orientation processes and follow-up to alleviate some of the problems.

Increasing the number of lay ministers working in parishes and expanding the permanent diaconate are two alternatives that appear to be in full use today. More than thirty-one thousand lay ecclesial ministers were working twenty hours or more a week in the church in 2008, and another ten thousand were in training. In 2009–10 CARA identified 266 active lay ecclesial ministry formation programs that were of at least two years' duration and that provided training for professional lay ecclesial ministry.

The permanent diaconate has been restored in recent years as a discrete office open only to men, including married men (who are prohibited from remarrying should their spouse die). The number of permanent deacons has expanded dramatically in the United States during the last thirty-five years, from 898 in 1975 to 16,649 in 2010, or nearly half the world's total of 36,539. According to the latest CARA figures, twenty-one dioceses in the United States now have more than two hundred deacons. Chicago, with 646, Trenton, with 442, and Galveston-Houston, with 383, lead all others. According to a CARA survey, 80 percent of the deacons are in active ministry. Some dioceses now have more permanent deacons than priests, and Gautier expects that to be the case nationally in the not too distant future.

Hoge's last two alternatives are to bring in more married priests from the Anglican communion, an option that seems unlikely to produce the numbers necessary, and to expand the pastoral provision allowing married Protestant ministers to become Catholic priests so that it covers married Catholic priests. Allowing married Catholic priests to return to active ministry, he said, has the potential to provide a quick boost in numbers. It is a suggestion, alas, that is as likely to be taken seriously in the Vatican as suggesting a woman for pope.

"In addition to these nine options, there is yet another," writes Hoge. "Do nothing. But it isn't very attractive, because present trends predict unhappy priests, unhappy lay persons, and institutional inertia."

The Catholic Exodus

Another area of Catholic statistics that seems to uphold the "bikini theory" is the concern over the number of Catholics leaving the church and the significance of that trend. In reporting on the In Search of the Emerging Church series, my travels took me to Cleveland, Newark, Albuquerque, Las Cruces, San Diego, San Francisco, Camden, and the Washington DC area. I often had off-the-record conversations with ordinary Catholics, more than a few times around a dinner table, and more often than not the conversation would turn to the numbers leaving the church. It was all anecdotal and usually about friends of a certain ilk—the "had it" Catholics, for lack of a better designation—who had reached the end of their rope with either boring homilies or what they perceived as single-issue politics, or a sense that the church would never fully accept women. Others were angry at the ongoing sex abuse crisis and what some viewed as a continuing abuse of power. The list of gripes, of course, could go on and on.

It was easy to develop the impression that the church is hemorrhaging people, some of its most involved and committed. A lot of mainline Protestant pastors in those cities would agree. Every diocese, it seems, has its parish of last resort for Catholics who are clinging to church membership by their fingernails. Every city of any size also seems to have its Episcopal, Lutheran, Disciples of Christ, United Methodist, Presbyterian, or Unitarian Universalist congregation that is the beneficiary of the Catholic fallout.

That anecdotal sense of things received a shot of credibility with the 2008 report by the Pew Forum on Religion and Public Life titled "Faith in Flux: Changes in Religious Affiliation in the U.S.," which showed that of those raised Catholic, only 68 percent remain Catholic. Fifteen percent remain Christian but now identify themselves as Protestant, with 9 percent members of Evangelical Protestant churches, 5 percent in mainline Protestant churches, and 1 percent in historic black Protestant churches. A total of 14 percent are now unaffiliated, while 3 percent had joined another faith.

The numbers sound foreboding. Those who have left Catholicism outnumber those who have joined the church by an almost four-to-one margin. Slightly more than one in ten American adults has left the Catholic Church after having been raised Catholic, while only 2.6 percent of adults have become Catholic after having been raised something other than Catholic.

For illustration's sake, consider that the adult population of the United States was 228.1 million in 2008. So, if one out of ten U.S. adults was a former Catholic, that 22.8 million would make ex-Catholics, taken as a denomination, the second largest in the country behind the Catholic Church, which lists 68.1 million members, according to the National Council of Churches' (NCC's) *2010 Yearbook of American and Canadian Churches.* The ex-Catholics would far outnumber the next largest denomination, Southern Baptists, who claim 16.2 million adherents.

The gloomy statistics don't end there. Forty eight percent of Catholics who are now unaffiliated, according to Pew, left the church before reaching the age of eighteen. The same goes for one-third of those now Protestant. "Among both groups, an additional three in 10 left the Catholic Church as young adults between ages 18 and 23. Only a fifth of those who are now unaffiliated, and one third who are now Protestant, left after turning 24."

In other words a great deal of the drain from Catholicism is occurring among those who are much younger than Vatican II–era Catholics and their longstanding debates over the direction of the church. A large majority (71 percent) of former Catholics who are now unaffiliated say the move from Catholicism occurred as a gradual drifting away. The same goes for 54 percent of those who left for a Protestant denomination.

What all of this means to the future of Catholicism isn't clear. If the numbers sound ominous, it is only recently that they have caught the attention of the Catholic hierarchy. In October 2010 a spokesperson for the U.S. Conference of Catholic Bishops, in answer to a question, told me that no one in the conference is studying the phenomenon. Archbishop Timothy Dolan of New York told an interviewer in 2009, "It scares the life out of me when I find out that the second most identifiable religious grouping on the religious landscape of the United States are people who say, 'I used to be Catholic.' We have to say, 'No, look, there is no such thing as a former Catholic. Your Catholicism is, as a matter of fact, in your DNA.'"[6] It was a concern he would list as a top priority when he was elected president of the National Conference of Catholic Bishops (NCCB) the following year.

One reason the trend has maintained a low profile might be that even though the church seems to be hemorrhaging members, its bottom line hasn't changed much. In fact, the 2010 figures by the NCC show the total Catholic population up 1.49 percent over 2009. How precise those figures are is open to question. The *Official Catholic Directory*'s 2010 figure was 65.6 million, some 2.5 million fewer than the NCC's total.

The important thing is that in the calculations of both organizations the Catholic population has been expanding steadily in real numbers. The reason given by everyone for the growth is immigration. In her assessment of the most current figures, The Rev. Eileen W. Lindner, editor of the NCC's yearbook, said that the "largest plurality of immigrants to the U.S. in the last 50 years have been Christian in their religious affiliation," and that the influx of "robust Christian communities among new immigrants" has profoundly affected the Christian faith community in the United States.[7]

Gray of CARA wouldn't get too gloomy over the losses or too giddy over the growth. What is happening, he claims, is fairly consistent with what has gone on historically. The reason the Catholic Church's numbers draw such notice when someone does a study is because the church is, by far, the largest denomination. In an extended essay on the CARA website, he points out that the percentage of those raised Catholic who eventually leave the faith—32 percent—is actually a far lower percentage than that of most mainline denominations. For example, according to Gray, of those raised Presbyterian, 59 percent have left that denomination; 56 percent of Anglican/Episcopal Church members have left; 54 percent of Methodists; 42 percent of Lutherans; and 39 percent of Baptists. Only Mormons (28 percent) and those of the Jewish faith (26 percent) have a lower rate than Catholics of people leaving.

What's more, he argues, the Catholic retention rate is especially remarkable in recent years because "the church, in the last decade, could not have had a bigger public relations nightmare than it had and the retention rate hasn't changed. Remarkably, Catholics have stayed, mass attendance hasn't declined, and the population continues to grow." In fact, in the Pew survey, only 2 percent of those who have left listed the sex abuse scandal as the cause.

Gray also believes that if those percentages remain stable, as they have for decades, the church will continue to grow significantly in the future simply because of the growth in both the native U.S. and immigrant populations. Researchers have known about the exodus of Catholics and others from their first denominations to another or to unaffiliated status for some time. Some of it may be explained by the decline in participation in civic and other traditional organizations that the general culture has experienced since the 1960s, he said.

What really concerns Gray, however, is the "sacramental data," that is, the numbers that show a falling rate in baptisms, some of which is related to a falling rate of fertility, but some of which is also linked to the exodus of Catholics. The drop in the number receiving later sacraments—first communion, first confession, confirmation, and marriage—is even more problematic, he said, because those numbers indicate that parents aren't following up with sacraments later in childhood. "Marriage is one of the [sacraments] most strongly affected. The number of marriages is so much lower than the number of the Catholics in church" would indicate. "It's not that Catholics aren't being married," said Gray, "it's that they are choosing to marry outside the church."

He noted that key generational differences also show a pattern. In the Vatican II generation, born between 1943 and 1960, 91 percent were confirmed after receiving first communion and first confession. Confirmation is seen as an important marker for showing decline in reception of sacraments. In the post–Vatican II generation, born 1961–81, or Generation X, the number confirmed had dropped to 79 percent. Among the Millennial generation, born 1982 or later, only 69 percent had been confirmed. Although the Catholic bottom line may be stable thanks to immigration, there is clearly a "lack of shepherding young Catholics into the faith," said Gray.

If loosening connections to traditional institutions explains a lot of the drift away from Catholicism and among other denominations, it doesn't explain everything. Among those former Catholics now unaffiliated, according to the Pew study, 56 percent said they were unhappy with teachings on abortion and homosexuality; 48 percent were unhappy with teachings on birth control; 39 percent were unhappy with how the church treated women; and 33 percent were unhappy with teachings on divorce and remarriage. Among those who became Protestants, 70 percent said they found a denomination they liked more; 43 percent were unhappy with church teachings about the Bible; and 32 percent were dissatisfied with the atmosphere at Catholic worship services.

Lower in the rankings of reasons for leaving (percentages ranged from low teens to mid-twenties) were the clergy sex abuse scandal; clerical celibacy; married someone from a different faith; dissatisfaction with clergy; and unhappiness with teachings on poverty, war, and the death penalty.

So, while the "churn" in the Catholic world may be no different percentage-wise from that of other denominations, the fact that the Catholic universe is so large means that the percentages represent millions for whom dissatisfaction with church teachings and practice were among the reasons for leaving.

The New Immigrant Church

Even in those places where the numbers aren't grim and the mood isn't experimental, the situation is hardly static. In the Archdiocese of Newark,[8] overseen by an archbishop who has a reputation as a staunch traditionalist and also has the rare situation of having more priests than parishes, many of the presumptions and practices of the past are quickly fading. The impressive, block-long sweep of the Cathedral Basilica of the Sacred Heart in downtown Newark is at once a symbol of the constancy of the church and a remnant of a previous Catholic age and of an earlier era of immigrants. Gone are the days of outsized brick-and-mortar dreams and a church built on the experiences and ambitions of Western European Catholics. This is the day of a new immigrant church made up of poor and often undocumented from around the world. The globalized church takes on an urgent reality in this beleaguered city. In the more than half a century since the cathedral was dedicated, the changes in the church in Newark have been so dramatic that the cathedral might be one of the few remaining elements that would be recognizable to those white men, steeped in Irish and Anglican religious experience, who initially conceived of it.

The Catholic community today in this city and many of its nearby environs constitutes, for the most part, a brown palette, where the shades range from light coffee to deep dark chocolate. The people are from everywhere; the diversity is overwhelming. In Newark, as in Los Angeles, Sunday mass is celebrated in more than sixty languages. In less than a week's period I met a pastor, a native of Uganda, who arrived in Newark by way of a Trappist monastery in Kenya; another pastor was from Southern Spain. Another associate pastor, a native of El Salvador, arrived fifteen years earlier as a teenager and illegal refugee and managed to become a citizen and then a priest. A small Latin mass chapel was run by a young Austrian priest, and an Italian was heading up the large representation of the Neocatechumenate movement in the archdiocese. In one rectory five employees hailed from five different countries, all first generation. Religious sisters, fewer in number perhaps than in the past, are leaders in ways they never were, effectively heading up parishes (though without title) and running extensive ministries and outreach to the poor.

The presumption in some parishes in the inner city is that a large percentage of the congregation is made up of undocumented immigrants. The immigrant detention center in Elizabeth, New Jersey, is a constant point of reference and ministry for some parishes and Catholic social outreach agencies.

Archbishop John J. Myers can view the cathedral's Vermont granite from a large porthole-type window in his third-floor office. With obvious pride he calls the cathedral "one of the great churches in the Western hemisphere." During an interview, however, the current reality of this densely packed archdiocese is at the forefront. Myers came to Newark from Peoria, Illinois, where as bishop he oversaw a diocese of twenty-six counties that had a total area larger than the entire state of New Jersey. In all of that real estate back in Illinois, there were only 169,375 Catholics, 12 percent of the population. It was easier to maintain order and keep track of things. Newark's 1.3 million Catholics make up 47 percent of the total population of the archdiocese, and that may be a low estimate given the large number of undocumented who come to church but don't register. Myers said the church works on a kind of don't-ask-don't-tell policy when it comes to undocumented immigrants. "The Lord said, 'Go and carry the Gospel to all nations. All the nations came to us,'" said Myers. "We get to learn to live with that."

Newark, anomalous as it may be in some ways, could hold answers for the future. This is not a church in a city that has permanently emptied out, as has occurred in so many other old inner cities. Instead, it is more a church in the city with an ever-shifting and very poor, often undocumented membership. The problem here is not lack of priests or population, said Myers, it's a lack of money. The archdiocese can't afford to keep pumping millions of dollars in subsidies into parishes that can't sustain themselves.

"I'll say a couple of things that we can foresee happening," said auxiliary Bishop Edgar da Cunha of Brazil, who heads an archdiocesan reorganization plan called New Energies. "One is we're no longer going to have the ethnic churches and national churches as we used to have. Now we have more integration. We have a parish that has Mass in Italian, Spanish, Portuguese, English, and Korean."

Part of the integration includes far more priests from other countries than was previously the case. "I think that integration brings the new dimension to the church. We have also seen, and we are working towards people seeing a wider view of church rather than 'My little world here. My parish is my little world and we are self-contained here.' We are trying to help people look beyond that parochial vision of 'It's just my parish, leave me alone with it.' We have people exchanging ministries and parishes exchanging ministries, reaching out to others. Suburban parishes are reaching out to inner-city parishes, and inner-city parishes are sharing ministries with other suburban parishes. There is that view of the church as more than just the small cluster of a parish."

The data and the experience of people in the pews are of a church undergoing an era of change for which there is no blueprint. "Pastoral leaders are living into the new realities that face them," says Jewell in a 2009 talk. "There is a palpable sense of longing for hope and support." In that hope they can call on the words of the U.S. bishops themselves, who have recognized some of the shifts under way. The greatest challenge in meeting the future, the bishops wrote in "Called and Gifted for the Third Millennium," their November 1995 pastoral letter, "is the need to foster respectful collaboration, leading to mutual support in ministry, between clergy and laity for the sake of Christ's Church and its mission to the world. This is a huge task requiring changes in patterns of reflection, behavior and expectation among the clergy and laity alike."

Lay people who are being cast in new roles and asked to take on new responsibilities "have a growing understanding," said Jewell, "sometimes more accurately described as the barest of glimmers—that the answers will not come from outside of themselves."

Chapter 3

THE SEX ABUSE CRISIS BEGINS

Tom Fox, editor of the *National Catholic Reporter*, was driving home from the Kansas City Airport in late March 2010, having just returned from Germany, when he punched the number into his cell phone for colleague Arthur Jones and said, "Dear God, Arthur, will this story never end?"

The Archdiocese of Munich—once headed by Archbishop Joseph Ratzinger, now Pope Benedict XVI—was facing a mounting revulsion against a priest, a serial pedophile, who had been approved for service in the diocese during Ratzinger's tenure, even though it was known that the priest had previously abused children. Fox had traveled there to report on the growing outrage over the revelations.

Fox and Jones can use such shorthand as "this story" and understand each other perfectly. The two of them, along with New Orleans freelance writer and author Jason Berry, probably have more experience covering the sex abuse scandal than any other journalists in the country. While the story blew up in a new way in 2002 with the revelations of abuse and cover-up by the *Boston Globe,* Fox and Jones first learned about the scandal in the early 1980s and the two, as *NCR*'s editor and Washington Bureau Chief respectively at the time, made the decision to run the first national story about the crisis in the issue of June 7, 1985.

Other topics—the civil wars in Central America, economic injustice, nuclear brinkmanship, and internal church debates over married priests, ordination of women, liturgy, the politics of abortion, and the church's stance toward homosexuals—would claim a fair amount of space in the pages of *NCR* over the years. No other single story, however, would so persistently demand attention or draw energy and time away from other reporting pursuits during the next twenty-five years as the sex abuse scandal.

"Sex abuse scandal" is a convenient journalistic tag that's attached itself to a much deeper, ongoing problem that has far more to do with power and authority and how they are used in the church than it has to do with sex. The scandal long ago ceased to be primarily about individual abusers and their wanton acts and became centered on the behavior of the hierarchy in particular and the Catholic clerical culture more generally.

The scandal doesn't claim any particular place on the liberal-conservative spectrum; it defies ideology and ecclesiological preferences. It is neither pre– nor post–Vatican II; it fits into no one's ideas of what a church should be or how its ministers should act. The reporting on the scandal bared the fact that a significant number of men who were charged with spiritual leadership of the Catholic community had egregiously sinned against its children. More important in terms of the scandal's longevity is the fact that the reporting also showed that bishops, the chief teachers of the community, in effect rejected their own teaching, hiding serial molesters and rapists of children and teens and often trivializing the claims of families and victims who tried to call attention to the abuse.

The bishops' repeated protestations to the contrary notwithstanding, a close reading of the record will show that in the U.S. church, at least, the bishops knew a lot about sex abuse, the dynamics of abusers and its dangers to the community long before the *Boston Globe*'s investigations.

Fr. Gerald Fitzgerald, founder of the Servants of the Paraclete, understood that sexual abusers should be immediately removed from ministry, not transferred from parish to parish or to another diocese. His view was circulating among bishops by the late 1940s.

Fitzgerald was consulted in the 1960s by the Holy Office, precursor to today's Congregation for the Doctrine of the Faith, about what he was discovering.

In that same time period he briefed Pope Paul VI about the problem in a private audience and through a detailed follow-up letter.

Pope John Paul II in 1985 was hand delivered a detailed report on the growing problem in the United States.

As noted above, that was the same year that the first extensive national story detailing reports from around the country was published in the *National Catholic Reporter* along with an editor's note and an accompanying editorial predicting the drain on the church's treasury and credibility if the bishops did not alter their manner of dealing with abusive priests and their victims.

Also in 1985 the U.S. bishops received an extensive "manual" outlining the scope of the problem and suggestions for how the crisis should be handled by three experts, including two priests and a civil lawyer. They did nothing with it.

The sex abuse crisis is not usually spoken about as a force that will shape the future of the Catholic community, but as the scandal continues to move across the globe, the diversion of time, money, and talent needed to deal with it already has had a deep effect on the life of the community. It has disrupted church life from the pews to the papal palace. In the United States alone, payouts to victims of priest abuse total more than $2.5 billion (*AP*, March 2010). No one yet knows the long-term effect of diocesan bankruptcies and downsizing of personnel, programs, and parishes along with discontinuation of ministries for lack of funds. It has become clear in the ongoing crisis that the scandal is not just an American problem but one that spans borders and cultures. The corruption that fuels the crisis—the sense of entitlement that pervades the hierarchy and its presumption that it is beyond accountability—seeps to the highest levels of the church.

It is essential to deal with the sex abuse crisis and the hierarchy's handling of it when considering the future because the crisis is, as I endeavor to show, symptomatic of deeper problems in the clerical/hierarchical culture. And those problems, which will have a lasting effect on the future, didn't just spring up in 2002 in Boston.

No matter what position one might take on any of the other issues confronting the church—whether you're all in for the most liberal post–Vatican II church imaginable, or you think that Latin and incense mark the path to heaven—the sex abuse crisis rises on the Catholic landscape as a monumental barrier to the future. There's no way to avoid it, and at some point the community will have to reckon with it honestly and in all of its dimensions.

Devising new rules to prevent future abuse and cover-up was essential to dealing with the immediate crisis, but rules don't begin to deal with the more fundamental maladies that surfaced when the abuse and cover-up were exposed.

The scandal has been analogized to a serious wound and to a cancer in the church. The terms are loaded with a sense of threat and danger, and we know that wounds and life-threatening disease do not just disappear because we wish to "get beyond" them. They need attention and treatment.

In that sense, the church is overdue for a reality check on both its diagnosis of the problem and what it is doing to treat more than just visible surface wounds.

Some of the loudest voices in the U.S. episcopal ranks, while diligent in condemning the abuse, argue that the hierarchy has been unfairly targeted. The bishops should take responsibility for their lapses, writes one cardinal, but on the other hand, he argues, the crisis "has been transformed into a scandal of church leadership," as if reporters somehow manufactured tales of episcopal cover-up.[1] Other bishops have pointed to abuse figures among schoolteachers, Boy Scout leaders, and parents themselves to show that the priesthood is no different from any other slice of society when it comes to the percentage of abusers it may have harbored. It has not been lost on the people in the pews that minimizing sin and its effects by comparing its incidence within Catholic circles to that in the wider culture is hardly a strategy bishops condone for the laity.

An often-repeated refrain among church leaders was that so little was known before the 1980s about the psychology of abusers that bishops were acting on their best instincts and on the best legal and psychological counsel available at the time.

There is undoubtedly a certain truth to that last claim—the psychological disciplines were less than precise in assessing the potential for recidivism among abusers, and psychiatry was less than unanimous on how patients should be treated. In fact, a great deal is still unknown about the disease and its myriad layers and manifestations. The truth of the disease's complexity, however, is often stretched to the point of transparency, and what emerges behind that stretched truth is quite another story. In many cases bishops made terrible decisions not so much because they lacked information but more because of whom they chose to hear, what warnings they chose to ignore, and what priorities they chose to act on. Further, these arbiters of public morality, who would instruct youngsters that they should examine their behavior if they're sneaking things or hiding what they are doing from parents and peers, certainly understood that keeping locked files, refusing to inform parishes of a priest's abuse of children or teens, and paying victims huge sums for their silence was a sure sign that they were engaging in activities terribly out of line with the ethos of a Christian community.

The following sections show that long before the 2002 investigation by the *Boston Globe,* church leaders had access to considerable information and warnings regarding the recidivism of those who sexually abused children and teens and the difficulty in treating them successfully.

I look at several developments in the crisis: the initial coverage by *NCR* and the analysis by editors based on that reporting; other documentation by church and legal professionals, as well as the early insights by the founder of the Servants of the Paraclete, an order dedicated to serving problem priests; the 2005 Philadelphia Grand Jury report and reporting on the scandal in that archdiocese; and details of the case of the late Marcial Maciel Degollado, founder of the controversial Legionaries of Christ. Those episodes in the long history of the crisis illustrate several disturbing realities, among them that church authorities had considerable information on the nature of sex abusers well before and as the scandal was breaking publicly; that those same authorities were deliberate and calculating in using civil law and the privileges granted the church by secular society to protect perpetrators of horrible crimes; and that a charming individual with access to lots of money could, despite a monstrous double life and a trail of abuse, bluff his way to prominence as a conservative champion of orthodoxy and a trusted friend of a pope.

I examine the scandal through the lens of an analysis of the clerical culture, particularly at its hierarchical level, in an attempt to understand how spiritual leaders could act with such callous disregard for the most vulnerable in the community. The examination includes a look at what appears to be a different view of the scandal developing among bishops in other parts of the world, some of whom see the crisis not as an attack engineered by enemies of the church but as a product, perhaps, of an ecclesial culture gone terribly wrong.

The Earliest News Coverage

The editors of *NCR* possessed no secret or advanced knowledge unavailable to bishops in 1985 when they decided to publish that first story in the paper's June 7 issue. However, the unsigned editor's note that preceded the story, as well as the editorial that accompanied it, displayed surprisingly comprehensive understanding of the scope and implications of the scandal. The editors outlined in detail steps that needed to be taken to assure the safety of children and to bring about legal action against perpetrators, many of which could be recognized in the action ultimately taken by the bishops as a group seventeen years later.

Two points that seem relevant to what the bishops knew and how they acted amid the crisis are often left out of the discussion. The first is that while little may have been known about the psychology of abusers and their capacity for deception and horrible behavior, the fact remains that sexual abuse of children has long been a crime. So it would seem that a bishop's decision to send a priest to treatment or continually transfer him to another parish or diocese rather than call the police, while perhaps done out of compassion, suggests a certain conviction that clergy are above the law. That seems especially the case when bishops were dealing with repeat offenders. Indeed, the fear that the church might lose its unwritten but very real special protections by civil law enforcement is referenced repeatedly in documents that have surfaced during litigation.

The second is that hiding serious sin, especially against the young, would seem a fundamental violation of the community's trust and of Catholic sacramental life. If bishops felt justified in hiding the molestation of children by priests, why should anyone else in the community be concerned with the social dimensions of their behavior? Why would the average Catholic feel compelled to be accountable to the larger community if bishops felt free to conceal what one psychologist, a former priest, aptly termed "soul murder?"

The reality is that the sex abuse crisis quickly moved from being about sex, horrible as the abuse is, to a scandal about institutional cover-up. It is that element—the deliberate, calculated, and ongoing hiding of the truth and denigration of those who attempted to bring the truth to light—that sets the church apart from other actors in the wider culture when it comes to its handling of sex abuse. Church authorities are supposed to condemn loudly the kind of behavior exhibited by many individual bishops and by the U.S. Conference of Catholic Bishops as a whole, not excuse and rationalize such actions.

It is beyond question that following the bishops' meeting in Dallas in 2002, during which they passed the Charter for the Protection of Children and Young People, the church established some of the strongest institutional measures possible to protect the young. In that regard the church has become a leader in implementing change and developing educational tools for protecting young people from sexual predators. It is important to note, however, that given the range of abuses uncovered, such a program is a minimal response and that those controls were instituted only after unprecedented public outrage at the church forced the bishops to take action. That has been the case at every step. Church officials do not divulge information. The only reason information comes out is because someone has forced the issue. There is no danger of overstating the case to say that without the persistence and dedication of victims like Barbara Blaine, who founded SNAP in 1989 and is now its president, and David Clohessy, national director of the organization, who has worked closely with her from its earliest days, a large portion of the truth of this awful chapter would still lie hidden in chancery file cabinets.

The story that appeared in 1985, written by Jones and based on the reporting of Berry about the infamous Gauthe case in Lafayette, Louisiana, and on *NCR* reporting in six other states (California, Oregon, Idaho, Wisconsin, Rhode Island, and Pennsylvania), showed the beginning of a national pattern of clerical abuse and cover-up by the hierarchy. The reporting contained shocking revelations, and the decision to publish it did not come easily. A front-page editor's note that ran in that issue reflects the deliberations that preceded the decision to publish. It said that the editors, "in a decision following considerable internal discussion, decided to publish the names of the priests involved, though not those of the boys and their families (except where the family names were already public). In each case these priests have already been named in open court or in legal depositions." Some cases had been mentioned in local publications. "That alone, however, is not justification for in-depth publication in the newspaper," the editorial continued. "Publication at this length comes in order to explain the extent of the serious nature of the problems involved." The details were chilling, and the paragraph introducing those details, while containing a narrative that would become only too familiar over time, was shocking at that point in church history: "Between 1972 and 1983, Father Gilbert Gauthe committed hundreds of sexual acts with dozens of boys in four south Louisiana Catholic parishes. He also took hundreds of pornographic photographs, which have disappeared. The priest, suspended by the Lafayette diocese in 1983, is now in a Connecticut mental facility." These were cases without precedent in U.S. law. Millions of dollars in damage claims were at stake, the story reported, and millions had already been paid out.

The piece that ran over more than four pages of the paper documented case after case of molestations, cover-up, and, in some instances, arrest and prosecution. The outline of a soon-to-be familiar pattern was clear in the accounts: Parents notified church authorities with allegations or suspicions of abuse only to be told that the church would take care of it, or that they were spreading vile rumors about a good man, or that they should be quiet about the matter.

A man in Portland, Oregon, told *NCR*, in an early indication of where Catholic anger and frustration would eventually be focused, that he was finding it more difficult to forgive Portland's chancery officials than he was the priest who sexually abused his son while the boy was a parochial school student. The father had been repeatedly frustrated in attempts to obtain funding for his son's counseling and other assurances from diocesan officials. He and others finally threatened a lawsuit, which led to a financial settlement.

The decision to publish that first story, to be the Catholic paper that would call attention to an ugly reality within the largest religious body in the world, pushed the twenty-year-old *NCR* enterprise to a defining moment. Fox recalls it as a lonely moment. "No other Catholic publication was going to do the story, and the major secular papers weren't going to touch it for fear of being labeled 'anti-Catholic,'" he said. It wasn't a popular story. People within the church accused the paper of seeking to destroy the institution or unnecessarily airing the church's dirty linen in public. "If you compare the reaction in the U.S. church and the wider community in 1985 with the public reaction today, there's a clear contrast," Fox said twenty-five years after the first story appeared. "When I read on National Public Radio on April 2, 2010, the *NCR* editorial calling on Pope Benedict XVI to disclose 'what he knew and when he knew it,' the paper received not derision, but support."

In 1985 the most serious immediate threat to the paper came from within. *NCR* board member Fr. Joseph Fichter, the renowned Jesuit sociologist, advanced a motion at a board meeting seeking a vote of 'no confidence' in Fox for publishing the material. It is to the credit of the other board members that no one seconded Fichter's proposal.[2] That show of support for Fox was also a resounding affirmation of the paper's basic mission. No editor after that would have to worry about ruffling the feathers of authority by reporting a difficult story or one that placed the institution in an unflattering light. It was understood that such stories were sometimes the product of the charge the paper's founders put to themselves: "To report the life of the church in the world . . . to press for as much information as can be had about events and their meaning."

Fichter resigned immediately and left the board. The Jesuit's reaction was understandable. As a sociologist and a priest, he could not accept that the numbers were as bad as the *NCR* story claimed. As the story advanced over the decades, of course, the numbers became much worse. The scandal took on international proportions and is yet without resolution.

Fox went on to become the newspaper's publisher and CEO, and in recent years returned as editor.

Seventeen years before the *Boston Globe* wrote about the Boston archdiocese's pedophilia crisis, and brought about the removal of Cardinal Bernard Law, the editor's note preceding that first story in *NCR* began: "In cases throughout the nation, the Catholic Church is facing scandals and being forced to pay out millions of dollars in claims to families whose sons have been molested by Catholic priests."

The note continued in bullet points that explained what was to follow in the article and advised: "Along with the rest of society, the church must examine the issues of child abuse, drawing most critical attention to those aspects of the problem involving church figures and structures that have victimized the young and their families."

The paper warned of the possibility of class-action suits from parents; exorbitant insurance premiums for all dioceses resulting from the current crop of civil and criminal cases; possible criminal liability of bishops who fail to take action; the loss of privacy for diocesan personnel files; cases testing the statutes of limitations in various states; and cases in the future based on the fact that church authorities "failed to provide a mechanism to safeguard the children after an initial complaint against a priest."

Seventeen years before the story was taken up by the major press, the editors of *NCR* concluded their note with this observation: "Yet the tragedy, and scandal, as *NCR* sees it, is not only with the actions of the individual priests—these are serious enough—but with church structures in which bishops, chanceries, and seminaries fail to respond to complaints, or even engage in cover-ups; sadly, keeping the affair quiet has usually assumed greater importance than any possible effect on the victims themselves."

The analysis was unusually prescient and outlined nearly all of the problems that would come to haunt the church to the present day.

A back-page editorial accompanying the June 1985 report laid out the scenario as the editors saw it from that initial investigation, and their observations would hold up as a characterization of the abuse saga for years to come: "Who's involved here, and what patterns of conduct emerge after events are looked at? Children, of course, are the most immediate victims. Traumatized, guilt-ridden, even suicidal, they are terrified by the idea of discussing what has happened to them with parents or other authority figures. Next, parents become victims, usually finding out what has happened to their children late in the game. Emotionally, they are tossed about by a variety of feelings: guilt for not having protected their offspring, anger at the priest who inflicted the harm and a sense of awkwardness for having to confront, in one way or another, a person they were trained to respect as a unique mediator of God's grace and love. Then, there are the ecclesial functionaries: the pastor, bishop and sometimes religious superior. In almost every case, these officials seem to follow an unwritten set of guidelines: Assure the parents everything will be taken care of. Caution them against getting an attorney, and by all means, plead with them not to go to the press."

If it seemed likely that parents might take legal action, the editorial continued, then bishops called in the priest and the diocesan attorneys but "never, under any circumstances, [would they] write or communicate with the parents." The bishops instead opted for "legal defense, not moral intervention."

The editors posed questions to the bishops: "What is this newspaper, or a diocesan chancery or a pastor supposed to advise the next parent who calls and says, 'I think my child has been molested?' Where can a parent turn and not be met with the pattern of episcopal evasion all too apparent in this week's accounts?"

The piece ended with suggestions, including more effective screening in seminaries and special seminary programs on sexuality to aid the development of emotionally healthy priests.

Principal among the suggestions was the development of "ministerial boards," much like the review boards that grew out of the 2002 meeting in Dallas, to deal specifically with clergy sex abuse. The editors recommended that the boards include psychiatrists, social workers, staff from facilities that deal with troubled priests, clergy, laity, and "at least one attorney." The boards should be able to make independent recommendations. "Most important, parents should have access to the board without previous consultation with their pastor or bishop."

While the behavior of some church leaders reflected behavior in the general society, the editorial said, "the church should lead social behavior, not reflect it, when it comes to seeking solutions."

Repeat sexual offenders among the clergy ranks "must be separated from the rest of society, as any offenders must be," the editors wrote. They also asked whether clerical offenders should be prosecuted under civil law and whether they should forfeit their priestly ministries or be sent into seclusion in a remote place or a monastery.

The realities were stark and disturbing, the solutions difficult, running up against ingrained habits and secrecy of the powerful clerical culture.

"It is only in tackling such traumatic realities," the editors concluded, "that the church becomes the example that benefits the society."

One can only wonder today what might have been different had the hierarchy at that time taken such questions seriously and acted on them rather than waiting for the 2002 blowup when the full force of the secular press, with its considerable human and financial resources, shined the light on the problem.

It is no mystery to Fox why it took the wider culture seventeen years to catch up with the story. "Today, the default position is that there is considerable clergy sex abuse that's gone on, and it's been documented and detailed to such a degree that it is a solid case," he said in a 2010 interview.[3] "But in 1984 and 1985, the default was that our priests were spotless, sanctified carriers of grace, celebrants of the sacrifice of the mass. There was a Bing Crosby, "Bells of St. Mary's" image to the priests. In that context the priest was able to say the victim is making it up and that the victim was trying to ruin his reputation, and he was readily believed." Such was also the presumption of the paper's readers, he said. Catholics of that era were educated to see priests as something other than ordinary lay people. Priests stood in the place of Christ, special mediators between the human community and the divine, and so it was not remarkable that many Catholics simply believed priests incapable of such horrible abuse. Perhaps there was the occasional bad apple, but not a pattern of abuse and cover-up that would widely implicate the leadership of the church.

Fox gives credit to Berry for drawing *NCR* into the story with his coverage of the Louisiana case. The first major *NCR* stories were based on Berry's reporting for a series that first ran in the *Times of Acadiana* in Lafayette, Louisiana. At the same time, *NCR* began hearing about other cases going to court or being settled in various parts of the country. "We had to overcome our own incredulity," Fox said, "because the assumption was that this couldn't be as pervasive as we thought, but the evidence kept emerging that it was."

Once the paper published the first story, it became inundated with accounts. Some weeks, Fox said, *NCR* would run a half dozen or so reports on different aspects of the crisis. There were times when he also became convinced that the sex abuse crisis was overwhelming everything else. "We were trying to figure out exactly what pedophilia was. It was a word that previously no one outside the psychological disciplines had heard of. At least a dozen times over the course of our years of coverage, I can remember saying, 'For the next three months we will simply not write about this.' And then something would come up that was so compelling, so outrageous, or so pathetic that justice demanded we cover it."

Other outlets, both Catholic and secular, "had to overcome their own incredulity, and then they had to face the consequences—what would happen if they as local papers took on the problem." In the early 1990s, Fox added, the major weekly news magazines began covering the crisis "and that began to chip away at the church defenses."

Fox became a kind of pariah in some church circles. He recalls attending a regional meeting of the Catholic Press Association where a bishop present let people know that he was uncomfortable being at the same meeting with Fox because of *NCR*'s coverage of the abuse crisis. Those attending became so upset at the obvious tension that they asked the two men to go off by themselves to have a conversation to see if they could work things out. Fox recalls that while he didn't necessarily convince the bishop of the paper's point of view, "we spent a couple of hours talking together and I thought that I was able to convey to him the truthfulness of our intent as journalists . . . that this was not being done out of malice but because this was a very, very important story for the church."

"A debt is owed to a brave little paper called the *National Catholic Reporter*," *The New York Times* declared in a 1993 editorial.

"Eight years ago the paper jumped into the story when much of the press was afraid to go near it." That was one of a number of accolades that would come the paper's way from other press outlets over the course of the paper's coverage.

NCR may have exhibited exemplary journalism, but the bishops weren't buying any of it. In answer to a question, Fox said that in all the years the paper covered the crisis, he never received a request from a bishop for a briefing on the matter or an invitation to discuss the issue. As is often the case in such circumstances, the messenger, not the truth conveyed in the reporting, became the focus of hierarchical anger. *NCR* was suddenly unwelcome on parish newsstands, a key point of exposure and bulk sales at the time, and Fox said that some bishops attempted to force the publication to remove the word *Catholic* from its name. Even so, it would continue to publish difficult stories with gut-wrenching descriptions of abuse and accounts of maddening official cover-up. The sex abuse crisis was, indeed, a cancer, and as continuing reporting shows, it has metastasized throughout the body of the church. It knows no boundaries, and it keeps running ahead of the efforts to contain or control it.

Other Early Warnings

By most accounts the vision driving Fr. Gerald Fitzgerald's ambition in 1947, when he founded the religious order Servants of the Paraclete, was to provide a place for treatment and healing of priests troubled by alcoholism and other substance abuse. Along the way he inadvertently became the founder of an order that dealt with priests afflicted by sexual disorders, particularly priests who sexually abused young people.

Not long after he opened a facility in New Mexico and word of the ministry started circulating among the hierarchy, bishops began to send priests who had sexually abused youngsters. Fr. Liam Hoare, vicar general of the order in 2010, said Fitzgerald, a deeply devout man who believed that the cure for alcoholism and other problems was prayer life and spirituality, never anticipated dealing with sexually abusive priests.

The priests showed up by bus and train, according to Hoare, and often the bishops never informed the Paracletes of the true nature of the priests' problems. "Back in the '40s," Hoare told a reporter, "nobody talked about this. You can't look at it through 2010 lenses."[4] In a 1948 letter to a priest who apparently had had sexual contact with youngsters and was seeking to return to Via Coeli, Fitzgerald responded that "it is now a fixed policy of our house to refuse problem cases that involve abnormalities of sex." That rule seems not to have remained absolute, since Fitzgerald continues to speak of the issue in correspondence with bishops and others in subsequent years. In that 1948 letter, however, he tells the priest of his hope of acquiring "in the not too distant future" an isolated island or mountain retreat, far from civilization, where "under the direction of a couple of saintly priests, the particular problem I envisage you as facing can be dealt with in a manner which is not possible here in a house of this nature."

Fitzgerald never got his refuge. In 1965, with Byrne's approval, he put a five thousand dollar deposit on an island in Barbados, near Carriacou, in the Caribbean that was for sale for fifty thousand dollars. But Byrne's successor wanted nothing to do with owning an island, and Fitzgerald, who died in 1969, was forced to sell his long-sought means for isolating priest sex offenders.

As he became more familiar with the problem of clergy sex abuse, Fitzgerald began to talk about the condition and its implications quite a bit. He corresponded with bishops and priests and wasn't hesitant to express his frustration with and disdain for priests "who have seduced or attempted to seduce little boys or girls." Fitzgerald's growing awareness of the problem and his strong convictions on the matter are contained in a cache of documents that include letters to numerous bishops, and to at least one Vatican dicastery, as well as to Pope Paul VI (a follow-up to a personal audience with the pope). The documents were unsealed in 2007 as the result of a court order obtained by the Beverly Hills law firm of Kiesel, Boucher & Larson. The documents had previously been used in a variety of cases to show that church leaders knew about the behavior of sex abusers long before the 1980s.[5] It appears from the documentation that by at least 1952, five years after he opened his ministry at Via Coeli, Fitzgerald was informing bishops of the need to remove child abusers from ministry. In a letter that year to the bishop of Reno, Nevada, Fitzgerald wrote:

"I myself would be inclined to favor laicization for any priest, upon objective evidence, for tampering with the virtue of the young, my argument being, from this point onward the charity to the Mystical Body should take precedence over charity to the individual and when a man has so far fallen away from the purpose of the priesthood, the very best that should be offered him is his Mass in the seclusion of a monastery."

He added that "real conversions will be found to be extremely rare. . . . Hence, leaving them on duty or wandering from diocese to diocese is contributing to scandal or at least to the approximate danger of scandal." In this particular case Fitzgerald's advice was ignored and the priest was allowed to continue in ministry. He was ultimately accused of abusing numerous children, and the church ended up paying out huge sums in court awards.

In a 1957 letter to a bishop that he addresses as "Most Dear Cofounder," presumably his friend Byrne of Santa Fe, he wrote, regarding those who abuse children: "These men, Your Excellency, are devils and the wrath of God is upon them and if I were a bishop I would tremble when I failed to report them to Rome for involuntary layization [sic]." He continued later in the letter: "It is for this class of rattlesnake I have always wished the island retreat—but even an island is too good for these vipers of whom the Gentle Master said it were better they had not been born— this is an indirect way of saying damned, is it not?"

He told a bishop wishing to place a priest who had a history of molesting young girls that the Paracletes had "adopted a definite policy not to recommend to bishops men of this character, even presuming the sincerity of their conversion. We feel that the protection of our glorious priesthood will demand, in time, the establishment of a uniform code of discipline and of penalties."

Fitzgerald acknowledged the special treatment that abusing priests received both from civil law enforcement and church authorities. "We are amazed to find how often a man who would be behind bars if he were not a priest is entrusted with the *cura animarum* [the care of souls]."

It is evident from the correspondence that Fitzgerald was in communication with the highest levels of the church and that Vatican officials were apparently concerned as early as 1962 about the problem of clerical sex abuse. In April 1962 Fitzgerald responded to an inquiry about abusive priests from the Congregation of the Holy Office, overseen by the powerful Cardinal Alfredo Ottaviani. The office was a precursor to today's Congregation for the Doctrine of the Faith.

In a wide-ranging letter Fitzgerald voiced his concerns about "immaturity" in priests the center was treating, argued for laicization of those who abuse children, and added, "we feel strongly that such unfortunate priests should be given the alternative of a retired life within the protection of monastery walls or complete laicization."

The following year Fitzgerald was granted a personal audience with the newly elected Pope Paul VI to inform him about his work and the problems he perceived in the priesthood. Personal audiences with a pope are difficult to come by in any age, and that the priest from New Mexico was able to secure one suggests that something important was afoot. In a follow-up letter to the visit, Fitzgerald wrote: "Personally I am not sanguine of the return of priests to active duty who have been addicted to abnormal practices, especially sins with the young. However, the needs of the church must be taken into consideration and an activation of priests who have seemingly recovered in this field may be considered but it is only recommended where careful guidance and supervision is possible. Where there is indication of incorrigibility, because of the tremendous scandal given, I would most earnestly recommend total laicization."

Like so much else in the U.S. church, Fitzgerald's vision was blindsided and nearly destroyed by a malady that was mostly hidden, though very real, at the time. The record that he leaves behind shows that he may have been naive in his wish for isolating offenders and treating them by spiritual means alone. It also clearly establishes, however, that he understood the intractability of the disease and its potential for damaging child victims and for compromising the church. Most important, it shows that he expressed his opinion widely to the U.S. hierarchy and beyond. Anyone who chose to hear received a bracing analysis of the problem. His analysis reached the highest levels of church governance when he was sought out for consultation by the Holy Office and Pope Paul VI about the problem he was discovering.

Warnings in the Mid-1980s

A trio of two priests and a civil attorney tried desperately in the mid-1980s to convince the U.S. hierarchy to take concerted action to act compassionately toward victims, to deal with abusers, and to confront the growing scandal head on.

Fr. Thomas Doyle, a Dominican and a canon lawyer working at the time in the Washington offices of the papal pro nuncio, Archbishop Pio Laghi, was one of the first priests in the country to become aware of the growing and national dimensions of the crisis. Another was Fr. Michael Peterson, a psychologist and then director of the St. Luke Institute in Silver Spring, Maryland, a facility that had experience in dealing with priests who sexually abused children. They were drawn together with a civil attorney, Ray Mouton, who was representing Gilbert Gauthe against pedophilia charges in Louisiana. The three eventually compiled a ninety-two-page document that bore the formal title "The Problem of Sexual Molestation by Roman Catholic Clergy: Meeting the Problem in a Comprehensive and Responsible Manner." It must be noted at the outset that one of the presumptions underlying portions of the document was that certain offenders could be rehabilitated to some level of ministry. Overall, however, the report served as a stern warning that an overwhelming scandal was about to break and that the bishops needed to take comprehensive and concerted efforts to get ahead of it.

The collaboration, detailed at length in Berry's *Vows of Silence,* grew out of each man's involvement with the Gauthe case. While much of this period has been dealt with elsewhere, two elements are significant to the questions at hand: what the bishops knew and when they knew it, and how those who sounded the alarm early on were perceived and treated by the bishops.

By his own description Doyle was a "French-cuff" conservative (theologically and politically), an ambitious and amply degreed young cleric who had a bishop's miter in his sights. He loved order, he loved being on the inside, he loved rules. The downside of being on the inside was, in his case, a loss of clerical innocence.

The Gauthe case began to change everything. Bishop Gerard Frey of Lafayette, La., had been warned about Gauthe's abuse of children several times after 1972. Gauthe ultimately admitted to having had sex with thirty-seven boys and was sentenced to prison. The priest had fondled the boys in the confessional, photographed them in sex acts, and had oral sex with them on fishing trips and in his rural rectory.[6] In 1983 three of the young boys who had been abused finally told their father, and he showed up with his lawyer at the chancery office. Gauthe was finally removed from ministry and sent for treatment.

The Gauthe case is now generally considered the beginning of the public unraveling of the nationwide, and later international, priest sex abuse crisis. It was the first time that a civil suit was filed against a diocese for failing to take necessary steps to protect children from a predator.

Doyle, Mouton, and Peterson were in constant contact as the crisis escalated in Lafayette and shocking reports of abuse by priests began surfacing in other states. The three decided, independent of any hierarchical request, to try to put in writing both their observations of the crisis and their suggestions for what might be done to help bishops deal with cases that the three "predicted would start to appear with increasing regularity." Their report went into extensive detail describing the crisis as it was unfolding and implications for the future. It covered civil, criminal, and canon-law questions, clinical and medical aspects of the sexual disorders involved, spiritual as well as public relations concerns, and suggestions for practical steps to be taken to deal with the crisis.

Among the central recommendations of the document was that bishops, as a national group, decide on a coherent strategy. "This is a very new and narrow area of legal jurisprudence which is developing with a very adverse effect upon the church's interests. In addition to the legal issues, there are unique canonical considerations and extremely complex clinical considerations which cannot or should not be addressed in a piecemeal manner," they wrote. Old cases of sex abuse "now carry consequences never before experienced."

Time was of the essence, not only because of the growing legal and financial problems but also because of growing media interest in the scandal. The document put the bishops on notice that the American Bar Association and other groups "comprised primarily of plaintiff lawyers are conducting studies, scheduling panel conferences, and devising other methods of disseminating information about this newly developing area of law." It warned that "potential exposure to the Catholic Church for the continuation of claimants coming forward in legal jurisdictions across the country is very great." They recommended that priests accused of abuse not be permitted to function "in any priestly capacity."

Awareness of sexual abuse of children was reaching new levels, the three wrote, and would continue to escalate in the coming years. "This increased awareness, widespread publicity, and the excellent educational programs available to children, which we all support, shall increase the reporting of such incidents and increase the likelihood that both civil and criminal actions shall be instituted against the offender and those sought to be held legally responsible with the wrongdoer."

The project envisioned by Doyle, Mouton, and Peterson would make "uniform assistance" available to any bishop who wanted it.

The document was by no means as radical a proposal as one Doyle might make today, convinced as he now is that the hierarchy's understanding of the church has "become so distanced from fundamental Christian values that bishops were willing to sacrifice the innocence of the most vulnerable for the protection of the institution" and that the hierarchical style of governance "enabled hierarchs and priests to live under the delusion that because of their holy orders, they are above the law."[7] At the time, however, the proposal, concerned as it was with protecting the image and reputation of the church, was groundbreaking in describing the problem, in seeking transparency from church officials, and in recommending a unified strategy in dealing with it.

Just how forward looking the document was would become apparent seventeen years later when the nation's bishops, having essentially rejected the proposal in part because autonomous bishops were not about to cede any authority to a national approach or to outsiders, would be forced by public outrage to do just that.

In one section the report starkly warns: "Every instance of sexual molestation of a child is a criminal offense" for which there are no provisions for plea bargaining. In another section the writers advise that bishops use caution in selecting treatment centers for priests because it was "especially important to understand that evaluation centers may be located in states having reporting laws which might prove problematic for the ordinary." They cited as example some states that had enacted legislation that "does not extend privilege of communication between a patient and his psychologist or psychiatrist to cases involving child abuse, including sexual abuse of children."

While the report warned of the legal requirements, it suggested communications between priest and bishop or priest and psychological counselor might yet be privileged from disclosure to law enforcement in some circumstances. It did not represent the full-throated, unqualified call that Doyle would later issue demanding that such priests be reported immediately to police. But Doyle was just awakening to the levels of deception that would eventually be revealed. His head was just beginning to turn, and blunt as he was in assessing what he was seeing, he still valued his status as an insider. He still had ambitions.

The information in the report, which was eventually sent to every bishop in the United States, was in part a call to new awareness of the problem. "We have been rather ignorant of the effects of sexual abuse of children by Catholic clergy over the years because it has never been investigated or studied in a systematic manner," the authors wrote. However, recent years had provided a significant sampling of adults in therapy because of abuse by priests, and professionals treating those patients were able to conclude that "such abuse has a profound effect even when it does not come to the attention of parents, family members, or the civil or church authorities."

It was also becoming clear to those treating such priests that suspension from priestly ministry or laicization should be a more frequent option for bishops. "It is imperative to clearly understand that transfer or removal isolated from any other action is far from adequate and could in fact lead to a presumption of irresponsibility or even liability for the diocesan authorities by civil courts. In short, those presumed to be guilty of sexual misconduct, especially if it involves child molestation, must *never be transferred* [emphasis in original] to another parish or post as the isolated remedy for the situation."

Peterson died in 1987. Mouton has moved out of the country. And as Doyle persisted in his examination of the scandal, realizing that it was, in all its ugliness, pointing to deeper problems in the clerical culture, his career track upward came to an end.

He was quietly moved out of the nunciature in Washington and decided to enlist as a Navy chaplain.

In 2004 Doyle, by then an Air Force colonel and openly critical of church leaders' handling of sex abuse, lost his "ecclesiastical endorsement" to be a chaplain, essentially ending his military career. Doyle was close to qualifying for a military pension.[8] The endorsement was withdrawn ostensibly over a canon-law opinion he had delivered regarding an instruction about daily mass and the manner in which the Blessed Sacrament was to be reserved. Doyle had no recourse to any form of due process, nor was he provided an opportunity to explain himself.

Archbishop Edwin F. O'Brien, who as head of the military archdiocese engineered Doyle's removal from the Air Force, became archbishop of Baltimore.

There is a price to be paid for defying the clerical/hierarchical culture.

Chapter 4

INTO THE DEPTHS OF THE CRISIS

I spent a chilly January evening in 2004 with a group of people who were conducting an outdoor memorial service on a lawn in City Park in New Orleans for fifty victims of sexual abuse by Catholic priests. The common thread among the victims was that they had all committed suicide, most when they were in their twenties or thirties.

Couples strolled by the quiet service, unaware of the sorrow being recalled, as the candles of the participants flickered; a group of young men, yelling in friendly competition, played a game of volleyball nearby. All around, life went on outside the small circle that had gathered for the service organized by victim advocacy groups SNAP and Voice of the Faithful.

I remember thinking at the time that the scene provided an apt metaphor for the larger picture: victims ignored for years, left to their own thoughts, their own recollections, their thin voices carried off on chilly winds.

The following day CNN leaked the figures of the first study by researchers at John Jay College of Criminal Justice. The study had found that some 4,450 priests had been "credibly accused" of abusing around eleven thousand children in the United States during a fifty-year period beginning in 1950.

Those figures were updated two years later because of new accusations and new revelations as the result of legal proceedings to at least five thousand priests and as many as thirteen thousand victims.

That first round of data was stunning. For years the language from the members of the hierarchy in reference to the crisis had see-sawed between apologies for their mistakes and misjudgments

and rationales excusing themselves of culpability; between con-
demnation of the acts of their priests and explanations that the
bishops simply didn't know the extent of the problem or how
deeply destructive it was.

Such defenses were unraveling now in the face of data, much
of which the bishops themselves had provided. Victims and their
relatives, like those who attended the memorial service in New
Orleans, could claim a modest vindication: they hadn't been imag-
ining or making up stories. Thousands of Catholic children and
teens across the country had been sexually abused, not infre-
quently in brutal ways, by the men their parents had taught them
to revere as representatives of Christ on earth.

Immediately after the report was leaked, the tussle began over
what the figures meant. Philip Jenkins of Penn State University
took a minimalist approach, deducing from the figures that "100
or so really intense serial pedophiles . . . account for most of the
cases" of abused children under the age of ten.[1] He said those who
argued that the rate of abuse had to be higher than that reported
were treating the most extreme cases of serial abuse as if they were
normal. Jenkins, who had written *Pedophiles and Priests: Anatomy
of a Contemporary Crisis,* believes that the crisis was overblown,
driven by the media and liberal Catholics who saw the scandal as
a way to impugn the hierarchy.

It is beyond dispute, however, that none of the figures presented is precise. Undoubtedly the John Jay studies, including one
on the causes of the crisis, will provide a standard base line of sorts
for historians and researchers in the future. But just as the home-
run figures of the steroid era in baseball are qualified, there is reason to approach the John Jay data with a healthy skepticism. Several significant cautions should be attached to the use of the data.
First, research and compilation of data by John Jay academics were
ultimately limited by how forthcoming bishops were in providing
the initial data. Further, in those instances when a diocese is required in legal proceedings to produce documents, the figures are
almost always greater than those initially volunteered, and the
sweep and nature of the abuse and cover-up more serious than any
statistical analysis could unveil. The findings of a second grand jury
in the Archdiocese of Philadelphia in 2011, five years after the first
had rendered a stinging rebuke of the church's handling of the

crisis, increased skepticism regarding the church's diligence. The second grand jury charged three priests and a lay teacher with rape and indecent assault. The grand jury also charged Msgr. William Lynn, former secretary of priests for the archdiocese, with two counts of endangering the welfare of children. It was the first time a diocesan official had been criminally charged in the scandal. The report alleged that he had permitted "dangerous" priests to be reassigned to ministries where they had access to children. An additional two dozen Philadelphia priests who had remained in ministry were suspended pending further investigation.

Finally, experts who work with victims, as well as victim advocacy groups, argued that the figure, representing more than 4 percent of priests during the period studied, is extremely conservative. Gary Schoener, a Minnesota-based therapist who had consulted on hundreds of church-related cases and who had worked closely with the Archdiocese of Minneapolis and St. Paul to set up systems to protect children, said at the time, "The big issue is that only a handful of sex abuse victims ever come forward." Consequently, he said, "you've got to change the 4,450 figure to a pretty horrific number."[2]

The fact that the figures were self-reported also meant that the numbers represented a floor and not a ceiling, said A. W. Richard Sipe, a psychotherapist and former Benedictine priest who has written extensively on the clergy sex abuse crisis and on other aspects of priesthood and mandatory celibacy.

Other ways exist, of course, to demonstrate the severe damage the crisis has inflicted on the church at the local level and how it has compromised the institution all the way to the papal palace. One of the distinctive elements of the crisis as it unraveled in Boston was the *Globe*'s success in obtaining papers previously sealed by the court. When Massachusetts Superior Court Judge Constance M. Sweeney granted the request of the *Globe*'s lawyers in January 2002 to unseal the documents in the now infamous case of Fr. John Geoghan, "the church's ability to deflect the issue began to crumble."[3] Geoghan was ultimately convicted and sentenced to ten years in prison for fondling a twelve-year-old boy in a public swimming pool. He was brutally murdered in prison while serving the second year of his term. At the time of his death Geoghan was facing civil lawsuits in which he was accused of sexual misconduct, ranging from fondling to rape, with more than 150 minors.

Before it was all over, the Massachusetts attorney general along with a group of state prosecutors, all Catholic, demanded and obtained records of more than ninety priests in the archdiocese who had been accused of sexually abusing hundreds of victims during the previous forty years. The documentation "showed that Cardinal Law and his top aides were repeatedly warned about dangerous priests, but continued to put these sexual abusers in a position to attack children."[4]

Most of the cases were beyond the Massachusetts statute of limitations for such crimes and could not be prosecuted. However, the shield that secrecy had provided was disintegrating. Where Law once could assure Catholics that what they heard about an abusive priest was either an aberration or manufactured by an anti-Catholic press, the people now could judge for themselves. The unedited language of the hierarchy, which showed little concern for the victims and went out of its way to justify accommodating and hiding abusers, was there for all to see in correspondence and depositions.

By April, when Law and others were summoned to Rome by Pope John Paul II, who was no longer able to ignore the crisis, the cardinal was advancing a far different analysis of the problem. He was no longer blaming others. "The crisis of clergy sexual abuse of minors is not a media-driven or public-perception concern in the United States, but a very serious issue undermining the mission of the Catholic Church," he said.[5]

Public furor combined with a public expression of no confidence by a large portion of archdiocesan priests, an extremely unusual and daring act for clergy, eventually forced Law from office, the only member of the U.S. hierarchy to be forced from office as a result of his administrative handling of the crisis. He was eventually assigned archpriest of the Basilica di Santa Maria Maggiore, one of four basilicas in Rome. Many of those within the hierarchical culture see the assignment as a punishment, a step down from a lofty perch as senior member of the U.S. hierarchy, a position from which he could influence a considerable amount of church life. Many outside that culture saw it more as a sideways move to a cushy job in Rome, where he retained his posts on six

influential Vatican congregations—high-level governing bodies—
including the one responsible for appointing bishops around the
world. Law had a reputation as a "kingmaker" who influenced the
possible choices forwarded to the pope for new bishops. It was, to
many, hardly a fitting punishment for someone who had left the
venerable church in Boston in chaos, with huge financial problems,
a demoralized clergy, and an angry and frustrated membership.

The documents in Boston, now catalogued and available for
public viewing on the website bishopaccountability.org, reveal a
sordid story of abuse of power and lack of concern for the most
vulnerable in the Catholic community that simply didn't match
the prevailing hierarchical narrative. Catholics, for the first time,
began to understand in a way that was not possible before the
documents were released that their presumptions about the good
intent and veracity of their leaders had been naive, that their trust
in the hierarchy's version of events had been deeply violated.
Catholics—and the new awareness was not lost on the wider public—began to see that their leaders were willing to betray, at a
fundamental level, the sacramental life that they preached if doing so was necessary to protect the institution and their own careers. They might still protest that they just didn't know as much
about sexual aberrations then as they do now, but the documents
show that they knew criminal activity was going on; that they hid
it from the faithful; that they paid families and victims hush money
in the hundreds of thousands, sometimes millions, to keep things
quiet; and that when confronted, lied about the scope of the problem and what they were doing about it. It was a story "ripped
from the headlines," but this time the principal actors in the criminal intrigue and corporate malfeasance wore miters and pectoral
crosses and presided over an institution that was supposed to be
a refuge from and bulwark against such evil.

It is easy in hindsight to see that Boston opened a new door to
understanding the depth and breadth of the abuse crisis that now
has become international in scope. At the time, however, many
half wished and half believed that it might be an outlier, an aberration in the big picture. Another major East Coast see, Philadelphia, would soon provide evidence that, difficult as it may have
been for some Catholics to believe, the behavior uncovered in
Boston was more normative than not.

In 2003, the year the U.S. bishops were pressured by public outrage to confront the problem of clergy sexual abuse during their June meeting in Dallas and Law was forced from office in Boston, a grand jury was empaneled in Philadelphia to investigate clergy sex abuse in the Archdiocese of Philadelphia.[6]

The investigation spanned three years, and the panel looked into some forty-five thousand documents from secret archdiocesan archives and took testimony from victims, priests, nuns, and diocesan officials, including Cardinal Anthony Bevilacqua. What resulted was a 418–page report, the most detailed and exhaustive examination of the dimensions and nature of sexual abuse by priests and its cover-up produced in the United States. It was issued September 21, 2005. A few years later, detailed government reports in Ireland would provide the same kind of documented portraits of abuse and cover-up in several dioceses in that country.

The effort in Philadelphia, however, represented a new moment in the ongoing attempt in the United States to get at the truth of the issue. Attorney Jeffrey Anderson of St. Paul, who has represented hundreds of alleged victims in cases against the church, termed the Philadelphia effort a "watershed" event. "This is the first time it has been comprehensively investigated and articulated," he said. "They [the grand jury] did something here that nobody has really done before."

The grand jury investigation in Philadelphia was the result of several factors, primary among them the determination of Philadelphia District Attorney Lynne Abraham, and the conviction of her staff, mostly Catholic, about the necessity of finding out what went on even if statutes of limitation prevented prosecution. The conviction grew as the investigation wore on.

The report, released in October 2005, said the investigators had found in the files accusations of "countless acts of sexual depravity against children," involving a total of 169 priests and hundreds of alleged child victims. The grand jury decided to concentrate on sixty-three of the cases.

The grand jury's report would reveal not only that the archdiocese had shuffled dozens of priests from parish to parish and that both Bevilacqua and his predecessor Cardinal John Krol had knowingly protected repeat sexual offenders, but that the archdiocese had reported an incorrect number to the John Jay investigators.

That lower number of sixty-three priests that the grand jury decided to investigate was nearly twenty more priests than the archdiocese had reported a year earlier to the John Jay investigators. According to an Associated Press report published February 26, 2004, the archdiocese had reported that allegations against only forty-four priests between 1950 and 2003 were found to be credible, 2 percent of the 2,204 priests that served during that time.

Richard Serbin, an attorney who represented abuse victims in several dioceses in the state, told AP at the time that the numbers reported couldn't be trusted. "The very people that have hid the scope and depth of this problem for decades are the ones that are producing the numbers," he said.

"Some may be tempted to describe these events as tragic," said the introduction to the grand jury report. "Tragedies such as tidal waves, however, are outside human control. What we found were not acts of God, but of men who acted in His name and defiled it.

"But the biggest crime of all is this: it worked," the report continued. "The abuser priests, by choosing children as targets and trafficking on their trust, were able to prevent or delay reports of their sexual assaults, to the point where applicable statutes of limitations expired. And Archdiocese officials, by burying those reports they did receive and covering up the conduct, similarly managed to outlast any statutes of limitation."

The investigators voiced regret at their inability to prosecute the priests and diocesan leaders. "We surely would have charged them if we could have done so."

The report emphasized that the grand jury "was not conducting an investigation of the Catholic religion or the Catholic Church. Many of us are Catholic. We have the greatest respect for the faith, and for the good works of the church. But the moral principles on which it is based, as well as the rules of civil law under which we operate, demanded that the truth be told."

The truth the panel uncovered was deeply disturbing. "When we say abuse, we don't just mean 'inappropriate touching' (as the Archdiocese often chose to refer to it). We mean rape. Boys who were raped orally, boys who were raped anally, girls who were raped vaginally. But even those victims whose physical abuse did not include actual rape—those who were subjected to fondling, to masturbation, to pornography—suffered psychological abuse that scarred their lives and sapped the faith in which they had been raised."

The sinister nature of crimes was exacerbated, said the panel, because "the abuses that Cardinal Bevilacqua and his aides allowed children to suffer—the molestations, the rapes, the lifelong shame and despair . . . were made possible by purposeful decisions, carefully implemented policies and calculated indifference.

"The evidence before us established that archdiocese officials at the highest levels received reports of abuse," the report said. The diocese, however, "chose not to conduct any meaningful investigation of those reports." Instead, officials chose to leave "dangerous priests in place or transferred them to different parishes as a means of concealment. . . . They chose to protect themselves from scandal and liability rather than protect children from the priests' crimes."

The grand jury was convinced that Bevilacqua, who holds degrees in both civil law and canon law, and Krol "were personally informed of almost all of the allegations of sexual abuse by priests, and personally decided or approved of how to handle those allegations."

The archdiocese reacted swiftly to the report, releasing a sixty-nine-page rebuttal charging that the grand jury had "a definite anti-Catholic bias" and had tried to "bully and intimidate" Bevilacqua, who, archdiocesan lawyers said, faced "hostile and unnecessarily combative" questioning from two and three prosecutors at a time.

Archdiocesan attorneys argued that the grand jury was unfair in speculating about the intent of documents used from the Krol era, since the cardinal had died in 1996 and was unable to defend himself. It criticized the secrecy of the proceedings and the power of the district attorney. The lawyers also said the "cruel and undeserved portrayal" of Bevilacqua was not supported by evidence. "The report takes excessive liberties with the facts, places unwarranted interpretations on the written documents, tortures Cardinal Bevilacqua's live testimony, and ignores much of what he said in order to cast him in the role of a leader insensitive to children and preoccupied with issues of legal liability," according to the response of the Archdiocese of Philadelphia to the report of the investigating grand jury.

The archdiocesan critique also charged that it was unfair to judge policies of decades ago by contemporary standards and that the grand jury failed to call adequate attention to steps the archdiocese had taken to improve its reporting practices and responses to victims. Most of those steps had been put in place following the 2002 Dallas meeting at which the bishops approved the Charter to Protect Children and Youth, which required formation of a National Review Board, a national Office of Child and Youth Protection, and review boards and educational programs at the diocesan level. Although the bishops could not mandate that dioceses follow the rules—and the Diocese of Lincoln, Nebraska, has refused to participate in any of the recommendations—nearly all dioceses and eparchies in the country have complied.

Abraham responded with a thirty-page rebuttal and by challenging the archdiocese to release the documents upon which the report was based. Her response accused the archdiocese of obstructing the grand jury's investigation "at every turn." As for its treatment of Bevilacqua, Abraham said that "any persistence in the questioning" of the cardinal "may have resulted in part from his evasiveness and claimed forgetfulness on the witness stand."

Bevilacqua, who was called to the stand to testify ten times during the grand jury probe, had been one of John Paul II's earliest appointments. He was named a bishop in 1980 and became archbishop of Philadelphia in 1987. During his tenures in Philadelphia and earlier in Pittsburgh, he faced contentious questions about his administration style and his oversight of diocesan funds. Bevilacqua would at times call attention to the fact that he held degrees in both canon and civil law, and he was a strident advocate of measures aimed at bracing up Catholic identity in church institutions. He was named a cardinal in 1991 and retired in 2003, the year the grand jury was empaneled, to the grounds of the archdiocese's St. Charles Borromeo Seminary.

"If the archdiocese believes that what we have said in the grand jury is false, then I call upon them to release the documents that they have been forced to turn over to us," Abraham said at a news conference later that September. "Open it to the light of day. No secret archives, no papal nuncio, no separation of church and state."

She continued: "If they think that we have falsified one thing, release the documents to the public. Let the press and public review them in their entirety, not through the filter of us or anybody else. That's what they [the archdiocese] can do to show that they are turning a page. If they think we've falsified or made things up, the answer is simple—release the documents. You'll see."

Cardinal Justin Rigali, who had taken over for Bevilacqua, immediately joined the critique, defending his predecessors and terming the report "slanted." He objected to its "prolonged explanations of abuse" and the "very graphic" nature of the depictions of abuse, adding, "I don't think it's of value to families."

In a September 21 letter to the faithful in the archdiocese, he said: "The report is very painful to read. The pain and suffering experienced by those who have been abused by clergy is great, and we must continually pray for healing for the victims." In the same paragraph, however, he said the report was "unjustifiably critical" of Krol, Bevilacqua, and others who worked in administration of the archdiocese.

His defense included the assertion that "in every single case of abuse reported to archdiocesan officials, action was taken based on the best medical information available at that time."

It was the same line of defense offered by Cardinal Law in 2001 as the details of the Geoghan case were becoming public. Law's attorney, in a letter in the archdiocesan newspaper, *The Pilot*, argued that Geoghan, "subsequent to the first complaint of sexual misconduct, was incident to an independent medical evaluation advising that such assignment was appropriate and safe."

No mention was made of the fact that Law and every other U.S. bishop in office in 1985 had received the report by Doyle, Mouton, and Peterson containing expert advice that advised a different course of action with repeat offenders.

Rigali's comments, constituting an ambivalent mix of acknowledgment, sorrow, and defensive rationales, typified the reaction of the hierarchy, particularly in those instances where abundant documentation was forced from chancery offices and locked file rooms to paint a substantial picture of how the church handled abusive priests.

If the grand jury report was based on tens of thousands of archdiocesan documents and days upon days of testimony from victims and church officials, what was left to say? The reports were unnecessarily too graphic and the interpretation of documents and testimony unnecessarily harsh? How does one speak about a priest raping children in a way that isn't graphic? The most unadorned description of the evil is an assault on all that is decent.

The problem, of course, is that the church in so many parts of the country—and more recently in other parts of the world—has had to acknowledge bills of particulars of the sort that was spelled out for the church in the Philadelphia grand jury report.

"These are the kinds of things that Archdiocese priests did to children," the report states on page three, then lists:

- A girl, 11 years old, was raped by her priest and became pregnant. The father took her in for an abortion.
- A 5th grader was molested by her priest inside the confessional booth.
- A teenage girl was groped by her priest while she lay immobilized in traction in a hospital bed. The priest stopped only when the girl was able to ring for a nurse.
- A boy was repeatedly molested in his own school auditorium, where his priest/teacher bent the boy over and rubbed his genitals against the boy until the priest ejaculated.
- A priest, no longer satisfied with mere pederasty, regularly began forcing sex on two boys at once in his bed.
- A boy woke up intoxicated in a priest's bed to find the father sucking on his penis while three other priests watched and masturbated themselves.
- A priest offered money to boys in exchange for sadomasochism—directing them to place him in bondage, to "break" him, to make him their "slave," and to defecate so that he could lick excrement from them.
- A 12-year-old boy, who was raped and sodomized by his priest, tried to commit suicide, and remains institutionalized in a mental hospital as an adult.
- A priest told a 12-year-old boy that his mother knew of and had agreed to the priest's repeated rape of her son.

- A boy who told his father about the abuse his younger brother was suffering was beaten to the point of unconsciousness. "Priests don't do that," said the father as he punished his son for what he thought was a vicious lie against the clergy.

Revelations of such repugnant behavior sets any bishop a horrific task: how to acknowledge the pain of the victims, the deep physical and spiritual damage that permeates the rest of their lives, while protecting those (either the current bishop or his predecessors) who knowingly allowed priests to go on ministering who had committed such awful crimes.

In Philadelphia for instance—and it is by no means an outlier in terms of the degree of depravity depicted in the report or in the hierarchy's manner of handling abusive priests—the documents showed that secrecy about the crimes was simply part of the system. Bevilacqua transferred Fr. Michael McCarthy in 1992, two months after the priest had been accused of "taking students from an archdiocesan high school to his beach house, plying them with liquor, sleeping nude in the same bed with them, and masturbating the boys and himself."[7]

According to the report, Bevilacqua had an aide tell McCarthy he would be reappointed a pastor after a sufficient amount of time had passed and that the new parish would be as far away as possible from his former parish "so that the profile can be as low as possible and not attract the attention of the complainant."

Another priest, Fr. Gerald Chambers, was transferred to seventeen different assignments in twenty-one years, and the records show that the church was running out of places to put him where his reputation for molesting children would not be known. One of his victims tried to commit suicide by slicing his throat and wrists and had been in and out of mental institutions for years, according to the report.

Fr. Nicholas V. Cudemo, described by Bevilacqua's vicar for administration as "one of the sickest people I ever knew," repeatedly raped an eleven-year-old girl. The abuse began in 1971. When she became pregnant in 1973 as a result o f the abuse, the priest took her for an abortion, and the physical and mental abuse continued. The victim, who has attempted suicide several times and whose husband told the grand jury that she still sleeps "in a position of fear with her arm covering her head," was one of a dozen alleged victims of the same priest. The victims included two current nuns at the time of the report. Formal complaints were filed with the archdiocese over the years, and Fr. Cudemo was even sued by his own family for sexually abusing his cousin.

According to the report, Bevilacqua refused to respond formally to the complaints or to seek out the victims. Instead, said the report, he called in the lawyers and "allowed [Cudemo] to continue in ministry with full access to children" until 2002, when the bishops as a national group were forced to confront the crisis.

Not only was Cudemo permitted to remain in ministry, but he was named pastor twice, of two different parishes, and in 1997 received a certificate declaring him "a retired priest in good standing with the archdiocese of Philadelphia." The certificate permitted him to continue working as a priest in Orlando, Florida.[8]

Rigali, who inherited the legacy of his two predecessors, Krol and Bevilacqua, was left with the unenviable task of having to face the elaborately documented truth of the matter while protecting their reputations, regardless of the record. Though a break in ranks has occurred on the rare occasion, it is an unspoken rule of the hierarchical culture that one does not speak ill of one's peers and patrons. So, while admitting "mistakes" and acknowledging that the "pain and suffering experienced by those who have been abused by clergy is great," he was also required to say that the criticism of his predecessors is unnecessarily harsh. Exactly what degree of culpability might be correct is never approached. What degree of responsibility for protecting the innocent of the community might be expected from religious leaders who demand meticulous accountability from the faithful in the most intimate of matters is never part of the discussion.

We can only wonder how deeply mired in ongoing deceit the church would have become, how many children would have been sacrificed to the institution's need to protect itself, how many more lives would have borne the scars of betrayal had not the combination of victims, lawyers, and publicity exposed what was going on. While it is quite possible that certain elements of the Philadelphia grand jury report were misinterpreted, that frustrated prosecutors may have gone a bit rough on the cardinal, or that sufficient emphasis was not given to the inadequacy of psychological insight of a given era, the data is indisputable: the brutality of the attacks, the lack of attention to what was going on with child victims, the secrecy and deliberate strategies employed to hide predators. In my experience of covering, assigning, editing, and commenting on stories from several vantage points during twenty-five years of this scandal, I don't know of a single incident in which a bishop voluntarily told his community about an abuser, about victims, about money paid for silence, even in the most abstract terms.

Any action taken—Law's banishment to Rome, removal of bishops accused of abuse, removal of priests, apologies, the Charter to Protect Children and Youth, formation of the National Review Board and establishment of a national Office for the Protection of Children and Youth, services to acknowledge victims and what they've endured—took place because public outrage had reached such a pitch that members of the hierarchy of the United States—conservatives, liberals, moderates, Paul VI appointees, John Paul II bishops—were forced to act.

In most journalistic attempts to deal with the imponderables of brutal degradation of children by priests and protection of predators by bishops, reporters are left with the unsatisfactory ending punctuation of the dry apology that has become required. End of story. There's no place left to go because all of the possibilities for reform, for a new way of doing things, lies within a hidden realm, a culture, as the next chapter will show, that remains distant from the experience of everyday Catholics. Those ordinary, responsible Catholics who come to adult understandings of responsibility and accountability, who realize that consequences attach to behavior, have also come to understand that their spiritual leaders live by other rules. No plebiscites exist in this hidden culture; no means for registering a vote of no confidence. In this secret society of men, no open means exist for holding priests and bishops accountable for criminal behavior and cover up.

Chapter 5

A PROBLEM OF CLERICAL CULTURE

The sex abuse crisis is not fundamentally about sex. The designation is a convenient label that has been applied to a deeper, ongoing problem that, at its core, has to do with power and authority and how they are used in the church. The sex abuse crisis is, more accurately, a crisis of the clerical/hierarchical culture "that can no longer maintain its superiority by dint of office or by claim of some ontological difference from the rest of humankind."[1]

Bishops, from the bishop of Rome on down, claim for themselves absolute authority over the most intimate details of the lives of Catholics within their domains. They are without peer or accountability within their territories. These are the men who (increasingly today) decide which individuals have permission to speak on church property, commanding that Catholics pay no attention to those deemed outside the fold. These are the men who can, with a bull or a bulletin notice, call into question a theologian's lifetime of work.

These are the men who can say they know the mind of God so perfectly that they are able to declare with certainty that millions of God's human creations, homosexuals, are afflicted with an "objective disorder" and thus are condemned to lives that can know no sexual intimacy lest they engage in "intrinsic evil." These are the men who tell married couples that there is only one way to prevent a pregnancy, no matter what other factors might bear on determining responsible parenthood in a given situation. They make clear to married Catholics who get divorced and remarry that they are unwelcome at the eucharistic table. These are the men who publicly announce that individuals and institutions are stripped of their Catholic identity, cast outside the community, because of agonizing decisions made in good conscience at the extremes of medical practice. They claim to be the sole and final arbiters in interpreting complex federal legislation, and they can declare that politicians who disagree with their tactical strategies be kept from the Eucharist.

These are the men who can marginalize, and in extreme cases have even excommunicated, the community's thinkers because they dare to ask a question about women's ordination or married priests. The same fate awaits those whose works of theology delve deeply into the questions that occur naturally and inevitably to those trying to live the faith and to witness within the mysteries of Christianity in an age of global pluralism.

These are the men with all of the answers, the certitudes that bind us all, they are the men who decide what can and cannot be said, with whom we can be intimate, how our marriages are to be conducted, what thoughts and questions we may or may not consider. And yet they ask us to believe that in the case of priests raping and molesting children they became detached from their moral moorings because of confusing information from outside experts. They ask us to moderate our outrage at what we learn about their behavior, rationalizing that the problem of child abuse exists everywhere in society.

The same men who decry the secularization of the culture, the diminishment of the transcendent in our lives, are the very ones who reduce the abuse of children to a threat, not to the foundations of human dignity that we say we hold so dear, but rather to their offices—to the presbytery and the episcopacy—and to the reputation of the institution. The bishops become practitioners of the relativism they so loudly condemn in others.

I am quite aware that the picture I paint above is without nuance and without an essential qualification: that most bishops are not out on the stump hurling anathemas. They have quite enough to do with the everyday administrative demands of running a diocese. I also know that more than a few of them wince at the hot actors, the ones who are eager to throw down the gauntlet, but that the culture in which they exist requires that they maintain silence. Princes of the church don't step on each other's toes. As a result, in recent years the loud minority has had little resistance in shaping the public narrative, in advancing what one commentator calls "Taliban Catholicism," as the norm. Their tone is often mimicked at the level of pastor and other positions of authority. I emphasize that I am not opposed to hierarchy and that I don't hate bishops. Quite the opposite is true. I am convinced that institutions are essential to the advancement of humans whether in the spiritual or secular realm. We are not angels; we don't communicate telepathically; we need one another; we need institutions in which to gather and support one another. We need communities that are not chaotic but are well ordered with solid, healthy leadership. We need leaders of integrity who understand and exercise an authentic use of authority, who understand prudence as an indispensable virtue. What we witness in our parish and diocesan structures today, I fear, is too often quite unhealthy.

It is probably important here to stipulate that I also am aware that all human institutions, even those that mediate the divine in our midst, are flawed. In the world of journalism, for instance, there have been plagiarizers and people who have manipulated sources and source materials to their own ends, passed on fiction as fact, or made other decisions that betrayed the trust of listeners and readers. We know about these because reporters and editors and general managers have been fired or publicly chastised, and their organizations have gone to elaborate lengths to explain where the culture of their enterprises had failed.

Business and politics have produced outsized scoundrels, but we often know about them because systems, imperfect as they may be, have held people accountable. So we've seen Enrons go under and Bernie Madoffs sent to prison. We've seen the Tom Delays and Dan Rostenkowskis, enormously powerful figures, hauled off to court; we've seen their colleagues censured, and we've seen presidents impeached, even forced to resign for betraying the public trust. Yet in the matter of the Christian community called Catholic, we are asked to submit to an absolute authority with no recourse for holding that authority accountable.

The Pew study referenced in an earlier chapter may document that the sex abuse crisis was not the immediate reason most people have left the church, but anyone who has spent any time at all among those who have left knows how corrosive the scandal has been to the ties that once held people within the community.

Anyone who has spent time within parish structures, among some of the most devoted workers, knows that in order to go on, those workers in the vineyard have to push the realities of the scandal to the background. It is a silent, hidden pathology that eats at the soul of the community in yet unknown ways.

The abuse crisis is a crisis of the clerical cultural, and evidence of the culture's inability to square off with the truth of it is piled up all around us. I am warned by a good priest friend of the dangers of using the term *culture*. He says *culture* is too broad a term, that it lumps all priests in the same category and doesn't allow for those, himself included, who have been railing, at least privately, against the cover-up behavior that he maintains resides in the realm of the hierarchical or chancery culture. Too many priests who are in the trenches keeping the church going and who have already been painted with the broad brush of scandal, he argues, are now being painted with the culture of the cover-up.

Using collectives always involves risks. Historians write of an early twentieth-century German culture that sought to exterminate Jews or of a Southern white culture that perpetuated slavery and built a legacy of lynchings, often preserved in photographs.

Neither characterization is fair to the many Germans who resisted and aided Jews or to Southerners who thought and acted differently.

Culture by its very nature, writes Fr. Michael Papesh, "is bigger than those who comprise it and blinds them to its contradictions." In *Clerical Culture* he defines clerical culture as "precisely the constellation of relationships and the universe of ideas and material reality in which diocesan priests and bishops exercise their ministry and spend their lives."[2] In its general sameness, then, the culture can also be different in details diocese to diocese and certainly from one country to another.

Clerical culture is something that most Catholics intuit and know when they see it, but it rarely gets defined.

The defense of bishops' behavior was first cast in the "few bad apples" argument that suggested that only a few priests had engaged in abuse and that the media was overstating and sensationalizing the problem. That approach was captured in the now infamous words of Cardinal Bernard Law, reacting to 1992 press coverage of the pedophile Fr. James Porter. "By all means," thundered Law, "we call down God's power on the media, particularly the *Globe*," referring to stories that appeared in the *Boston Globe*.[3]

We then went through the tortured apology stage, best exemplified by the words of Cardinal Edward Egan in a 2002 letter to parishes in New York: "If in hindsight we also discover that mistakes may have been made as regards prompt removal of priests and assistance to victims, I am deeply sorry."

Cardinal Roger Mahony has managed as of this writing, through seemingly endless legal maneuvers, to escape complying with an agreement worked out by the courts to hand over thousands of documents dealing with sex abuse in the Los Angeles Archdiocese and his handling of the matter. In 2009 he articulated another strain of hierarchical rationale for time and again placing known molesters in the proximity of children: "We have said repeatedly that . . . our understanding of this problem and the way it's dealt with today evolved, and that in those years ago, decades ago, people didn't realize how serious this was, and so, rather than pulling people out of ministry directly and fully, they were moved."[4]

And then there is the repentant cardinal, deeply aggrieved over the "tragedy" of priestly abuse who must, however, note that the real danger in all of this is latent anti-Catholicism: "Priestly abuse of children and young people is a great tragedy of unbounded proportions and bishops must take responsibility for it; but it is also an occasion to unleash the anti-Catholicism that has never been far beneath the surface in U.S. history," wrote Cardinal Francis George of Chicago.[5]

In the same section of his book, George, an influential figure who was president of the bishops' conference from 2007 to 2010, makes another odd conjunction of claims. "The priestly sex abuse scandal has been transformed into a scandal of church leadership, of church authority," he writes. "Deservedly so, for bishops have failed, but also deliberately so," placing the blame for the shift largely on the major secular media, especially *The New York Times*.

"For some," he continues, "the only safe Catholic, the only good Catholic, is a Catholic who is at odds with the bishops." He castigates "self-styled prophetic voices in the church today," characterizing them as "pro-abortion, pro-contraception, pro-divorce, pro-gay marriage—pro any of the other items on the long list of sexual and culture freedoms claimed today. That is the voice of the dominant culture, and those who speak it receive their reward, at least in the opinion pages of *The New York Times*."[6]

It's a confusing outburst, at the least, but the tactic is clear: discredit anyone who might call bishops to account in the matter of their handling of the scandal by lumping them indiscriminately with all of the evils and cultural strains that are seen as threats to the church while simultaneously equating such questioners with anti-Catholic elements of a past era.

One presumes that the National Leadership Roundtable on Church Management, an impressive group of lay professionals that formed in recent years in the wake of various church crises, sexual and financial, was not trying for irony when it invited Bishop Arthur Serratelli to a 2010 session offering "a blueprint for accountability."[7]

Serratelli offered what amounted to a blueprint for avoiding accountability, an unintentional parody of the hierarchical culture's list of rationales for its handling of the crisis.

He began by hauling up a much-debated line from a 1973 homily of Pope Paul VI in which the pope said: "From some fissure, the smoke of Satan has entered the temple of God." Serratelli suggests that it is a reference to the "disquiet, dissent, and dissatisfaction" that followed the Second Vatican Council. It is safe to say, without going into any extended exegesis of a minor papal statement, that the jury's still out on exactly what the pope intended by the comment and that those on the Catholic left and right have used the quote to their own purposes in the years since.

Significant in this case is that Serratelli uses it as a point from which he draws a straight line through the debates that have followed the council, which he views as the start of the unraveling of all vestiges of authority and decorum within the church. He sees a weakening of authority that "in recent times has only increased because of the perceived betrayal of trust by church authority in dealing with clergy abuse in terms of sex and money." One infers from his language that a betrayal of trust never actually occurred but was only "perceived," although later he talks of the sin of the certain church leaders, without getting into details or saying what consequences such bishops should face.

His point becomes clearer as the line he draws gathers data from recent CARA studies showing that the majority of sex abuse cases reported "actually took place between 1969 and 1979." Without going through an exhaustive list of qualifications that would have to be attached to the bishop's presentation to draw it somewhat close to reality, it is enough to repeat what has already been noted here and is widely accepted in other quarters: that reports of sexual abuse often lag behind the event by decades; that the number of cases often cited is based on self-reporting that has been shown, in those instances where documentation has been obtained through legal processes, to be much lower than the actual count; and that the history of the Servants of the Paraclete and research by Richard Sipe, presented in his book *Sex, Priests, and Secret Codes,* among others, show that sexual abuse of minors occurred in the church well before the U.S. 1960s culture influenced anyone.

Serratelli gives the obligatory acknowledgment: "In no way can we dismiss, condone or gloss over the financial misappropriation of some of our priests, nor the sexual abuse on the part of others, but"—there is usually a telling "but" to these admissions—"we need to be aware that these are not just Catholic problems."

As evidence, he recounts that a "Sam Miller, a Jewish businessman in Cleveland, gave a talk before the City Club in Cleveland. He gave his audience some statistics that showed 10 percent of Protestant ministers admitted to acts of pedophilia, while only 1.7 percent of Catholic clergy had been guilty of it."

Where Mr. Miller obtained his information is not established, nor does the bishop question the use of figures that, certainly on the Catholic side of things, are simply incorrect. The data collected by the John Jay study clearly shows that more than 4 percent of priests were credibly accused, a figure that most who work in the field consider conservative.

Serratelli raises the protests against the Vietnam war as damaging to all forms of authority and claims that "from the 1940s to the '60s, many university students were exposed to cultural relativism, and in the water of cultural relativism, there was spawned a loss of respect for moral restraint." He cites anthropologists Ruth Benedict and Margaret Meade, who, he said, revealed to the world that other cultures existed with moral codes different from the code "accepted by everyone in the United States" and that "shortly afterwards, people began to think [the code accepted in the U.S.] didn't have any legitimate authority whatsoever.

"The authority of morality in this country was thrown into question, just as the authority of the state and federal government. Thus, the '60s was a period of a general breakdown in respect for authority, both political and moral. It was a time when moral rules were ignored and America threw herself into the orgy of the sexual revolution."

Serratelli draws his line directly from that orgy of sexual revolution to the sex abuse crisis, asking, suggestively, "Did those times at all play into the fact that as statistics show, the period after the '60s was the same period that were the highest reported cases of sexual abuse by clergy?"

What is important here is not the jumble of anthropological speculation and questionably used statistics, nor, by the way, is it the bishop's invocation of former New York Mayor Ed Koch to back up his point that the press was unfair in its treatment of the church. What is significant in the larger picture is the need, almost desperately expressed in his speech, to deflect blame, to see the causes everywhere else but where, to most outside the clerical culture, a great deal of it lies. His speech is revealing of the determined efforts of U.S. bishops to not engage in any introspection about what they did and why they acted as they did. No unsettling questions need be directed toward the hierarchy.

The case is increasingly made in informal circumstances that Catholics should simply go about doing what Catholics do and pay no attention to the bishops. Some point to the studies that show that young people are detached from institutions in general and from organized religion in particular and don't much care what bishops have to say.

Cardinal George himself expresses the wish for a Catholicism without the contentious left-right split and one in which adherents pay less attention to the bishops. He describes an idyllic and docile faithful for whom Catholicism is a quieting, centering influence.[8]

He is equally dismissive of liberals and conservatives.

Liberals, he said, are critical of authority "although they'll use it when they're in power." Conservatives are less critical of authority "but equally dependent upon it."

Each side, he said, is unhappy with bishops for either possessing authority or not using it enough. "Both of them are defining themselves vis-à-vis the bishops rather than vis-à-vis Christ, who uses the bishops to govern the church. It's not a Christ-centered church, as it's supposed to be; it's a bishop-centered church."

He admits that the bishops played a role in creating the problem and says they are working on what the bishop's proper role should be, particularly in governance.

George sees as a third option a "simple Catholicism" that is neither liberal nor conservative. It is a Catholicism, he said, that one sees "in the lives of ordinary Catholics who just take for granted that we go to Mass, we say the rosary, without thinking very much about it. We contribute to Catholic charities and we take care of our neighbor in very spontaneous ways." That manner of religious practice, he said, was the Catholicism of his youth in Chicago. Of course that was a time before women began to seek greater roles and responsibilities throughout society and across religious institutions. It was an era when gays were still closeted. It was a time before lay people were spoken about in an entirely different way from previous eras in both canon law and the documents of the church.

George expresses the desires of many for an easier, more organic relationship within the church from pew to chancery. He wishes for a less contentious means of living and expressing what it means to be Catholic. One suspects, however, that if bishops are "trying to work through" what their role is, what it means to be in relationship with and central to a Catholic community "without controlling everything," certainly lay people are asking similar questions. How do they embrace a new sense of vocation, of priesthood even, when the cardinal's idea of being "just Catholic" involves a pre-conciliar passivity requiring they remain distant from the processes where decisions are made that affect their lives? How do lay people take a more active role in the church and its outward ministries when the evidence suggests, time and again, that their work can be upended and destroyed at the whim of a new pastor or a new bishop?

Perhaps if the cardinal's ideal is that lay people simply ignore bishops and concentrate more on Christ, a reciprocal arrangement might be struck. But ignoring one another wouldn't be very Christlike and would only call attention to a kind of dysfunction that already pervades the ecclesial structures.

The point is, in a hierarchical organization, bishops, and how they lead, matter, which is why the culture of leadership matters. The sex abuse crisis and concomitant financial crises have brought increasing pressure for change and reform. The culture, it appears, can't hold.

Fr. Donald Cozzens, writer in residence at John Carroll University, has written with unusual candor and insight from within the culture. In *Faith That Dares to Speak* he claims that today "we are witnessing in the institutional church the *unraveling of the last feudal system in the West*" (emphasis in original). In the ecclesial version of feudalism, the pope, as sovereign or king, "grants benefices"—dioceses—to bishops who "in turn promise obedience, homage, and loyalty." The bishops then grant benefices—parishes—to their priests, who also promise "obedience, homage, and loyalty to the chief shepherd of the diocese." And, finally, the parishes, fiefdoms for the pastors, are doled out with the widely held understanding that some of them are considered "plum assignments," others a form of banishment.

Ancient feudalism's economy depended on the promise of land for protection. In the church's version, "the church offers an economy of grace, promising salvation through the 'economy' of the sacraments. A subtle transaction takes place between parishioners and the clergy understood as keepers of the sacraments. In return for practicing one's faith, that is, for leading a life of moral rectitude and orthodox belief, and in return for obedience to the teaching office of the church and for its financial support, Catholics are granted the assurance of divine grace, of salvation itself."

If the culture is unraveling, it is doing so, as Cozzens sees it, "in fits and starts." It also appears today that the more pressure the culture feels from outside to change, the greater the resistance in some sectors. So we see an increase of the accoutrements of royalty and of certain court behaviors. Websites now refer to bishops as "your grace," and the more familiar designations of "your excellency" and "your eminence" don't elicit the awkwardness they might have some decades ago. We see an increase in lace and yards and yards more silk than has been the case since before the council. Capa magnas, long flowing capes suggestive of royalty of an earlier age, are making a comeback. The princes of the church who are so disposed designate their own chapels where traditionalists gather to worship. The leaders sometimes process from rectory to church under canopies held aloft by young seminarians and priests, who also are called on to attend to the trains of the prince's elaborate capes. In these ceremonies there is much vesting and de-vesting while sitting in "throne" chairs, all done against a backdrop of murmured Latin.

Commentator Eugene Kennedy has likened such goings on to Civil War re-enactors. There is a theatrical quality to it, as if someone has found a cache of props in a theater closet and set out to remake the past. The grand displays can make an easy target for those in the Catholic community not inclined toward such worship preferences and liturgical regalia. However, for committed traditionalists—and even others not so committed but who feel a lack of transcendence in some of the worship forms available in ordinary parishes—such displays bring reassurance and spiritual comfort. They connect people to a sense of awe and reverence, to the notion of timelessness about the church, and to the reassuring conviction that faith equates to certainty, that faith means one has all the answers one might need to navigate life's vicissitudes.

It is unfortunate that such preferences get caught up in all of the internecine Catholic debates. Bishop Walter Sullivan, retired bishop of Richmond, Virginia, once made a genuine and laudable gesture to traditionalists within his diocese. Sullivan, one of the most liberal members of the hierarchy at the time, granted permission for a Latin mass parish—which continues to this day—and even dusted off his Latin to say the first mass. What he did was a show of graciousness, an acknowledgment that some of his people were hurting deeply, feeling that the mass they had known all their lives, the ritual that for years had grounded them in their faith, had been ripped from them. What Sullivan demonstrated was that the Latin mass need not be a point of battle.

Tolerating the celebration of the old Latin mass is not suggesting that it is the wave of the future. I have yet to meet a pastor who feels his job or his parish is threatened by the presence of a Latin mass chapel nearby.

At the same time, one can't ignore what is represented in those rituals. They embody, in the implied and overt ecclesiology, the very ideas about priesthood—the distance of the clerical culture from those in the pews, the symbols of office, power, privilege, and dominance held within a society closed off from other mere mortals—that provided a rich seed bed for the clergy sex abuse scandal.

Cozzens cites Bishop Nestor Ngoy Katahwa of Congo during a 2001 Vatican conference on the episcopacy. As "princes of the church," the bishop said, "we are more at ease with the powerful and the rich than with the poor and the oppressed. And the fact that we maintain sole legislative, executive and judicial powers is a temptation for us to act like dictators, more so inasmuch as our mandate has no limitations."

The Maciel Case

The most dramatic modern example of the kind of corruption that can take hold in a culture of isolated privilege and unlimited power is the case of the late Fr. Marcial Maciel Degollado, founder of the once-powerful order, the Legionaries of Christ.

The Legion, as it is also known, is crumbling today. At the start of 2011 it had handed over its publication, the *National Catholic Register,* to the Eternal Word Network enterprise. It was selling schools, its priests were abandoning it for diocesan postings or other orders, and defections reportedly were heavy from its lay arm, Regnum Christi, which ran many of the schools. Fundraising, which Maciel once achieved at breathtaking rates, had tanked. The Vatican had ordered an investigation and a long process of rehabilitation of the order was under way. The prospects were daunting. The challenge was to remake a religious order "built on the 'charism' of a founder who sexually abused child seminarians and fathered out-of-wedlock children, including two sons who claim they are incest victims."[9]

Why did it take church officials from 1997, when nine former priests and seminarians first went public with their charges against

Maciel, until 2006 to admit the truth? The nine decided to step forward after they were stunned to hear John Paul II refer to Maciel as "an efficacious guide to youth." The former members of the Legion, interviewed in the United States and Mexico by freelance journalist Jason Berry and Gerald Renner, then religion writer for the *Hartford Courant* newspaper, said that Maciel had molested them in Spain and Italy for three decades, beginning in the 1940s. Several recounted how Maciel told them he had permission from Pope Pius XII to seek their assistance in obtaining sexual relief of physical pain.

The men weren't after monetary compensation; they merely wanted the Vatican to discipline Maciel and to prevent him from gaining access to any other young seminarians.

Maciel, however, was in favor in the Vatican. He was bringing in young seminarians and ordaining lots of priests. At one point his order existed in twenty countries and boasted five hundred priests and twenty-five hundred seminarians. Maciel was charming and had established a lay organization that viewed itself as a kind of "shock troops" of conservative piety and orthodoxy of the purest sort. Maciel and his organization represented Catholic identity on steroids. And he raised money, millions upon millions. He knew how to use it, too. He spread cash and gifts around the Vatican the way, in other venues, lobbyists and tycoons grease the political skids. He was a capable operator who lived a monstrous double life and was able to scam everyone from the rich widow and the local pastor to the Vatican secretary of state and the pope himself.

Few knew better the levers of the culture and how to work them to his own ends. His displays of piety were elaborate, and he used the language of humility and holiness to bind his underlings to absolute secrecy. Secrecy was essential because his trail of deceit went back decades and had been flagged earlier by church officials, but he always managed to resurface in a stronger position.

Cracks in the culture appeared from time to time. Bishops complained about Maciel and the Legion. One petitioned the Vatican on behalf of a priest who had been abused and finally found the courage to leave the order to become a diocesan priest. The testimony of the former priests and seminarians constitutes a powerful indictment of Maciel and the cultish aspects of the order. The Legion was banned from or faced severe restrictions in at least seven U.S. dioceses.

Canon lawyers within the Congregation for the Doctrine of the Faith thought the accusers had a strong case, but all procedures abruptly stropped in 1999 without explanation. What became clear in the years since is that Maciel had protectors in very high places. He traveled with the pope on some of his journeys, and, as late as 2004, John Paul honored the Legion by entrusting it with the management of Jerusalem's Notre Dame Center. John Paul II also praised Maciel that year for sixty years of "intense, generous and fruitful priestly ministry." In a letter posted on the Legionaries website the pope wrote that he wanted to join in the "canticle of praise and thanksgiving" for the great things he had accomplished and said Maciel had always been concerned with the "integral promotion of the person." The Legion was clearly John Paul II's idea of what a religious order and Catholic expression should be.

That same year, however, Cardinal Joseph Ratzinger, head of the Congregation for the Doctrine of the Faith, ordered the case reopened, and a thorough investigation, including interviews with accusers in several countries, was undertaken. In 2006, with Ratzinger now pope, Maciel was finally disciplined.

Maciel could count on staunch supporters in powerful conservative circles in the United States, including Fr. Richard John Neuhaus, editor of *First Things* magazine, who roundly dismissed the accusations and once declared that he was "morally certain" the allegations were false.

The story containing the initial accusations ran in the *Courant* on February 23, 1997. Less than two weeks later, on March 8, Neuhaus wrote: "One cannot help but be greatly impressed by both the discipline and the joy evinced by so many young men who have followed the vision of Father Maciel in surrendering their lives to Christ and His Church. I confidently pray that your apostolate will survive and flourish long after these terrible attacks have been long forgotten."

The conservative, now-defunct *Crisis* magazine urged the *Courant* to "withdraw its false article and apologize to Father Maciel, the Legionaries of Christ, and faithful Roman Catholics." William

Bennett, former education secretary and federal drug czar, who has written extensively on personal and public morality, weighed in: "The flourishing of the Legionaries is a cause for hope in a time of much darkness. I look forward to continuing my involvement with and support of the Legion of Christ."

Mary Ann Glendon, a Harvard law professor, disparaged the "revival of long discredited allegations" that she said "would come as a surprise were it not for the fact that the U.S. is currently experiencing a resurgence of anti-Catholicism." She said that Neuhaus's "meticulous analysis of the evidence" should have "put the matter to rest once and for all." She recalled sitting next to Maciel for several weeks during a Vatican event and said, "I simply cannot reconcile those old stories with the man's radiant holiness."[10]

One might disagree with the ecclesiology and religious ideology of *First Things* and the defenders of the Legion, but they represent a sophisticated strain of Catholic intellectual endeavor and serious and at times eloquent discourse on faith and its interaction with and place within the wider culture. How then were they so duped?

George Weigel, a leading conservative voice at the Washington-based Ethics and Public Policy Center, was a staunch defender of Maciel early on. After Maciel's fall he was one of the first to come out on the *First Things* website strongly critical of the Legion. He called for a "root and branch examination" of the order and wondered if the Legion could be reformed after the order rid itself of "those complicit in the Maciel web of deceit." Yet he continued to defend John Paul, never wondering how the pope himself might have abetted the deceit. He argued that the pope "may well have been ill served by associates and subordinates who ought to have been more alert to the implications of [Maciel's] cult of personality." Weigel had abundant access to John Paul II. He interviewed him ten times for his 1999 biography, *Witness to Hope,* which avoided any mention of the scandal that had erupted in the United States. In 2002, after the revelations in Boston forced John Paul to address the crisis, Weigel flew to Rome to serve as an ad hoc papal adviser. In his most recent book on John Paul's legacy, *The End and the Beginning,* Weigel asserts that "it was revealed after the pope's death that Maciel had long led a double life of moral dissolution." The fact of the matter, of course, is that numerous and credible accusations of that double life had been given extensive publicity long before John Paul died. In *The End and the Beginning*, Weigel allows that the pope "could be deceived." However, argues Weigel, it was the pope's virtues, the very elements of his personality that shaped his greatness, that allowed him to be deceived. It was John Paul's "profound disinclination to humiliate, or make a spectacle of, someone else; his intense dislike of gossip; his occasional tendency to project his own virtues onto others; and his determination to find something good in another's actions or words" that paved the way for his occasional "misjudgments about personalities, including clergy and senior members of the hierarchy who ought to have been disciplined or compelled to retire."[11]

The bishops' moral compasses were thrown off kilter by bad information, and John Paul's flaw was an excess of virtue.

"Certainly there was more to it than a few errant functionaries," said an *NCR* editorial commenting on how Maciel could have fooled so many for so long. "The myth of Maciel fit John Paul's idea of what church should be—grand, conspicuous, highly regimented, filled with loyal priests who would not question authority, rich in personal heroics, and larded top to bottom with pious practices and rules that helped maintain order." It was a vision held dear by those in the United States who ardently defended Maciel and the Legion.

The Maciel myth fit the John Paul II myth, and John Paul's acolytes in the United States couldn't imagine such an enormous disconnect in what they considered a seamless and holy narrative. All of those young priests they saw attracted to the Legion, all the full seminaries, the spiritual disciplines, the piety, the robust orthodoxy, the rigorous approach to sexual issues, the regimented ranks of lay followers, all embraced and celebrated and rewarded by their bigger-than-life pope. This was the newly reclaimed old Catholicism; this was certainly the future, the direction the church should be heading. After the truth about Maciel became irrefutable, Neuhaus wrote in *First Things* on May 19, 2006, that "one of the many factors that entered into my moral certainty regarding Fr. Maciel's innocence was my great respect for John Paul II and his repeated statements of support for Fr. Maciel." Personality cult piled on personality cult.

Neuhaus, using a tactic often employed by those defending the clerical culture amid the sex abuse crisis, condemned the journalists who broke the story. He wrote in *First Things* in March 2002: "Berry's business is Catholic scandal and sensationalism. That is what he does. Renner's tour at the *Courant* was marked by an animus against things Catholic."

In a clear reflection of the culture they defended, a culture with its quietly negotiated system of payment and reward, John Paul and his most ardent acolytes were able to see only the trouble that fit the script. They were unable to hear the cries of the victims.

Different Views Emerge

What Peter Isely remembers about driving to a coffee shop in the suburbs north of Milwaukee in November 2009 to meet Fr. James Connell was that he really didn't want to go.[12]

Isely, a victim of clergy abuse and a founding member of the Survivors Network of those Abused by Priests, known as SNAP, had been to so many meetings. "I was tired. I was tired of the whole thing."

"How can I put this?" he asked. "I usually get calls from priests, or priests come up to me in town, and they say, 'Thanks, if it weren't for you guys nothing would change.' But they would never do something publicly."

So he thought this would be another of those meetings where perhaps there would be a bit of understanding that wasn't there before, an experience of the other person as something more than a collar or, conversely, as something more than a protester.

This meeting, however, would end up being different from the rest. And it would be different, Isely said in retrospect, because Connell dared to ask a critical question of himself. It was a question that might, in the asking, sound remarkably obvious, especially for a minister of the gospel. But it was so unusual that Isely said he's never heard of a Catholic cleric asking it of himself in the context of the sexual abuse crisis.

What makes the question all the more intriguing is that it occurred to Connell the same day he learned that Isely and other members of SNAP had called for his removal from the archdiocesan review board because, the group alleged, he had been part of a cover-up of a notorious case of sexual abuse during his time in the chancery office in the 1990s.

October 13, 2009, was an agonizing day for Connell. The accusation, which he still denies, stung. The archdiocese contends that Connell, at the time he was vice chancellor, documented the offenses of the late Fr. Lawrence Murphy, who was believed to have molested as many as two hundred boys at St. John's School for the Deaf between 1950 and 1974. According to the archdiocese, Connell's documentation was aimed at permanently removing Murphy from the priesthood.

The victims' group, however, charged that Connell failed to notify the deaf community of Murphy's history. Those conflicting claims, and whether it was Connell's responsibility to notify the deaf community, remain unresolved.

The morning that he heard about the charges, announced by Isely in a televised news conference on the steps of the cathedral in Milwaukee, Connell had to make a trip from Sheboygan, where he is pastor of two parishes, to Milwaukee to visit the sick child of parishioners. He said he was "torn apart by lots of emotions."

As he left the hospital to return to his car, the question that had been bubbling below the surface all morning burst through: What if I had been a victim of sexual abuse by a priest?

On the drive back to Sheboygan he said he prayed the rosary and felt a calm come over him. The question has stayed with him, and since that day he has come to consider "the minor bruising" he received as incidental compared with the suffering of those who have been abused.

He said he came to understand that "something else was going on, another door was opening. That TV moment may have been a moment of God's grace, too."

"During the ensuing days," he wrote in his open letter, "I found my empathy for [abuse victims] growing as I focused on their struggle for truth, justice, healing and peace. I also began to wonder how the lives of survivors would be different today if they had never been abused by a priest."

That moment led to a phone call to Isely and their meeting.

Isely is a psychotherapist, a clinical social worker with a degree from Harvard Divinity School and experience in working with victims of clergy abuse. Around 2002 he gave up that dimension of his work when he decided to become a more committed advocate for victims while maintaining a small private practice. Isely was abused by a priest while a young student in a seminary school.

"Rape and assault is a violent parody of human love and human consent to love," said Isely. "However God made the universe, he made it in a way that would require our free consent to him and to consenting to his absence here, as we find in the book of Job and as we find on the cross, the horror of that absence.

"I've seen almost 20 years as a victim, and as survivors begin to speak, a remnant comes forth to ask: Where can we place our witness to change the culture and stop the next assault? That is why Fr. Connell is so important. Because what he is doing and what he is trying to do may stop the next assault of a child."

The sixty-seven-year-old Connell had an unusual path to priesthood: a master's degree in accounting (certification he maintains to this day), a senior-manager-level position at the big accounting firm Peat Marwick Mitchell & Co., and a failed marriage that he describes as "more my fault than hers." Whether all of that had anything to do with his ability to see things differently is unknown, but asking the question about what it would have been like to be a victim of clergy abuse forced him to consider a perspective that a lot of victims would say has been missing from all the other church activity, however laudable.

From that perspective, Connell has criticized the LaCrosse, Wisconsin, diocese for making it more difficult for the review board there to determine whether a priest is credibly accused of abuse. The standards of evidence being used, he said, go well beyond those required by the U.S. bishops' charter and by civil law. "Some priests or deacons could still be in active ministry who would not be there if the correct standard of proof were used," he said.

He has organized regular discussions with victims and with priests, and he has shown up, unsolicited, at a SNAP demonstration. He has spoken out to his brother priests in the diocese, arguing that the church "cannot be healed from the poison of the priests' sexual abuse scandal until three questions are discussed publicly. Who knew what? When did they know it? And, what was done with the information?"

Connell's is a relatively fresh voice on the abuse issue in the United States, and his questions, arising from his personal contact with those who have been abused by priests, are rare evidence of a change of view within the clerical culture. He has reached a new starting point for consideration of the crisis, as he recounted in a January 2011 presentation to members of the Milwaukee Archdiocese Priests' Alliance: "Whether committed by force or by seduction, every act of sexual abuse of a minor by a priest is a crime, both in civil law and in church law. No doubt, most people understand the term 'statutory rape.' Indeed, from teenage years onward, people know that sexual activity between an adult and a minor is wrong, legally and morally. So, in discussing sexual abuse of minors by priests we are not talking about the actions of a schoolyard bully. We are talking about the actions of a criminal. This must be the starting point for addressing this crisis."

Looking at the issue through the lens of his new questions, he comes upon a particularly searing one for the hierarchy. He told his fellow priests that a parishioner had commented to him that "parents would never allow their children to be near an abuser, no matter the status of the statute of limitations or the advice of psychologists. Why did bishops not behave as parents? Why did they not protect the children?"

Connell has reached the conclusion that the issue today "is not about current protocols, nor is it about the volume of data that has been provided to the courts. Rather, it's about the response of the church in the early years of the priests' sexual abuse crisis, and how the response in those years continues to impact life today for some victims/survivors, as well as for the church community and the civil community."

What effect the pastor of two parishes in Sheboygan, Wisconsin, might have in changing the hierarchical culture remains to be seen, but in statements, speeches, interviews, and at least one pastoral letter, bishops in various parts of the world beyond the United States have begun raising similarly provocative questions about what happened. Their questions extend to whether something intrinsic to the Roman Catholic Church—perhaps its clerical culture, its manner of governance, the way its leaders exercise authority, or a combination of these—has either caused or abetted the priest sex abuse tragedy.

From South Africa to Australia, Austria to Ireland, prelates are suggesting that perhaps deeply ingrained habits that have become inherent to clerical and hierarchical behavior, yet are inimical to the message the church proclaims, have contributed to the depth and scope of the scandal.[13]

The discussion that is emerging from church leaders in other parts of the world is markedly, and in some instances dramatically, different from the responses and analyses of the problem that have been advanced by bishops in the United States.

One of the more formal and extensive examinations was issued in May 2010 by Archbishop Mark Coleridge of Canberra and Goulburn, Australia, in a pastoral letter timed for Pentecost titled "Seeing the Faces, Hearing the Voices: A Pentecost Letter on Sexual Abuse of the Young in the Catholic Church."

Coleridge declined to be interviewed, responding in an email that he invited reference to the letter, but that he had otherwise decided to allow the pastoral to speak for itself, adding, "For the moment I may have said enough."

Coleridge's pastoral outlines his growing awareness of the problem—from meeting with and listening to victims to reading transcripts of trials and working in the Vatican. That awareness eventually led him to a point of view that at first he had rejected, that priest abuse of children was "cultural rather than merely personal, at least in the Australian situation."

"I came to think that the problem was in some way cultural, but that prompted the further question of how; what was it that allowed this canker to grow in the body of the Catholic Church, not just here and there but more broadly? I would part company with some answers to this question, because they seem to me ill-informed, one-dimensional or ideologically driven. There is no one factor that makes abuse of the young by Catholic clergy in some sense cultural. It seems to me rather a complex combination of factors which I do not claim to understand fully, even if I now understand more than I did."

Among the elements Coleridge listed that may have contributed to the culture that allowed the crisis to fester and grow are the following:

- "Poor understanding and communication of the church's teaching on sexuality, shown particularly in a rigorist attitude to the body and sexuality."
- Clerical celibacy, while not itself a factor in Coleridge's estimation, "may also have been attractive to men in whom there were pedophile tendencies which may not have been explicitly recognized by the men themselves when they entered the seminary."
- "Certain forms of seminary training which failed to take proper account of human formation and promoted therefore a kind of institutionalized immaturity."
- "Clericalism understood as a hierarchy of power, not service. . . . It was a fruit of seminary training that was inadequate at certain points, and it is almost inevitable once the priesthood and preparation for it are not deeply grounded in the life of faith and discipleship."
- "A certain triumphalism in the Catholic church, a kind of institutional pride, was a further factor. There is much in the Catholic church, her culture and tradition about which one can be justifiably proud. . . . But there can be a dark side to this which leads to a determination to protect the reputation of the church at all costs."
- "The church's culture of forgiveness, which tends to view things in terms of sin and forgiveness rather than crime and punishment."
- A "culture of discretion" that "turned dark when it was used to conceal crime and to protect the reputation of the church or the image of the priesthood in a country that has never known the virulent anticlericalism of elsewhere."

While Coleridge had the opportunity to watch the scandal unfold from several vantage points—he spent several years working at the Vatican's Secretariat of State before being appointed a bishop in 2002—others caught in the crossfire of the controversy have also issued strong, if much briefer, statements.

Bishop Donal McKeown, auxiliary bishop of Down and Connor in Ireland, commented following the release of the government report on sex abuse in the Dublin archdiocese: "What I am looking forward to is the church in Ireland seriously taking on that agenda [for reform], committing itself to a process that will develop us into a church that is transparent, that is open and accountable."

Bishop Willie Walsh of Killaloe, in advocating for reform, told the *Irish News,* "If some structures which we have put up over the years and over the centuries have to be taken down, then so be it."

In an April 22 statement, Irish Bishop Jim Moriarty of Kildare and Leighlin said he was announcing his resignation because he had been part of the governance of the Dublin archdiocese "prior to when correct child protection policies and procedures were implemented. Again, I accept that from the time I became an auxiliary bishop, I should have challenged the prevailing culture.

"The truth is," he said, "that the long struggle of survivors to be heard and respected by church authorities has revealed a culture within the church that many would simply describe as unchristian. People do not recognize the gentle, endless love of the Lord in narrow interpretations of responsibility and a basic lack of compassion and humility."

The term *culture* appears in many of the analyses advanced by the bishops mentioned here. It is never precisely defined, but it is often used in a way that assumes Catholics understand its meaning.

An example is contained in the statement issued by the Irish bishops, from their December 2009 conference, responding to the evidence of widespread abuse and cover-up detailed in the Murphy Report, the result of a government investigation into the Dublin archdiocese: "We are shamed by the extent to which child sexual abuse was covered up in the archdiocese of Dublin and recognize that this indicates a culture that was widespread in the church. The avoidance of scandal, the preservation of the reputations of individuals and of the church, took precedence over the safety and welfare of children."

Archbishop Diarmuid Martin, a Vatican official much of his career who was appointed to Dublin in 2004, has been an unusually forceful advocate of full disclosure. He has also sought, unsuccessfully and behind the scenes, the resignation of a number of Irish bishops, including two of his own auxiliaries who were implicated in past cover-ups.

Following release of the Murphy Report, Martin told The Associated Press that his colleagues in the Irish hierarchy "must tell 'the entire truth'" about decades of church cover-up of abuse or face broader investigations by the government. To that end, he willingly handed over seventy thousand pages of documents related to abuse and cover-up. In an interview on Irish television he said he had read many of them over a weekend and at one point became so disgusted that he threw them to the floor.

In the wake of those revelations Martin has emphasized both priest training and formation of laity for pastoral work. During an April 4, 2011, talk at Marquette University Law School, Martin said that he was working on plans to have seminarians, prospective deacons, and laity training to be pastoral workers "share some sections of their studies together, in order to create a better culture of collaborative ministry. The narrow culture of clericalism has to be eliminated."

Martin expressed discouragement at the reluctance within the church to undertake "a painful process of renewal."

While expressing optimism that ultimately the future of the church would be guided by the Holy Spirit, he said that on a personal level, "I have never felt so disheartened and discouraged about the level of willingness to really begin what is going to be a painful path of renewal and of what is involved in that renewal."

In his talks and other statements Martin is not specific about the practical steps he might envision in that renewal. Perhaps he stays away from specifics because raising the specter of renewal in such terms can also raise a host of complications. While he believes the future of the church in Ireland "will see a very different Catholic church," he said he worries "when I hear those with institutional responsibility stress the role of the institution, and others then in reaction saying that 'we are the church.' Perhaps on both sides there may be an underlying feeling that 'I am the church,' that the church must be modeled on my way of thinking or on my position. Renewal is never our own creation. Renewal will only come through returning to the church which we have received from the Lord."

But before any renewal can occur, people have to be aware of the need for it, and Martin lamented "the drip-by-drip, never-ending revelation about child sexual abuse and the disastrous way it was handled. There are still strong forces which would prefer that the truth did not emerge. . . . There are signs of subconscious denial on the part of many about the extent of the abuse which occurred . . . and how it was covered up. There are other signs of rejection of a sense of responsibility for what had happened."

In an April 2011 talk at Marquette University Law School in Milwaukee, Martin said that although he has been criticized for handing over documentation to the state investigators, he believed then that he "was doing the right thing and I was more and more convinced I was doing the right thing the more I read those documents and as I met with some of those who were the victims of abuse and their parents and their spouses and their children."

He said he was angry at the church leaders for failing the weakest in the community. "I still cannot accept a situation that no one need assume accountability in the face of the terrible damage that was done to children in the church of Christ in Dublin and in the face of how that damage was addressed."

Different Response in the United States

To the ears of U.S. Catholics the candor of Coleridge and Martin, especially the latter's cooperation with civil authorities, would ring as a starkly different approach than that taken by most U.S. prelates. But the assessments of the several government investigations that have been conducted into the activities of various dioceses in Ireland are strikingly similar to those made by the few grand juries and the National Review Board appointed by the U.S. bishops in the wake of the explosive revelations in 2002 about sex abuse and the church cover-up over decades in the Boston archdiocese. The conclusions are in agreement about fundamental points: the church failed to report crime to civil authorities and in most instances acted to protect the interests of the institution and the priesthood rather than act in the best interest of those abused.

Martin seems to reject the familiar hierarchical defenses when he writes that while sexual abuse of children by priests "constitutes only a small percentage of the sexual abuse of children in our society in general," that fact "should never appear in any way as an attempt to downplay the gravity of what took place in the church of Christ. The church is different; the church is a place where children should be the subject of special protection and care. The Gospel presents children in a special light and reserves some of its most severe language for those who disregard or scandalize children in any way."

Similarly, he turns on those who critique the church's response in terms of public relations. "There are those who claim that the media strategy of the church in the archdiocese of Dublin following the publication of the Murphy Report was 'catastrophic.' My answer is that what the Murphy Report narrated was catastrophic and that the only honest reaction of the church was to publicly admit that the manner in which that catastrophe was addressed was spectacularly wrong; spectacularly wrong 'full stop'; not spectacularly wrong, 'but . . . ' You cannot sound-bite your way out of a catastrophe."

Conceding that sexual abuse of children may have been viewed differently in past eras, Martin nonetheless wonders how the church could have turned its back on children. "It is hard . . . to understand why, in the management by church authorities of cases of the sexual abuse of children, the children themselves were for many years rarely even taken into the equation."

The questions that Martin and other bishops are beginning to pose echo the questions that have been posed for more than two decades in a variety of formats by advocates such as David Clohessy and Barbara Blaine of SNAP; by Fr. Thomas Doyle and Richard Sipe in their books and in countless columns and articles; by church observers and writers such as Eugene Kennedy, Peter Steinfels, Margaret Steinfels, David Gibson, Scott Appleby, Sr. Joan Chittister, Mary Gail Frawley-O'Dea, Russell Shaw, Rod Dreher, lately George Weigel, and the list could be extended much further. This thick cloud of witnesses to the scandal, people whose lives and careers cross all manner of ideological and theological boundaries, may not come to the same conclusions on remedies, but they are asking many of the same questions. Central are questions about accountability, transparency, trust, and truthfulness. The hierarchy is left with a difficult choice because it stands to lose a great deal in terms of privilege, exclusivity, and the perquisites inherent in the old way of doing things should it choose to open up the culture to deeper examination; at the same time it has even more to lose in the long run in terms of trust, credibility, and moral authority if it doesn't.[14]

As convinced as I am that detailing the record and pursuing the truth of the sex abuse matter is essential to the long-term health of the Catholic community, I am just as aware that spending as much time as my job required amid the weeds of that toxic patch can give one an excessively gloomy view of the church. That's why in the spring of 2008 I decided to get out from behind the desk to go breathe in the walk of faith that I knew was occurring beneath the cloud of scandal and despite the many intra-Catholic squabbles.

Some years ago a bishop from a very rural diocese who was known for experimenting with church practice (he had to, there weren't nearly enough priests to do things the conventional way) told me that if I wanted to see the future of the church, I should go look in the margins of things, not in the downtowns of the big archdioceses.

His advice was on my mind when I headed to New Mexico.

Chapter 6

TRAVELS ON THE MARGINS

New Mexico

It is unlikely that New Mexico would be the first option that comes to mind should discussion turn to the future of the church in the United States. If, however, as many indicators suggest, the future church will have to do more with less, will have to move from the unsustainable models of the past to something more modest and reliant on lay ministry, New Mexico may not be a bad place to investigate.[1]

The state has about it an austere, out-of-the-way character, with its long stretches of desert and horizons of abraded, reddish mountains. The landscape along Route 25, which runs the length of the state from north to south, can be evocative of the biblical quality of unseen significance. This land of hidden prospects might hold some answers for the future.

The church here has a history that arches back four hundred years through struggle and eventual resolution among the indigenous culture and Spanish missionaries and colonists. This is not the Irish church; it is not the church of immigrants striving to make it in a WASP culture. It has never had the money or other resources to heap up great monuments of granite and marble. It is a humble church, even today, but one rich in examples of hard-earned successes.

Fittingly, the Catholic Center in the Santa Fe archdiocese, located in Albuquerque, near the geographic center of the state, is a modest structure on a campus that includes a high school.

In Las Cruces, a diocese that sprawls along the state's southern border, the Diocesan Center has the low-slung look of a typical strip mall installation. It would be difficult to gin up a great deal of hubris in such an environment, especially when one wall of the main corridor of the center is lined with the haunting, iconic wood engravings of Fritz Eichenberg, whose work was popularized by Dorothy Day's *Catholic Worker* newspaper.

A third diocese, Gallup, describes itself as a mission diocese within the multicultural Southwest. It covers areas of northwestern New Mexico and northeastern Arizona.

In many ways the church in New Mexico stays close to the ground and to the people. It never has had an abundance of "homegrown" priests. Because of the great distances between places (people in the chancery office say the drive from the eastern to the western extremities of the Las Cruces diocese takes about ten hours by car) Catholics traditionally have had to fend for themselves in a way that those in parishes of the Northeast, for instance, have not.

No great Catholic institutions have arisen here, so Catholicism has had to inject itself in different ways into institutional life. At the University of New Mexico, for instance, Richard Wood founded the Southwest Institute on Religion and Civil Society, to which he brings a background steeped in Catholic social tradition. That tradition is strongly reflected in the institute's programs and research topics.

"The things that other places worry about are the way things have always been here, and we've survived," said Dominican Fr. Matthew Strabala, director of the Dominican Ecclesial Institute, a collaborative effort among the Dominicans who run the Aquinas Newman Center at the University of New Mexico, the archdiocese, and lay participants. "That's not to put everything in the negative. There's something about the style of church here; it's as old as the hills."

Quite a bit older, in fact, some priests here like to point out to friends from places like New York and Philadelphia, than Catholicism on the East Coast.

Out of that history has come "a balance, a collaboration, between the different dimensions of it—the Spaniard style and the Pueblo spirituality—and life does just move at a different pace here," said Strabala. "It's the older-style Spanish Catholicism, where it's much more community based. It's not as instinctively hierarchical," he said, as is the church in other parts of the country.

It is easy to get the impression that this is one of those places where theology and necessity are meeting to fashion something new, the shape of which is not yet clear. In the summer of 2009, Dominican Sr. Bernice Garcia, seventy-two, was keeping things together at St. Francis Xavier Parish in a poor neighborhood in downtown Albuquerque. Her title was parish administrator, but by any other name (canonical precision notwithstanding) she was the pastor. Ten years ago a visitor here would not have encountered a woman holding that position. Garcia never dreamed as a little girl growing up in this parish that she would one day be the equivalent of its pastor.

Sarah Nolan was a sophomore at the University of San Francisco at the turn of the millennium. She was a long way from her home in southern New Mexico and had already moved through progressive stages of personal change—from a fascination with science and wanting to be an engineer to interest in marketing to undecided—when she found her window to deeper faith and a life's work steeped in the church's social justice tradition.

Though separated in age by at least two generations, and worlds apart in life experience, Nolan, twenty-eight at the time of the interview in 2009, and Garcia represent some of the strong impulses within the Catholic community that are shaping its future: the growing role of laity in the church, especially women, despite prohibitions against ordination of women; the conviction reinforced by the Second Vatican Council that Catholics, by virtue of their baptism, have an essential part to play in salvation history; and the rising awareness throughout Christianity of the social dimension of a life of faith.

Nolan may have been feeling a bit adrift in her second year at the University of San Francisco, but the Jesuits had a new way of focusing a young adult's attention. Nolan had joined one of the new Living and Learning Communities the Jesuits had established on campus. Members lived on the same floor of a dormitory. They prayed and reflected together as a community, and they took a class together.

The class she attended that began to change her life dealt with globalization. A video shown during the first class opened with a scene of the Organ Mountains, a southern New Mexico landmark she knew well. It is a rugged range said to have received its name from early Spanish colonists who thought one of the formations resembled the stacked pipes of organs in European cathedrals.

Nolan recalled, "And then they showed the mountain range that went from El Paso to Juárez, the Sangre de Cristo Mountains. And then they started talking about the *maquiladoras,*" the factories that were springing up just on the other side of the border in Mexico, places that often were described as sweatshops, with terrible working conditions and low wages, where products were manufactured cheaply for consumers in the developed world.

The documentary dealt with wrenching issues along the border: women being killed trying to get to work, divided families, and the dangers of illegal migration. "After class, I sat with my roommate and I bawled. I was just crying, and I couldn't figure out why it had affected me so much. I think after some reflection I realized I was just really angry. I was angry first of all at what was happening—the realities that were uncovered to me. Second of all, I was angry because no one had taken the time to teach me or to tell me what was going on in my own hometown. . . . I was mad because I had to move two thousand miles away and pay a private institution to teach me what was happening in my own backyard. That moment was for me my first kind of conversion experience."

She didn't leave things at the anger stage.

She began to dig a little bit deeper into the why of her anger and the why of the conditions she was learning about. "I started doing a lot of justice work. I worked with the School of the Americas Watch on campus. I was working on United Students Against Sweatshops. We started our Peace and Justice Coalition." She went to Washington to lobby, and she began to realize the distance between "the people I was organizing and doing justice with" and "the people I was going to church with."

Church was important to her, an anchor in San Francisco and at university, places dramatically different from her home. "I could go to mass and I would feel like home because it was the same. I could go and I knew the routine, I knew what the words meant, and I knew it just felt familiar, so I would just dive into mass."

She was invited to become more involved with liturgy planning and began to learn the deeper significance of liturgical elements and practice. "I was just fascinated by it, so I started taking more theology courses, and then I started taking more Latin American history courses."

She spent five months in El Salvador in 2001–2 in a Jesuit program. She lived and worked in community "and saw these Catholic women organizing cooperatives because their families didn't have enough meat, so they had a soy cooperative where they would make soy products.

"I saw finally what I had realized was missing at the University of San Francisco, where the justice and peace work was over here, and the faith work was over there. I realized what was missing was what the women and people in the community were doing in El Salvador. . . . They were utilizing their faith and their faith formation as a lens for their justice work. There was like a switch that went off in me. I was like, 'Oh, it doesn't happen in a vacuum. Both don't happen separately. It's because we're Catholic that we do this justice work.'"

When she returned, she was convinced "there has to be something of that equivalent for the United States and for our communities." During the months she spent in El Salvador, she kept thinking about Las Cruces and the surrounding towns and villages of the Mesilla Valley. Married now and the mother of a young child, she's doing "faith-based community organizing" back in southern New Mexico, gathering religious leaders across denominational and political boundaries "to negotiate the interests" of the region.

New Mexico ranks at the wrong end of many national lists: forty-eighth in high school graduation, second in teen pregnancy, low on the list in children's health. The counties of southern New Mexico fall even below the state rate, she said, while "most of the money and power is in northern New Mexico."

"Who is speaking for the residents of southern New Mexico and who is able to focus all the needs and interests? I think it's our churches and our congregations." It is there, she said, that values and needs align. She has formed a PICO affiliate for the region, Comunidades en Accion y de Fe (CAFÉ). One by one she has involved members of the clergy from a variety of denominations across southern New Mexico. A number of Catholic priests have become involved.

From immigration issues to poverty to homelessness to feeding people through ubiquitous food banks, she is putting liberals in touch with conservatives, evangelicals with Catholics, connecting African Americans, Hispanics, and Anglos, and doing the painstaking work of figuring out how they can work together.

There is tension over some issues, particularly immigration, between some Hispanic and white pastors "because they don't know each other." So she stepped up her efforts, with the help of a Catholic priest and Methodist minister, to meet individually with other pastors "to engage them a little more deeply before we bring them all together again."

And then there is the occasional surprise, like the rabbi at the local reform synagogue who said his biggest concern was the need to work on immigration, even though his congregation is mostly retired, white, and not from New Mexico. The rabbi explained by recalling Jewish history and its multiple exoduses. He said he viewed the immigration centers as "modern-day concentration camps." His problem was that he didn't know any immigrants, and that's where Nolan came in. "There's this desire to be in relationship with people who are directly affected by the problem so that they can not only get to know people who are going through this problem, but so they can also have a path for their theology" and apply it to the realities that people are going through.

How does she see a solution to the seemingly intractable immigration issue?

"My stance is very much a Catholic one, where countries have rights to secure their borders" but at the same time a responsibility to minimize harm. "And right now, people are dying in our desert trying to cross. Families are being separated.

"I think long term we're going to have to legalize many of the people who are already here. It is unrealistic for us to think that people are going to have to return to their native country and then come back. There has to be some kind of compromise. As a church, we need to be prepared for that conversation and we need to start preparing our congregants to have this discussion because if we think health care is a divisive issue in our congregations, holy cow, just wait until immigration."

In El Salvador, Nolan learned that religion there did not remain a "mountaintop experience." She was told there to "go back down the mountain. Don't pitch your tents up here. Go back down and use what you're learning and what we're teaching in your struggles for dignity and respect."

Now she's doing that beneath the Organ Mountains, and she's discovered that "people are experts on their own lives. They know what's going on, and if we're willing to listen to them and be in relationship with them, we would know the solutions so much easier. . . . We put people in relationship with one another—people who are afraid of losing their healthcare and people who don't have healthcare; people who have been citizens their whole life and who maybe came here generations and generations ago, and people who are just new to this country. They need to start knowing each other, so that's what we're trying to do here in southern New Mexico."

On a Wednesday morning in late August 2009, Sr. Bernice Garcia sat in the back of a small chapel on the grounds of St. Francis Xavier parish as people wandered in for 8 o'clock mass. It was celebrated by a husky young priest, a member of the Franciscan Friars of Renewal, a relatively new order based in New York, who prayed many of the prayers in Spanish but spoke the homily in English.

His sermon finished, Garcia stood at the side of the chapel and summarized the main points of the priest's reflections in Spanish for the mostly Spanish-speaking congregation.

This is church in New Mexico, at times cobbled together with the help of outsiders, expressed almost always in two languages, simultaneously steeped in tradition and pushing the edges of new forms of organization. Garcia is a member of the Grand Rapid Dominicans of the Sacred Heart, but she grew up in New Mexico in the parish where she was pastoral administrator until the summer of 2010, and she's spent much of her career here as an educator and leading other parishes.

She embodies the mix of old and new and considers herself traditional. Yet she holds views that are hardly traditional. She was deeply affected by the Second Vatican Council. "It gave us permission to move forward," she said, recalling the era before the council when "mother superiors made all the decisions. The biggest thing that happened was in our apostolate. That was the most important thing." Prior to Vatican II, she said, sisters were sent, "and sometimes when you're sent, you don't commit. You're sent and so you think, 'I have to be here.'" It's different when you have to find your own job. "You had better do that job. I think we have served better. Then, we also opened up. There was nothing that wasn't available to us."

She remembers being interviewed in those early years after Vatican II and asked the question: "What do you think a sister should not do?"

"I thought, 'Well, she probably shouldn't be a bartender.' And then I thought, 'Bartenders are probably the best psychologists in the world. People sit and tell them their whole story.' I couldn't think of any legitimate job a sister couldn't do. We have sisters who became hairdressers. They do it for us, and they do it for the homeless downtown. They listen, and they have brought people back into the church. So we preach. Wherever you go, you can preach."

The traditionalist in her is sometimes trumped by the needs of the community. "I do what needs to be done," she said. "That's how I preach. That's how I live my charism."

She said she'd never thought, as a novice, that she would one day be running a parish. "I've never wanted to be a priest either, but I think, 'Why can't women serve as priests?' I think we should have married men first, because we have deacons already. It could easily happen. If the pope said, 'Let's ordain married men,' it could happen because so many of them are already working in churches.'"

And that pragmatism surfaces in other ways. Once a priest objected because she was blessing people. "I said, 'Heck, I'm baptized. Baptized people can bless. I bless holy water. I bless the people and whatever articles they bring.' It's better that than saying, 'Wait until Sunday,' because they're not going to wait until Sunday. They're not going to remember. Things need to be done when they're needed."

In fact, her position at St. Francis Xavier grew out of such need. There were no priests available, and the archdiocese needed someone to run the parish, so she was appointed. She was, in the summer of 2009, one of four women in the Santa Fe archdiocese who were pastoral administrators. Whether the role of women will expand in Santa Fe is an open question. Archbishop Michael Sheehan, when asked how the archdiocese would deal in the future with the growing priest shortage, responded that male deacons would probably occupy pastoral administrator spots in the future.

That apparently was not Sheehan's intent when he had to replace Garcia. In June 2010, hampered by knee and hip problems and barely able to walk, Sr. Garcia retired. She said the bishop at first urged her to stay on. She said the archdiocese interviewed several other religious women in an attempt to replace her, but none could commit soon enough to take the position. A permanent deacon has been hired to take her place.

The issue of religious women being replaced by deacons can be a point of contention. Religious sisters and other women I spoke to in my travels see the trend as another irritating gender issue within the church. Bishops were fine with religious women and even lay couples when no other option existed, they claim, but as soon as enough permanent deacons, another layer of ordained male clergy, become available, the religious women and lay people are replaced.

If deacons figure to be a significant part of the future, the Santa Fe archdiocese has a good jump on it. Sheehan points out with some pride that permanent deacons now outnumber priests, a group that includes a substantial percentage of foreign priests. The breakdown, as it stood in 2010, was telling:

- Of 86 active diocesan priests, 14 were foreign.
- Of 91 religious order priests, 17 were foreign.
- Of 220 ordained permanent deacons, 187 were active, 10 more than the number of priests.

A reality today, said Deacon Steve Rangel, director of deacons and of pastoral outreach for the archdiocese, is that while the faith remains constant, the church keeps changing. "The church here adapts and makes whatever modifications and changes are necessary because the centermost part of it is our faith. It is like a leaf going down a stream. There may be boulders and other obstructions, but the leaf will find the path. It follows the flow; it doesn't fight against it."

Several hours to the south, in Las Cruces, some of the adaptations are apparent. The chancellor in 2009 was a lay man, Wayne Pribble. He previously owned and operated a psychological and psychiatric clinic in Indianapolis. Since leaving the chancellor's position in 2010, he and his wife are running the diocesan retreat center.

The vice chancellor in Las Cruces is Debbie Moore, who began working for the diocese in 1984 as a secretary in the ministries office.

They are two members of a chancery staff that is nearly all lay people and religious sisters. In an interview Bishop Ricardo Ramirez pointed out that at the time there was no full-time priest at the pastoral center. "The vicar general is not here full time. Our chancellor is a lay man; our vice chancellor is a lay woman. I'm the only one that's full time, and even I am part time because I'm out a lot."

Las Cruces is one of the poorest dioceses in the country, located in a state that in 2007 was ranked forty-fourth in household income. As much as 20 percent of the diocese's funding comes from outside, primarily from the U.S. bishops and the Extension Society. This close to Mexico (half the state border's Mexico, the other half, Texas), immigration issues color everything. Catechists have to be aware in their planning not to ask youngsters to travel to gatherings that will require going through highway immigration checkpoints. Being a member of the church here is a no-questions-asked proposition. Illegals are welcomed. Ramirez says he is proud of the U.S. church as a whole in its efforts to "welcome the stranger."

In conversations people often acknowledge, without prodding, the pervasive poverty if only so they can talk about how rich they are in other things, those intangibles that arise out of their history and experience.

History's current chapter in a border region like Las Cruces is dominated by the experience of immigration, a reality that has become an integral part of the social infrastructure here. The church finds itself smack in the middle of all the tensions. If church workers have to be aware not to send undocumented kids through Border Patrol check points, they might also be called on to minister to future Border Patrol members who attend the national training center in Artesia, within the diocese. The Catholics among them are bused to one of two small parishes in that area.

Ramirez believes the law should be changed. "It must change just out of humanitarian concern. It's so un-American for our country to be doing what it's doing with families of the undocumented, and with families separated, with even spouses not able to be together or with their children, or children with their parents—that is unpardonable.

"And then there have been reports about the way some of these detainees are treated. They're not criminals, they're not dangerous, they haven't committed criminal acts of violence, but they are treated as if they were."

At the same time the bishop believes borders have to be secured, and if law enforcement is an inevitable part of the mix, he prefers the Border Patrol to local police. He said he is "very impressed" with the training prospective members of the Border Patrol receive over a six-month period. "They have to be fluent in Spanish if they want to get out as Border Patrol officers," he said. Also, they are trained in immigration law. They become almost immigration lawyers when they come out of there. . . . That's why I don't like local law enforcement officers—police departments, sheriff's departments—doing that work. They haven't had the training that these other fellows have had."

Las Cruces is not just materially poor, as a diocese it's low on priests, too, which has forced it to develop strong lay ministries. Lay ministries always teeter on the fence between theology and need. Where lay people are in demand because of a shortage of priests, the theology of lay ministry, the lay person's sense of calling, the language of the priesthood of the people is always close at hand. But even in a region of great need, as is the case with Las Cruces, the temptation is to swap out lay leadership should a priest become available. Lay leaders throughout the country will tell you that one of the unspoken conditions of employment in the church is a constant sense of uncertainty. Are they called, and is there a strong theology of lay ministry? Or is the call limited to times of need?

Ramirez said he's "learned some hard lessons over the years" regarding lay employees. "We would have a lay person running the parish and all of a sudden we found a priest. 'Oh we found a priest!' So immediately [the priest] was sent to take over. We hurt that lay person; he or she just had to move out of the way, and we will never do that again."

Now, he said, whenever a lay person is asked to take over the running of a parish—and the same goes for a permanent deacon or a woman religious—he or she receives a contract. "We assign them first," said Ramirez. "They get a term. Like a priest gets a six-year term, the lay person or pastoral life coordinator will be assigned for two years, three years, four years, five years—whatever it is—and we respect that."

He even sees the prospects for permanent positions in the future, "especially in small parishes and small missions that are very hard for us to get a priest for. I think in the future, there will be permanent situations."

It is arguably easier to envision such a future in a place like Las Cruces than in other dioceses because parishes here have been run by lay women, religious sisters, and a lay man who was not a permanent deacon. Ramirez said the church is also affected by the success of Protestant evangelical Hispanic churches. "They are powerful, they're smart, they're articulate, and it's not just that they entice people by helping them materially or by being nice to them. They have something to offer; they have something to give."

He describes that something as "charism," and "passion," "the excitement of the gospel, and they're able to put it across."

He finds evangelical preaching inspiring and asks, "If they can do it, why can't we do it? We have the fullness of truth, we have the fullness of the life of the sacraments. We have so much more. Why can't we be as excited or even more excited? I really think with the Hispanic people, there's a lot of great potential that we have not begun to even tap into. We're talking about people who have very, very strong faith. I mean, the Latino people are fundamentally people of faith."

Handing on the faith is key, he said, and he sees promise among some of the deacons in the diocese who are "wonderful preachers."

"Somewhere along the way, they were encouraged to do what they're doing. . . . I tell the priests, 'Make sure that this deacon preaches at least once a month. Hand him over the speaker's stand. Let him preach. Let him do his stuff,' and some of them are doing wonderful work."

New Jersey

South Camden

A statue situated under a stained-glass window on a side of Sacred Heart Church in South Camden might hold a key to understanding this most unusual place and its legendary pastor. It is a striking bronze sculpture of a clean-shaven young man holding a piece of bread, a fish cooking on a spit nearby.

The pastor, Fr. Michael Doyle, calls it "Breakfast on the Beach with Jesus after the Resurrection." It's one of his favorite scripture stories. The statue was done by a friend, the late Fr. Leonard Carrieri, an Italian priest and Missionary of the Sacred Heart, who lived in the parish. Carrieri had started sculpting in his late fifties and, like so many others, was drawn to do some of his work in this corner of South Camden, where redemption can seem to occur at a breathtaking pace.

You begin to feel this place lure you to an awareness of a reality that is counter to the one that hits you in the face on the drive from outside the city, through the city's burned out neighborhoods, past despairing clumps of young people on street corners and stoops, through the smell of neglect.

Writing about the misery of Camden is the easy part. The evidence in this most broken of American cities is everywhere. In 2002 it was the target of the largest municipal takeover in the history of the country—a $175 million project that essentially allowed for preempting the failed local government—and the initiative has foundered. A 2009 series on Camden by The *Philadelphia Inquirer* started with a description of the city as "so broke, so unable to perform the basic functions of government" that it can't even begin to think about repairing a century-old brick sewer system that leaks into people's homes.

"The glory of it, or the attraction of a Camden," says Doyle, a poet, a peace activist once arrested for stealing draft-board records (and ultimately acquitted), and a native of Ireland, "is the fact that there's so much there to be transformed. The human being has a great love for transformation, and loves to take something and bring out of it what's there."

One morning in August 2009 we stood before Carrieri's statue, this young Jesus with a look of near wonder on his face, gazing beyond his left shoulder as if he hears or sees something interesting in the distance. And from one viewing angle, in the background was another statue, a much more traditional rendering of the Sacred Heart, a full-length, bearded figure in post-resurrection robes.

That seems to be one of the bits of magic about this place. Doyle isn't about taking anyone's church away, but rather expanding everyone's idea about what a Catholic Christian community can be. And it's all done with a bit of Irish whimsy, with a deep sense of how art gives life, and with such a profound connection to humanity that he doesn't need glossy brochures or mission statements to get the point across.

Doyle has been pastor at Sacred Heart a long time, thirty-five years, and he turned seventy-five the year I visited, setting off speculation about when he'd be forced to retire and about what will happen at Sacred Heart should he leave. As of this writing, he's still there and going strong.

If the future of the church will be lived out, as many experts predict, in circumstances of greater scarcity—both in terms of material wealth and numbers of clergy—then Doyle's experience might be instructive. At a time when parishes are leaving the inner city and Catholic schools are closing by the score, Sacred Heart and its elementary school are thriving.

The school more than survives because for decades Doyle has been sending out monthly letters (forty-six hundred at the moment) to sponsors all over the country. He insists on using stamps; he won't hear of metered postage. He started a sponsorship program twenty-five years ago, asking people to give three hundred dollars to a child in Camden. He's never changed the amount, just widened the circle of donors, and in 2008 he raised $700,000.

The parish thrives because it has attracted young people who have taken up bold and inventive ministries and because Doyle has succeeded in incorporating middle-class parishioners from Camden's suburbs into his poor congregation.

The primary objective, said Doyle, is not to be a church to help the poor, but to be a church "to honor the poor."

A bit of food, a bit of art, prayer, photographs everywhere of visitors, famous and little known. It begins to add up. A children's chapel was remodeled in recent years, about the same time that the Heart of Camden, a parish-based nonprofit that "takes over abandoned houses and transforms them into livable housing, and then sells them" was building a greenhouse for a young urban farmer. Things here connect one to the other until you understand, by dint of all the activity and people gathering around, that this is an extraordinary parish.

The children's chapel is handsomely done, and there's a huge rock at one end of it—and another story. When they were digging out the plot for the greenhouse, this huge rock emerged, said Doyle, and he asked workers if they could haul it the block or two to the church and slip it through the chapel windows, which were in the process of being replaced. Of course they could. Things just get done around here, a real contrast to the rest of Camden.

Doyle asked the workers if they could carve out a level spot on the top of the rock to accommodate a chalice and other sacred vessels. They could. So he has an altar for liturgies for the little ones. "I can stand up here and slap this rock," he said, "and tell the children that this rock is older than Moses!" An idea about creation comes into clearer perspective in the basement of Sacred Heart Church.

The walk around the parish continues, and one gets caught up in an intricate web of stories—of efforts and people, of mission and conversion, of endless despair being constantly transformed.

Just outside the children's chapel is a large room, a cafeteria that has been outfitted as a temporary theater in which plays and other performances are staged. In the not too distant future, such productions will be held in a far more professional setting in a theater that the parish is building across the street from the church. The pastor has also had a poet's walk constructed. Someone gave him a brick that supposedly came from one of Henry James's homes in Ireland, and that inspired a brick patio of sorts, fittingly next to the theater, with an arched gate in front and the names of literary figures inscribed in the bricks that make up the walk.

The theater idea began with one of many "dear friends" of Doyle and of Sacred Heart. When conversation turned to the possibility of building a small theater, the friend said he'd take care of the bulk of the fundraising. Someone else tore down the existing structure for nothing, and several unions volunteered labor, and so it goes around here. The theater site received a sort of special blessing when actor Martin Sheen (he was here to narrate a video, "The Poet of Poverty," about Doyle and the parish) orated from the bottom of the pit before construction began.

"What the world needs now is inspiration," said Doyle, in explaining the theater, "and whatever inspires will save. Camden people may be poor, but put them on a stage and they own it."

A brick, a conversation, a need, an encounter, anything is likely to trigger Doyle's imagination, a very Catholic imagination that spills out all over the neighborhood and in all directions. Some of it is very visible, like the peace monument constructed on public land at an intersection just across the street from the church, or the church itself and the public art that surrounds it, or the courtyard setting that he sees as a peaceful space for meditation.

Some thirty years ago Doyle was talking to a poor man who lived in a home nearby. The man told Doyle that he was being forced to move because the landlady was selling the house. Doyle asked for her name and called her and asked how much she needed. She told him twenty-five hundred dollars. "So I gave her thirty-one hundred. I gave her six-hundred more than she asked for it—and then I took the house over." He put the man back into the house and said, "Just give me so much per month and in three years, you'll own the house." And that's what happened.

Doyle realized then that "there wasn't a huge amount of money sitting between rental and owner, and we set out to create owners. If you want to have a neighborhood, you've got to have owners. That was no big, genius thought of mine to start the Heart of Camden. It was simply a guy having to move, and out of that came the Heart of Camden." So far, the organization has rehabbed and sold about 130 homes.

The list grows. "I was talking to the bishop [Joseph Galante] one day," said Doyle, "and he said, 'We've got to work with youth.' I said, 'There are three words to go with that: gym, gym, gym.' A gym is what you need. You've got to get kids into something where they're brought under a roof and play basketball, the boys and girls, and they connect with coaches that help them and so forth." At that point, the Heart of Camden was involved in transforming an old movie theater into a gym.

A former convent was being remodeled into a Center for Transformation "with a view to bring the church into deeper connection with environmental transformation."

There's a thrift shop selling used clothing that was faltering until the poet pastor came up with a business plan: sell diapers cheaper than anyone, but put them at the back of the shop. It worked. "They come for the diapers and then they buy things for 50 cents. . . . It's a ministry to people. They can get good clothes."

At the foundation of it all is liturgy and ritual: for those killed by violence each year, for pregnant women, for the unveiling of a new statue, and Sunday mass. Doyle holds that church is a place to "forget about the head and the intellect. Come with your soul. Come there and be a child and let your soul be lifted. That's what I think about, and then I preach. I say to them, 'I am preaching to you, just going over ground so maybe you have a better idea. I'll go over the ground of the readings and maybe you, if you'll just stay with that, you'll have a better idea than I have in that way.'"

He's not here to give answers, he said, but to "provide help and facilitate the possibility that those attending a liturgy would enter into moments of lift to God. That's it."

North Camden

When Fr. Jeff Putthoff comes into a room, the equilibrium shifts; things move toward him. He is a huge presence with a booming voice and a big laugh. If the Jesuits had a heavyweight division, he'd be in it. He has a personality to match his size, enormous energy, ambitious dreams and ideas that spill out so rapidly and with such enthusiasm that even when he's sitting still he seems to be in constant motion.

You've seen it before—it's the same gene pool, perhaps, as that of the hard-driving CEO who commands corporate legions or the kid-entrepreneur who's yanking down seven figures. They possess that combination of self-assurance and willingness to disassemble old presumptions that leads to new insights and bold new ways of doing things.

But it's Putthoff's questions—they, too, are outsized—that really set him apart. They run to such un-CEO-like queries as "How do we best know God?" They fuel an entrepreneurial spirit that is at the service of youth who are trying to manufacture different endings than expected to lives that begin in some of the most wretched and despair-riddled circumstances in the country.

Welcome to Putthoff's world in Camden, New Jersey. It's a three-story row home transformed into a technology training center with the unlikely name Hopeworks 'N Camden, an almost naively buoyant bubble floating amid the burned-out squalor of surrounding blocks. I'm back on the margins, but once again, rather than feeling off center and out of it, I sense that I am in the thick of both the type of circumstance and the questions that point to the future.

The forty-four-year-old Putthoff's questions, though aimed primarily at the purpose of religious life, particularly the Jesuits, could easily be applied to the larger church. His ministry in the guts of one of the poorest American cities in a way is his declaration about the future of the church as well as his answer, for the moment, to unsettling questions he poses to himself about what it means to be a priest and to be a Jesuit. They become pointedly pressing questions in this era of dwindling numbers and resources, a time he refers to as a period of "diminishment."

Putthoff sat for an interview in late summer in the ground-level front office of Hopeworks on a day when the school was conducting a technological scavenger hunt that tested trainees' skills. He was stamping participants' "passports" as tasks were completed. Putthoff rests easily in paradox, this child of the Midwest and product of Rockhurst High School, an elite Jesuit institution in Kansas City, Missouri. In his pre-Jesuit priest days he also had a private pilot's license. He carts to Camden master's degrees in

English, theology, divinity, and is one course shy of a master's he's still working on in organizational dynamics. Putthoff thinks placing all of this talent and education in North Camden is "one of the greatest things the Society of Jesus does . . . and we should be very proud of that—and not in an arrogant way. I don't think we say that enough. So all of this resource has been spent on me, and I'm here to do this, and I'm here because we have a common mind. We share our monies and our resources. That I could come here and start a nonprofit not at a regular executive director's salary but at a priest's salary, that's a great gift."

Such gifts, however, are disappearing from Camden. Until recent years, he said, there were several Jesuits in Camden, and they ran a parish that had medical, legal, and social-work clinics, as well as a school. Putthoff was an associate pastor. He's the only Jesuit remaining in the city, the parish abandoned, he said, because the Jesuits determined they didn't have the personnel to keep it open. It has since merged with two other parishes in a diocesan realignment that has nearly halved the number of parishes in the diocese.

"Jesuits are shrinking," he said, and that reality leads the Society of Jesus to ask such questions as, "How do we take the three people who can teach in high school and make them present in our institutions? And so we can't even look at a possibility like Camden."

He believes the order may be asking the wrong question. "There's this sense that we don't have enough in our tank to do this. I don't agree with that premise. I don't believe we were founded to staff institutions. We were founded to follow God and all that that means. The Jesuits were all about that, and the first companions were only a handful of guys. So that's what I'm talking about. There's a disconnect from that spirit and that mission and the reality we live today."

It's not that he dislikes institutions or thinks them unimportant. But he thinks that Jesuit institutions such as St. Joseph's Preparatory School in Philadelphia have enjoyed what he describes as "150 years of a treasure, which is Jesuits in the society, and now at the end of 150 years they want to say: 'What do we do?' And what's worse is it's not the institution saying this, it's the Jesuits."

His point is that after 150 years of Jesuits tending to the institution, it ought to be able to move into the future on its own.

The society taps into strategy instead of purpose, he says, and the strategy answers the question: "'How do we keep St. Joe's Prep or any other Jesuit institution alive?' But that's not the question. The question is our purpose, which is the kingdom of God, which is to connect to a God of hope, to be people who witness to this incredible . . . living Bread, this incredible sense of a God who is alive." I begin to hear echoes of Franciscan Fr. Richard Rohr from the desert in this desperate city, in the kind of urban core that the "new monastics" call the new desert.

In the end, he asks: "Is diminishment an opportunity or a scourge? . . . What is the wonderful change that is presented to us in our diminishment? I think sometimes we have a reaction to change that's just 'pull back, retrench.' I would just say that what's exciting for me about diminishment is that it opens up some possibilities for new ministry or new connections with people we traditionally wouldn't serve because there are not enough guys to hold the whole the way we used to."

In Camden alone there's a list of possibilities for alternative ministries: teaching at community college or the local branch of Rutgers University, prison work, the work he's doing with marginalized youth. "The need is huge here," he said. At the same time, he believes the old institutional models, both those of the order and of the larger church, don't allow that kind of flexibility. Jesuits, he said, "have been taught to believe that the provincial can discern the will of God and then tell you" what it is. "That doesn't work in today's world. Nobody does that. No one believes that one person can hold all of the truth. The truth is way too big. Business today is understanding that—that's why you need all this consultation. That's why I think we're really struggling with an authority structure that is trying to wrestle with a postmodern world, a world where there are lots of truths and differences, which is great because we have a spirituality that can embrace that."

All the questions about authority and leadership need not get caught up in analysis of roles, he said. The question boils down instead to how one orients oneself to God. "Can I hold all of God? In some mysterious way we say, 'You can and you can't. It's like revelation, it's all known and yet we can't understand it.'"

"A wonderful paradox?" he's asked.

"It is. It totally is."

The questions about truth and versions of the truth lead him to a hi-tech analogy. He recalls a recent homily in which he talked about "how cool a GPS [global positioning system] is—you just plug it in and you go. It's almost as if you can't get lost anymore. But here's the wild thing: I had three masses one day, and I needed to put a check in the bank between masses. My GPS tells me the bank is seven miles away. I go tootling off to the bank and, on the way back, on the very corner where I turn in to go to the church, is a bank, my bank. It wasn't in the GPS. But I found that so wonderfully refreshing. It isn't all locked in, and I drove right by that. I had to have seen that, but my mind didn't take it in because I knew, by God, that the truth was seven miles away.

"I'm serious about the GPS—I love it because of the certainty of it, but we can get lost in our certainty. If you get so certain, you really get too rigid."

Jersey City

Our Lady of Czestochowa Church was packed for the 12:30 mass on Mother's Day. Four families waited at the rear of the church with their infants, who were to be baptized. In the congregation there were dozens of young families with young children and scores of young singles.

Fr. Tom Iwanowski looked out familiarly on a congregation whose primary membership is made up of people between the ages of twenty-five and fifty, a demographic that most religious leaders would covet. In little more than a month he would be moving on from this community where he had arrived fourteen years ago, at the request of the previous archbishop of Newark, with the simple mandate to "go and change the direction of the parish."

Change it he did.

The story of the transformation of OLC, or Our Lady of the Waterfront, both tags now popularly used to refer to the Jersey City parish, is a tale simultaneously of how disruptive change can be, of the ease with which the Vatican's attention can be turned toward relatively unimportant local matters by a vocal minority, of the professional skills and enormous work it takes to be a successful pastor today, and of the arbitrary nature of Catholic existence where the character and work of a community can be undone in an instant.

That latter point was perhaps the most compelling matter the day of my visit. It hung over everything. What will happen, was the prevailing question, when Fr. Tom leaves?

The question was probably much the same for the few Poles who still inhabited the parish fourteen years ago: What will happen when we get the new guy?

By most accounts I heard, both at the parish and around the archdiocese, the parish fourteen years ago, a traditionally Polish community, was on its final legs. It was a moribund place with few parishioners, a physical plant in disrepair, not a lot of money and dwindling collections, and little presence in the wider community.

In many ways what happened when Iwanowski arrived fourteen years ago is the tale of many nationality parishes in the Northeast in recent decades: reality checks everywhere are showing that the numbers—of members, of the collection, of the bank account, of funerals, of baptisms, of new parishioners—simply won't work. There is no future in these places.

Iwanowski was assigned to the parish by now retired Cardinal Theodore McCarrick in 1995. By 2000 Iwanowski realized there was little need for a Polish mass, especially since St. Anthony's, a Polish parish that gave birth to OLC in 1905, was just a mile away.

"What happened is some Polish activists and some other people who were not happy with the parish . . . said I had transformed OLC into a community center for yuppies and that I had miniskirted nightclub singers singing and that I was a Unitarian," said Iwanowski, during an interview in a conference room at the parish following mass. The language was amplified by extreme right Catholics and at least one of their publications, and people began showing up for protests. They called Iwanowski an "ethnic cleanser."

They protested weekly for nearly five years and created such a stir "that I was investigated three times by Rome, twice by the Congregation for Clergy, once by the papal nuncio, and then Cardinal Josef Glemp came to see me," said Iwanowski. Glemp at the time was the archbishop of Warsaw and primate of Poland.

Ultimately, peace prevailed and the parish prospered, but it took the support of Archbishop John J. Myers, who had a reputation as a staunch conservative and who took over for McCarrick in 2001.

"When he came in 2001, they were protesting and they thought, 'OK, now Myers is coming. . . . He would get rid of me.' Well, Myers gave me a second term for six years and was supportive" even when the activists took their protests to the cathedral in Newark. Myers intervened with Rome. "He refused to give in," Iwanowski said, "and he also came here for mass. He was 100 percent supportive of me and what we were doing here, that we were moving in the right direction."

The right direction didn't occur without another considerable gamble.

When Iwanowski arrived as pastor at age forty-six, the average age of parishioners was between sixty-five and seventy. The church had no readers, no eucharistic ministers, and no music program. "It was just going through the motions and acting as if it was 1950, but it was now 1995. They really did not see what was going on around them. It was a matter of trying to get people to see what was there and to make the changes that were necessary."

This little church is located a few hundred feet away from the intersection of Sussex and Warren streets in Jersey City. Iwanowski bounded into the intersection to show a visitor that if you look straight South on Warren it looks like the Statue of Liberty is floating there, right at the end of the street. Look east on Sussex, and you can see the emptiness in the Manhattan skyline that used to be the towers of the World Trade Center.

The larger point beyond that geographical curiosity is that the church is also within easy commuter distance of New York City and, like nearby Hoboken, it holds a significant attraction for young people anxious to make their mark in the Big Apple while avoiding that city's exorbitant rents. Jersey City is part of what the Archdiocese of Newark has dubbed the Waterfront, and it has nothing to do with Brando-esque thugs and corruption. This waterfront, as Iwanowski discovered, is teeming with young people waiting for an invitation to something.

"I recognized that the liturgy is most important," said Iwanowski. "I always say that people are judging the homily, the music, the sense of welcome, the liturgy in general. They don't hold up numbers, but they're always making a judgment. I knew it was silly to try to bring people in because the liturgy was so bad it would just drive people out."

So he took the plunge and hired musicians, who at the time cost him four hundred dollars a week against a collection that was only twelve hundred dollars on a good Sunday. "It was a risk to do that, but I knew that we had to have good music. Then I established readers, eucharistic ministers, and then we started to get the church known in the neighborhood."

As early as 1996 the parish had a website—way ahead of the curve for most institutions at the time, especially churches. He initiated an event called Spring on Sussex Street, which the parish put on for ten years—a street fair "just to get people to know that the place wasn't closed, just so people knew there was life in the building."

The parish followed that with a program called Festival of Christmas Song, an outdoor festival of Christmas music, again "so the neighbors would know we were there."

The neighborhood took notice. The people began to arrive. They were young, working in finance, technology, the arts. They lived in apartments and commuted to Manhattan by ferry or the PATH train. If that earlier era was anything like today, they marveled at Iwanowski's capacity to remember names and the ease with which the short but focused and well-delivered homilies roll off his tongue. People keep talking about the gifts he has for remembering names and preaching.

Iwanowski laughs a bit at that assessment. If there is a gift involved, it is the gift of hard work. The self-described shy pastor does remember names, but it hardly comes naturally. He explained that from the beginning of his ministry here, whenever he met someone, he wrote the name on a small card and later entered it into a diary he kept. He was still doing that in the months leading up to his sabbatical. Before Sunday masses began each week, he consulted the diary to refresh his memory.

"Sometimes I'll see someone and I'll forget the name. I'll run back to my room and check the diary to get the name."

When people joined the parish, they met with Iwanowski for at least forty-five minutes, and he took their picture. The photos were entered into a parish data base of sorts that he consults—

names with faces. In those meetings he said, "I find out about you, and it changes our relationship because now I know you and you know me."

Good music. Well-trained readers and ministers. A sense of welcome. And then there's the homily.

Iwanowski wrote a great deal to his parishioners. Each Sunday in the bulletin he published a "Pastor's Column," a kind of overview of what's gone on around the place. It was filled with names and appreciation for things that people on the staff and volunteers did to make events, liturgical and otherwise, possible. He also wrote a brief box in the bulletin each week on stewardship, tying the idea of giving time, treasure and talent to the weekly readings or a theme of the season. Each Wednesday parishioners received an email from the pastor titled "Looking to Sunday." It is an artfully presented, inspirational reading based on the coming Sunday's readings. One sent out just before I arrived contained four thoughtful paragraphs on the nature of prayer. Iwanowski has continued publishing the email reflections as pastor of St. Joseph Parish in Oradell, New Jersey.

All of that thinking and writing and his own reading of preaching aids and scriptural reflections feed into his sermons, which he completes by 10 p.m. every Friday because that's when he calls a dear friend he met in seminary. Every week he goes over the homily with his friend, who left seminary before ordination. "And he tells me whether it's good or bad." Sometimes the friend tells him to start over, sometimes "he gives me a star."

At Our Lady of Czestochowa, Iwanowski also passed the homily around to people on staff or other friends to get reactions before he delivered it. He did all of that because he thinks the Sunday liturgy, especially the homily, is the most important thing he does in terms of contact with his entire congregation.

"The homily and the celebration of the liturgy, what more important things can you do? That's where you're going to see the most people. That's the most important thing you do in terms of preaching the word and celebrating the liturgy."

At the time of his leaving he shared the apprehension of many of his parishioners because he knew that the vibrancy of the parish depends on a kind of evangelism peculiar to this place. His young parishioners may have been deeply committed to the parish and may have worked hard at volunteering and sustaining ministries, but they didn't stay around very long. Careers took them elsewhere, or they began to have children. It's difficult to find affordable two- and three-bedroom apartments here, so young families end up leaving.

Iwanowski estimates that his congregation turned over, in large part, every three to four years. He said he sometimes felt like a college chaplain trying to maintain continuity while also recruiting new congregants each year.

Iwanowski had advocated, as part of the Waterfront Ministry Task Force, "that when we change people and parishes change, that you need to pick people who have the sense of what needs to be done. . . . The person who is replacing me should come in six months to a year ahead of time. He would learn what is going on and then transition seamlessly, but we're horrible in terms of that."

When he left, he had the satisfaction of leaving behind a thriving parish with a school, 425 families, a Sunday collection that had risen from twelve hundred dollars a week to between six thousand and seven thousand dollars a week, a Christmas collection that brought in $127,000 in 2008, and an Easter collection that garnered forty-four thousand, both well above the goals set. And the plant that was deteriorating has been rehabbed throughout, including the church, at a cost of several million dollars.

The pastor had gone through a bit of development himself.

"I've come to recognize that the most important way that I experience the presence of Christ is in the celebration of the liturgy, which the people are key to. . . . I always say, the power is in the pews—they are the people of God. I think I've grown more comfortable with people because I've recognized them as the presence of Christ. I think I've come to love people more."

Chapter 7

OF RUMMAGE SALES
AND THE NEW COSMOLOGY

It may be difficult to see how the manner in which the church handles parish closings, the priest shortage, or the sometimes bitter debates among its members relates to a bigger picture.[1] For people at ground level, pursuing faith can seem an immediate matter of survival. Navigating troubled ecclesial waters in search of the community that "fits," whether it's a parish with good liturgy and preaching, a group intent on preserving Latin ritual, or people forming a eucharistic community with lay leaders, can be exhausting work filled with uncertainty. What's happening on the ground, however, often is the result of, and reflective of, much larger forces at work. Phyllis Tickle would say that those competing tensions, the anxieties of the era, are among the signs that we are squarely amid a grand shakeup that occurs on a twice-a-millennium basis to institutionalized Christianity. In *The Great Emergence* she argues that this phenomenon has been "sending intimations of itself" and "slipping up on us for decades in very much the same way spring slips up on us week by week every year."[2]

Her treatment of the Great Emergence deals largely with U.S. Protestantism and with a phenomenon that has generated its own universe of communities, literature, and theology. However, her thesis—that we are experiencing an emergence of huge proportions fashioned by forces ranging from the printing press to further advances in science and technology, from biblical studies to various realizations about space and time that have infiltrated our religious certainties—serves as a larger frame for an investigation of what is emerging in U.S. Catholicism.

127

Tickle, founding editor of the religion department of *Publishers Weekly* and author of more than two dozen books, cites Anglican Bishop Mark Dyer's observation that "the only way to understand what is currently happening to us as 21st-century Christians in North America is first to understand that about every five hundred years the church feels compelled to hold a giant rummage sale." Another way to put it, as Tickle does early on in her book, is that "about every five hundred years the empowered structures of institutionalized Christianity, whatever they may be at that time, become an intolerable carapace that must be shattered in order that renewal and new growth may occur."

Dealing in 500–year cycles, give or take a few decades, means that the last "garage sale" occurred in the sixteenth century with the Great Reformation; five hundred years back from that was the Great Schism; and five hundred years before that "takes us to the sixth century and what once upon a very recent time was labeled as 'The Fall of the Roman Empire' or 'The Coming of the Dark Ages.'"

Through all of these periods, Tickle writes, three things have always occurred:

- a new and more vital form of Christianity emerges;
- the previously dominant form of Christianity "is reconstituted into a more pure and less ossified expression of its former self"; and
- "every time the incrustations of an overly established Christianity have been broken open, the faith has spread . . . dramatically into new geographic and demographic areas."

Perhaps an even more important point for Catholics—if, indeed, Catholicism is going through the same experience as the rest of Christianity—is Tickle's observation that the central question the faith faces while making its way through the turmoil of each of these periods is: Where is the authority? There have been various answers, from *sola scriptura* to papal infallibility. But the answers of one era give way to the alterations and refinements of the next.

Each time the previous story is "broken" (think, for instance, of how Copernicus and Galileo disturbed Catholic cosmology and scriptural certainty) and "the common imagination dispelled into a thousand wisps of half-remembered and now ludicrous fantasy," there emerges "an adjusted, largely new story and an adjusted, largely new, imagination." Emerging along with the new story and imagination are the advocates to articulate and promote them. In the doing, authority finds a new locus.

In Tickle's theory, America contributes enormously to the current emergence by virtue of its religious diversity and the way we no longer live just objectively in a pluralistic culture where religious freedom is guaranteed but, more significantly, and increasingly, as we moved from a rural to an urban culture, in close proximity with one another. The breakdown of old barriers has occurred over time as a gradual process, beginning with "people swapping stories and habits, people admiring the ways of some other people whom they liked, people curious and able now to ask without offense." All of the swapping back and forth was aided not only by our physical proximity with one another but also because we lived in a media age. "Newspapers, magazines, radio, television, and in one mighty burst of glory, the Internet, saw to it that ideas flew about like bees in an overturned hive."

If one is tempted to dismiss Dyer's earlier assessment as predictably Anglican (or more narrowly, U.S. Episcopalian), with its distaste for some of Roman Catholicism's absolutes and with its tolerance of revolutionary ordinations of women and gays, Tickle claims that the Roman Catholic Church was actually way ahead of most in anticipating the questions of the current emergence.

In fact, she writes, "approximately one quarter of today's 'emergents' and 'emergings' are Roman Catholic, not Protestant, in background and natal formation." Those Catholics will be found in a range of denominations and independent communities. What Tickle describes is an unofficial but deeply ecumenical dialogue about *emergence* and what it means for individuals and denominations. The high representation of Catholics (both those still within the church and those who have left) leads Tickle to conclude that any treatment of the period leading up to the Great Emergence "must acknowledge the presence and enormous formative impact of both Vatican I and Vatican II on Roman Catholicism in particular and on re-traditioning and emergent/emerging Christianity in general."

"Vatican I was a recognition that things were changing," she said in an interview. "Vatican I was trying to hold the line" by establishing authority in the principle of papal infallibility." Much of Vatican II was to accommodate or enable or advance what was happening" with its push away from Latin to a common tongue, "more lay leadership and encouragement of greater use of daily offices by laity." The groundbreaking document *Nostra Aetate*, the statement on Catholicism's relation to non-Christian religions and particularly its rethinking of the church's relationship to Judaism, "was a recognition that changes were happening. Rome was the first large body of Christendom that responded in any way that recognized in some organized way that change was afoot," she said. And church leaders at that moment met "to see how they could reposition the church to accommodate the changes."

A characteristic of these times of upheaval (also called hinge periods) is "a heavy anti-clericalism." And this period is no exception. "The last time it was indulgences, this time it's sex," as in gender disputes, celibacy, and the mess of the sex abuse crisis. Though what will emerge is yet unknown, she said that "Rome doesn't have the authority any more," as it may have in the past, to orchestrate every detail of every movement as the church progresses toward the future. And that means, she said, "the authority's got to be somewhere else, but where?" She believes that Christian scriptures will continue to provide one point of authority and another "is going to be community. Self-organizing principles are too much a part of what is happening culturally and politically to say it is not going to be part of what is happening" in religious circles.

Different forms of community, often heavily laced with monastic elements and disciplines, have already emerged in Protestant and ecumenical circles, she said, and increasingly she knows of Catholics who for various reasons of disenchantment or disagreement with the institutional church are gathering in communities outside the official structures. The church, following the Great Schism, sought to locate authority in a single place, the papacy, she writes, with appointed cardinals around the papal throne, "a religious expression of the system of kings and lords growing up in the centuries of pre-Reformation culture."

If, as she contends, the governance of the Christian church, in its broadest sense, often reflects and/or influences the political structure of the secular realm, then what does the future portend in an age not of kings and lords but of ever-growing pressure for democracy and broad participation?

In the future, Tickle writes, emergent Christians will likely locate authority in both scripture and community. She compares the notion to "what mathematicians and physicists call network theory. In this case, the Church, capital C—is not really a 'thing' or entity so much as it is a network in exactly the same way that the Internet or the World Wide Web or, for that matter, gene regulatory and metabolic networks are not 'things' or entities. Like them and from the point of view of an emergent, the Church is a self-organizing system of relations, symmetrical or otherwise, between innumerable member-parts that themselves form subsets of relations within their smaller networks, etc., etc., in interlacing levels of complexity."

There are no markers, of course, pointing neatly to some future. But on the road, hearing story after story of anxiety over parish closings and what will become of the church as the number of priests keep falling, I hear hints of what Tickle describes as the future—a Christianity that is "relational, non-hierarchical," and "democratized . . . as an analog for the political and social principles of authority and organization that will increasingly govern global life during the centuries of the Great Emergence."

One priest tells me that the future of Catholicism is "experiential and relational" and that the "most fundamental Catholic thing is community." Another tells me, "Take time, our new understanding of the mystery of time, our new understanding of the mystery of space and a more humble acknowledgment that God remains fundamentally mystery to us." All of it, he contends, "is creating a perfect storm, with winds blowing every which way."

Around tables and in circles of conversation with lay Catholics and women religious deeply invested in what becomes of the Roman Catholic Church, there is a certain determined resignation as the questions swirl. Catholic life may be, in many ways, an arbitrary venture. Will the next bishop upend all we've done? Will the next pastor appreciate all we've built over the past two decades?

Will our parish go on the chopping block because there aren't enough priests? But almost invariably these people already have a fall-back position in other small communities, some sacramental in a canonical sense, some not, that keep them both tethered to the church and hopeful for the future.

Whether this is part of the Great Emergence, of course, remains to be seen, but given all of the change and the turmoil, it is not a far leap to say that at least a minor emergence is upon U.S. Catholics.

From the Desert

If the notion of an emerging church first took root among Protestant leaders and thinkers who began asking questions and engaging in conversations that spanned denominational boundaries and old enmities, it is being nourished in part by the peculiarly Catholic tradition of contemplation.

"I am invited to teach contemplation more to ecumenical settings, evangelical churches, and Protestant churches than any Catholic churches because they [Protestants] know they don't know," said Fr. Richard Rohr, founder of the Center for Action and Contemplation in Albuquerque, New Mexico. Rohr, a member of the Franciscans' New Mexico Province, is a kind of one-man ideas industry, a prolific author and a much-sought-after speaker around the globe. He has often mined the insights and wisdom of a range of academic disciplines as well as other religious traditions to advance new understandings of Christian faith and spirituality. During a long interview sitting at a small table outside his center he described himself as a "popularizer," but that minimizes the breadth of his work. His questions regarding the future of religious institutions, including the Catholic Church, as well as his extensive work with men's spirituality, are often on the forward edge of what eventually become broad discussions.

One of the more ambitious undertakings of the center was a conference in March 2009 entitled "The Emerging Church: Christians Creating a New World Together," a meeting of a thousand people, about half of them Catholic, by Rohr's estimation, the rest mainline and evangelical Protestants and other Christians. The point of view of the conference might well have been summarized in the title of a talk given by Brian McLaren, a Protestant pastor, thinker, and lecturer recognized as a leader of the emerging church movement: "The Historical Jesus: What You Focus on Determines What You Miss."

Indeed, Rohr believes that the contemplative tradition, the third of what he describes as four pillars of the emergent church and his point of entry into the discussion, is precisely the sort of tradition that allows one to see "with a different set of eyes" and perhaps shift the focus a bit to see other parts of history and tradition that one might be missing.

The great mystics such as Teresa of Avila and John of the Cross "in their own way are saying that the lowest level of consciousness is 'either-or, us or them.' As you advance, you become more 'us and them,' not 'us or them.' You see things non-dualistically," he said. "That's going to be the more important thing that I would like to communicate, that really another word for contemplation is non-dualistic thinking. That's what makes people able to be merciful and forgiving. You can't love your enemies with a low-level dualistic mind. It's impossible, you don't have the software to know how to do it. So we tell people to love their enemies. Normal Catholics can't do that with the software that they've got." Catholics, he said, were never taught they need "a different consciousness to understand the gospel. That's my grand assumption in everything I'm doing anymore," and much of what he does involves teaching contemplation.

Contemplation may be undergoing a revival of sorts, especially among younger Catholics and Protestant evangelicals who are discovering the discipline, but the first pillar supporting the emerging church, according to Rohr, is "honest Jesus scholarship. Not a seminary-trained Jesus scholarship, where you begin with your conclusions—Lutheran conclusions or Catholic conclusions or whatever they are—and then you just learn an understanding of Jesus that's going to keep the church going." The movement, he said, pulls on the recent "wonderful outpouring of honest Jesus scholarship from feminists, from black people, from poor people, from just honest, even white, male scholars."

The second pillar is a rather broad recognition across denominational lines of the centrality of peace and justice issues to the ministry of Jesus. "They are much more front and center for Jesus than the issues that most churches make central, most of which he never talks about. For example, why did we make abortion and gay marriage the litmus test of whether or not you were Christian? Those were not the litmus tests for 1,900 years. How come they are now? Where did this come from? I don't want to just make those two the issue, but it seems to me a classic example of smoke and mirrors," he said. "We don't want to look at the issues that tell us to change our lives, our consumer culture, our greedy culture, our prideful culture, our wealthy culture from the papacy to the episcopacy to the priesthood and all the way down. We're such a part of the system we can't critique the system."

The central place given to peace and justice issues is so pervasive, he said, that there is a quiet consensus he perceives globally on the matter. "There's no central office anywhere teaching the Emerging Church Doctrine. That's what tells me this is from the Holy Spirit."

The final pillar is the one still most in process: "finding the vehicles for this kind of vision." What kind of community structure, he wonders, will allow this to happen yet not be in competition with organized religion but instead be "complementary and happily on the side? This is what's happened to groups like us," he said, referring to the center. "Our conferences are bigger than ever in the last years. Why? I think people want to retain their Catholic identity" while pursuing a view and spirituality that encourages "integrative" rather than "oppositional" thinking.

Tickle was one of the principal speakers during that first gathering, and Rohr agrees with her observation about authority. "For religion to be religion, it always has to appeal to some kind of absolute or final authority. So the question of where does your authority come from, as Jesus is asked, is always going to be there. My intuition, and it might be totally wrong, is I think the new authority is going to come from nature or the cosmos, the natural world.

"I know when Catholics first hear that," he said, "it sounds new age-y, but it seems to me that's the primary Bible as the Franciscans believed." That Bible, he said, has existed for 15 billion years "and has an inherent authority reflected in Romans 1:20, 'God is revealed to things through the mind, to things as they are made.'"

The rediscovery today of the natural world, of "things as they are beyond our technology and mental constructs," will become the new authority "that we're going to be forced to appeal to, especially as we continue to destroy this planet, and we realize this is the one thing we all have in common: that we're all standing on and eating off this same earth."

The natural world was an authority that appears to have been agreed upon by indigenous people around the planet, said Rohr. "We used to use the word in philosophy class: *facticity.* This is the 'what is.' We were always looking for the facticity. Here it is: These trees, this grass, and that sky. How can you beat that for ultimate authority? This names what we all better be obedient to. . . . This is demanding obedience and a response from us far more than any mental construct from a pope or scripture."

It is the new cosmology that sees that the Bible was written in the "last nanosecond of geological planetary time. As I love to say to crowds: Do you really think God wasn't talking for the first 14 billion years or whatever it is? They get that. They really get that. Let's listen to this talking. As a Franciscan, I find that so rooted in our early experience, although we lost it, too."

Rohr is one of the bright stars in a constellation of Catholic thinkers and writers, speaking from beyond the staged ideological wars, whose frequent-flier miles and national and international bookings would rival those of most celebrities. Rohr and Sr. Joan Chittister, who have appeared together in the past and who appeal not only to a wide swath of Catholics but who also have a strong crossover appeal to other denominations and women and human rights activists, are booked well into the future. Another is Oblate Fr. Ron Rolheiser, a best-selling author in great demand as a speaker. At one point or another, the three have crossed paths, with at least two of them headlining the same conferences or speaking engagements.

For Rohr, the new cosmology also recognizes that the old conception of natural order, the up-and-down universe from which hierarchical examples of leadership are modeled, no longer applies.

"It doesn't work," he said, "and we've got a system [in the Roman Catholic Church] that totally depends on up and down." That model, he said, "is summed up in the need to define the world in terms of superiors and inferiors, and the white, male system always does that. There are always superiors and inferiors. You just see Jesus paying no attention to that. Nowhere is it probably symbolized more graphically than in the Roman Catholic Church, which has all these scriptures about the least of the brothers and sisters, and the little ones deserving the greatest care, when in fact, what we do is dress up the big ones. We idolize and quasi-worship the big ones."

If Rohr's answer to a kind of institutional stalemate—the infighting that eludes resolution—is to move toward non-dualistic thinking, Rolheiser speaks of "getting underneath" the divide that always seems to be on the surface when he faces a Catholic crowd. "That polarization will be front and center, whether it's spoken or unspoken. The tribes are there, and they're sizing you up, they're sizing each other up. What that tends to mean is that the ecclesial questions become central. They're not necessarily our deep longing questions at all. They're about who has power, who should be ordained, how's the pope handling the sexual abuse crisis, and so on."[3]

In an interview with NCR he invokes a giant of modern Catholic spirituality writers, the late Henri Nouwen. "His premise was that what's most deeply personal and private is also most universal. He'd name this kind of deeply private, guarded experience, often chaotic experience, lonely experience, and even sinful experience, and people would say, 'This guy's nailed it. This is how I'm feeling.'" It is another way of saying that important as dogma might be, it rarely converts, it isn't the stuff that holds communities together or that gets at "deep longing questions."

Rolheiser, like Rohr and Chittister, may preach beyond the bounds of denominationalism, but intrinsic to their separate approaches is the realization that humans live in real space and real time and, ultimately, have to choose a community within which to nourish and practice their faith. One of the reasons he's Catholic, Rolheiser said, "is that I think we have the richest intellectual tradition.

"The early church fathers used to say this, and it's still a great line: 'God wrote two books. God wrote the Bible, and God wrote nature. You have to learn how to read both.'" Catholics, he said, have had "1,700, 1,800 years of working at that second book."

All three speak from within the tradition in which they have been informed and nurtured, even as the trajectory of their thought often stretches the traditional in different directions. Each has been reared within the confines of the institution, in fact, shaped by some of its most rigorous disciplines as members of religious orders. Yet their words reach beyond the borders of Catholicism, filling the space of an almost post-institutional dimension. Like Sr. Thea Bowman, the spirituality they speak of is infused with decades of study and meditation within the institutional structures of Catholicism, and yet it is not aimed at creating a property exclusive to or wholly owned by the Catholic Church. The questions they entertain—and they are many—are not designed to lead one in a circuitous path back to a church that contains all wisdom and all the answers. Their conceptions of God, more inquiry than certainty, are aimed at loosening God from the boundaries of our imaginations, not at creating a God that fits our horizons and ambitions. Struggling with the enormous problems and challenges posed by a pluralistic age doesn't mean, for them, rejecting pluralism.

Echoing a central theme of the emerging church, Chittister says the journey is the important element and "explains, as well as anything, I think, how it is possible, necessary even, for me as a Roman Catholic to stay in a church that is riddled with inconsistencies, closed to discussion about the implications of them, and sympathetic only to invisible women. The fact is that I have come to realize over the years that church is not a place, it is a process. To leave the church may, in fact, be leaving part of the process of my own development. And so, intent on the process of grappling with truth, I stay in it, when, for a woman, staying in it is full of pain, frustration, disillusionment and, far too often, even humiliation. Both of us, this church and I, have need to grow. The church needs to grow in its understanding of the Gospel and I need to grow in my understanding of myself as I strive to live it. It is, in other words, a journey of conversion for both of us."[4]

Chittister, whose activity and persistent questions on behalf of women in the church have brought her into conflict with several levels of hierarchy, uses the image of Jesus—sparring verbally with Pharisees, weeping over Jerusalem, teaching in the synagogue and presiding at the Holy Thursday meal—as a model for contending with contemporary church authorities and with rules that make no sense to her. In those circumstances we see a Jesus proclaiming truth regardless of the cost; dealing "with the depression that comes from failure, from rejection . . . trusting the truth, living with the faith and hoping to the end."[5]

In a November 2009 talk in Kansas City, Missouri, Chittister described the evolution of her ideas about God as "faced with one question after another, the questions of what it was to be a woman, what it was to step into outer space, what it was to see goodness where once I had been told only faithlessness abounded, I became more and more convinced that God was to be found in other places" than the traditional habitats and identities. It was, indeed, "the search itself that could possibly save me from the worst consequences of the small, parochial, nationalistic, chauvinistic God I had once known and been taught to fear."[6]

"Suddenly a confluence of things around me began to converge newly in my own spiritual life," she said in this Kansas City talk. "I began to see God grow or maybe I saw me grow and couldn't tell the difference. So I have abandoned God the stern father who had no time for human nonsense and little time for women either. I have abandoned God the cloud sitter who keeps count of our childish stumblings towards spiritual adulthood in order to exact fierce retribution from humans for being human and I have seen all those fragments of the face of God dissolve into the mist of the impossibility of a God who is not Godly."

Those were the gods that never really existed, she said, "and must never exist if God is really God." But what replaces such small ideas? Who replaces them?

"I have become sure that if all I know about God is that my God is the fullness of life and the consummation of hope, the light on the way and the light at the end, I will live my life in the consciousness of God and goodness everywhere. Obscure at times? Yes, but never wholly lacking. Now God, at this stage of life, that old rascal, is doing it again. I am moving in my heart from God as a trophy to be won or a master, however benign, to be pacified, to God as cosmic unity and everlasting light."

Chittister speaks for a wide constituency of women, Catholics and members of other denominations, whose conceptions of God have moved beyond the images of their childhood catechesis. Her extensive work on behalf of women's rights around the globe, her contact with women of other denominations and faiths who are asking the same questions and facing the same resistance to change that Catholic women encounter within the church, have given her a particularly acute sense of the dimensions of the shifts underway.

She is one of the higher profile and recognizable voices within Catholicism giving expression to the faith of our fathers and mothers, to understandings of religion and spirituality that build upon but are not limited to tradition.

Many believers, wholly occupied with life's more immediate demands, never get beyond the first lessons and images of childhood religious instruction. Whatever answers and images register at an early age remain the answers and images for a lifetime. That usually means a Christianity of certitude, a notion that is, itself, a contradiction, of course. At the same time, the Catholic community is fortunate to be dragged along, as it always has been, by those who have the time and capacity, the vocation, for engaging the larger questions and issues. In many ways today Chittister, Rolheiser, Rohr, and others like them, visionaries well schooled in the community's history, serve as mediators between the academy and everyday seekers. They provide access to the expanding territories of spirituality and a reliable new map to a land, once neatly bordered and fenced, that now rolls out beyond our horizons.

Static teaching in a moving church

The shifting plates beneath the Catholic landscape can produce tremors as subtle as Newark Archbishop John Myers's acknowledgment that parish boundaries have become meaningless or disruptions as momentous as the realization that in the pluralistic information era, ideas and questions are no longer bound by borders, national or ecclesial. From Tiananmen Square to Tahrir Square, information flows regardless of governments' wishes. The same goes for the Catholic group in the Southwest United States that gathered at a Protestant church to view videos of a speaker, who happened to be a bishop in good standing, that another bishop had banned from the diocese. Increasingly Catholics are finding ways around the institutional "no."

They're learning that the Protestant congregation down the street or the conference room at the local hotel will do just fine for their programs. In my own experience, a small group wanting not to do battle with the local bishop while also wishing to bring in speakers we knew would be problematic if hosted by a Catholic parish began a small group called Topics to Go. The "organization," an informal committee of four or five at any given time, planned for speakers and held most of the sessions at a local Unitarian church. During the several years of its existence, crowds averaged between 250 and 350 on Saturday mornings. The sessions were held from 9:30 to 11:30. People attending kept donating funds so that we could continue to bring speakers in, put them up at a home or a local hotel, and pay them a stipend. My experience is not unique. I know of others organized by Jesuit alumni or Voice of the Faithful that have done the same. And, of course, bishops don't control the book publishing and electronic communication markets. The writing, publishing, speaking, and inquiry go on and on and finds broad, receptive markets.

It is an uneasy tension that currently exists with so much in question. In many ways what we're experiencing is a new expression of that ancient tension between charism and authority, between the Spirit's sometimes unpredictable leading and the need for institutional order. To talk of an emerging church or emerging Christianity is to speak of something that owes a great deal to tradition but that seeks its shape and bearing in ways not yet fully formed.

That may be the nature of emergence—that whatever it is never arrives all laid out with clear boundaries and with easily identified markers so everyone knows who's in and who's out. That may also be why the language of those who take the prospect of emergence seriously is so loaded with movement and an impression of travel. From Vatican II, which spoke of a pilgrim people, to the image of journey that is so prevalent in contemporary spiritual writing, the concept of church is anything but static. A second conference organized by Rohr's center and focused on the emerging church was titled "How We Get There Determines Where We Arrive." It is more than a clever play on words. The journey, it turns out, is the place, and the sojourners don't expect that all the answers will be waiting, like an award for finishing, at the end of some religious obstacle course. The idea stands in contrast to those who want to re-square all the lines and fill their faith with certitude. The movement of an emerging church, the uncertainty of it all, is necessarily in conflict with the notion that the church is changeless and that eliminating the progress since the end of the council in 1965 is a way back to some unspecified era of doctrinal purity.

There was no "golden age" in the church, as Rolheiser points out. In those past eras when, indeed, belief in God came easier to a greater percentage of the population, it was belief in a God and attendant religious practice that we would today judge seriously flawed. "They believed in God easily but then struggled with superstition, slavery, sexism, unhealthy notions of fate and predestination, excessive fears of eternal punishment, and legalism."[7] The god of their imagination and understanding is not the one we know or worship today.

In the religious constructs that grew out of such notions of God, they "burned witches, waged religious wars, slaughtered innocent people while thinking themselves on a crusade for Christ, forbade scientists to look through telescopes, and, further back still, sacrificed humans, mainly children, on altars."[8]

For scholar George Weigel, an influential and popular voice in conservative circles, the debate in contemporary U.S. Catholicism is between those who advocate a dissent-riddled "Catholic light" point of view and the practitioners of a robust orthodoxy personified by the late Pope John Paul II and the episcopacy he was able to reconstruct with appointments made during his quarter-of-a-century reign.

Such a stark dualism, of course, does an injustice to the far more complex story of the church in the post–Vatican II era and looks past the severe institutional upheaval and shrinkage in the West that occurred under John Paul's appointees. It is, however, a convenient journalistic device staking out two of the more distant poles of the narrative. Those two disparate poles are valuable in exploring an iconic moment of the post–Vatican II church in the United States, the 1968 debate that erupted with the release of *Humanae Vitae*, the encyclical that restated the church's opposition to artificial means of birth control. That event is viewed by both sides as a defining moment in the evolution of the post–Vatican II church, but for different reasons. Conservatives see it as a major step toward the dissolution of authority and obedience within the church; those on the liberal side view the widespread rejection of the teaching as a bracing expression of the *sensus fidelium* and a sign of maturation of the laity.

Both sides are correct. The rejection of the Vatican teaching on birth control by a vast majority of U.S. Catholics certainly diminished the authority of the hierarchy and allowed laity to think outside the framework that had been established for them during years of memorizing questions and answers from *The Baltimore Catechism*. If Sunday homilies and the hellfire-and-brimstone sermons of the occasional parish-mission preachers were any indication, sex was that area of life most productive of occasions of serious sin for the lay person. As Fr. Andrew Greeley has pointed out, when couples realized that disobeying a longstanding, central obligation for married Catholics did not immediately bring down the wrath of God, and when they discovered overwhelmingly sympathetic priests in the confessional, something significant occurred in the adult U.S. Catholic psyche.[9]

This wasn't as new an act of defiance as many believed. Greeley's studies debunked the "myth that at one time the good, pious lay people did not practice family limitation, but had large families and trusted in God." In fact, Greeley asserts, the size of Catholic families in the United States diminished from 4.3 members to 3.8 between 1870 and 1940. He attributes the perception of large Catholic families to "a mathematical paradox: Many more people come from large families than there were large families. Thus, the descendants of large families are overrepresented in the population compared to the number of families in which they were raised."[10]

In any event, and whatever the means used to limit family size (Greeley only suggests, without getting specific, that some means was used) with the well-recorded reaction to *Humanae Vitae*, a taboo was broken. If previously it had been broken in the privacy of a couple's bedroom, now the world knew that Catholic couples were disregarding the birth-control mandate.

And thus was launched the fundamental dynamic for Catholic debate in the United States over the next few decades. Most of the debate focused on matters sexual: birth control, though the significance of that issue faded to background because most simply ignored the teaching and moved on; homosexuality, an issue in which the church tries to maintain the "hate the sin, love the sinner" approach while simultaneously decreeing that the orientation itself is a disorder; and abortion, the politics of which for some is a litmus test of true Catholicity. Add to those the internal gender/sex debates over married clergy, female clergy, and divorced and remarried Catholics. Given the roster of the most enduring debates in contemporary U.S. Catholicism, the uninitiated might reasonably conclude that the majority of our sacred texts deal with matters of sex when, in fact, quite the opposite is true.

The issues remain prominent because they provide easy measures for determining loyalty and fidelity. It is around these matters that the terms *orthodoxy* and *heterodoxy* so often fly. To these issues is applied the either/or language that can quickly separate those who are in from those who are out, the obedient from the dissenters. They provide an arena for the exercise of authority, for clear lines. If we are able to identify "intrinsic evil" and disorders within this ground, then other matters—torture, poverty, militarism, huge discrepancies between rich and poor—become secondary.

The obsession with sexual issues and the unending debates they provoke are the rolling tremors that keep reminding us that something deeper is being disturbed. One need look no further than the controversy surrounding the birth-control encyclical to discover the more profound upheaval. For while the debate over birth control quickly devolved into the language of fidelity and obedience, of far greater importance was whether the rationale underpinning the encyclical's conclusions was valid.

Fr. Charles Curran became the lightning rod for the anger that boiled over among those who considered dissent from the teaching, especially by a theologian at a pontifical university, a betrayal of the church. Curran, then a professor of moral theology at the Catholic University of America, was the public face of dissent in an episode that has been amply recounted and analyzed elsewhere, including in his own autobiography, *Loyal Dissent*.[11] Among peers he maintained the highest profile in opposing the teaching, and he organized colleagues in composing a widely publicized written response to Pope Paul VI, but he was hardly the most radical in his criticism. The public protest by professional theologians, however, was unprecedented in the modern era and eventually grew to more than six hundred scholars in the sacred sciences.[12] The encyclical's use of natural law underpinning its logic was assailed from all sides, including by theologians who agreed with the conclusions of the document.

The statement from Curran's group said that the conclusions of *Humanae Vitae* were "based on an inadequate concept of natural law: the multiple forms of natural law theory are ignored and the fact that competent philosophers come to different conclusions on this very question are disregarded."[13]

Among those who criticized the use of natural law in the document was Germain Grisez, a widely respected theologian who did not dissent from the document's conclusions. But Grisez, much before the release of the encyclical, "had begun to argue that the entire effort to derive moral principles (the *ought*) from the sheer facts of the physical universe (the *is*), as the older style of natural law had attempted, was a doomed project."[14]

Theologians more liberal than Grisez, Jesuit Fr. Richard McCormack among them, attempted to strike a balance between maintaining (1) the pope's authority as a teacher by virtue of office as well as Christ's promise to always be with his church and (2) the common-sense understanding that "no Catholic theologian could claim that the authority of official teaching was totally independent of the arguments advanced to explain it."[15]

A decade later, Massa points out, another Catholic University professor, Joseph Komonchak, a centrist in his approach to controversial issues, would make a similar observation about the deficiencies of relying solely on Jesus' promised "'aid of the Spirit' in guiding the teaching of the church." Komonchak cited Vatican II as an example of teaching that relied on a "front loaded" approach incorporating free and open debate as an alternative to teaching that relied solely on the authority of the magisterium.

Christ's promise of aid, Komonchak said, did not excuse church leaders from employing "the most plausible theological explanations in presenting and interpreting Christ's message in history." On the contrary, he argued, "the intrinsic necessity of theological reasoning in the magisterial process should also mean that it is not illegitimate to ask of an authorized teacher: 'Why do you teach this? How did you arrive at this conclusion? How is [this teaching] related to the central truths of the gospel?'"[16]

This was the shattering of the carapace that sent reverberations down into the pews. Baring the limits of such use of natural law— this "unacceptable identification of natural law with natural processes," as McCormack described it—was a new phase in the maturation of Catholic theology that had the effect, intended or not, of calling attention to the fact that a papal pronouncement could be sorely lacking in its reasoning and logic.

Curran paid the clerical culture's price for being the public face of theological dissent: he was forced from his position at Catholic University in 1986. Since 1991 he has been teaching at Southern Methodist University in Dallas and has continued to publish and lecture widely.

Some may yet lament the fact that most Catholics don't heed the birth-control teaching, but of at least equal consequence to the institution is the hierarchy's loss of credibility in the wake of a teaching judged flawed by so many theologians and rejected by so many in the pews.

And the loss of credibility was not only among laity. Studies by Greeley showed that before *Humanae Vitae* was issued, 67 percent of responding priests reported they wouldn't refuse absolution in confession to someone practicing birth control. Five years after the encyclical was released, that number had risen to 87 percent. Additionally, 60 percent of priests surveyed rejected the teaching.[17]

It is rare that internal conflict of the sort experienced during the birth-control encyclical debates should become so widely publicized and discussed. Theology doesn't normally hit the streets in such a big way. One force that made the matter accessible to lay people was a commission, appointed by John XXIII and continued and expanded by Paul VI, to consult on the matter. The group included lay members, such as Pat and Patty Crowley of Chicago, among the founders of the Christian Family Movement. In the end, the majority of that commission, including several world-class theologians as well as bishops and cardinals who were brought on to block the majority report, recommended changing the law. But members of the curia who objected to any change had the pope to themselves in the aftermath, and when the final document was promulgated some months later there were some very surprised members of the majority.

Few outside the commission knew of what became known as the "Majority Report" until journalist Gary MacEoin, in Rome at the time, got wind of it and persuaded those who had obtained a copy that the perfect place to publish it would be this new, upstart weekly paper in the United States called the *National Catholic Reporter*. The document was authenticated and published on April 19, 1967, and ignited a discussion that went on from the Catholic academy to the Catholic dinner table and beyond for quite some time.

Authority was being relocated. If the proponents of a changed law lost the battle for a different kind of encyclical than finally appeared, they at least had been at the table and had been heard and could relay the story of the proceedings. Their vote may not have counted in the Vatican, but a different sort of plebiscite occurred on the ground. The vast majority of Catholic adults voted their dissent by ignoring the teaching. In the end, however, it remains an unsettled state of affairs. Ignoring a teaching is one way of assessing or reacting to authority, but it does nothing to rehabilitate or affirm legitimate authority. The search is still on for the twenty-first century's authentic expression of authority.

Chapter 8

IN SEARCH
OF AUTHENTIC AUTHORITY

Where is the authority? The question echoed loudly, if not in that precise language, as the dust settled on the birth-control controversy. While that episode only began to define the whole of what happened in the aftermath of the council, it contained the elements for creating the perfect theological/ecclesiastical storm. If the Barque of Peter survived the tempest, the crew was seriously rattled and the pope elected in 1978 set about immediately devising ways to quell any further storms.

Much has been written already about the effect of Pope John Paul II's appointments to the episcopacy on church life in the United States. I have no intention here of going over that ground in any detail. It is enough for the purposes of discussing the emerging church to point out that in the aftermath of the birth-control debacle—as lay people and religious women and some priests continued to ask difficult questions and to press issues discomfiting to the hierarchy—we began to see a revival of some expressions of episcopal authority that had fallen into disuse for a brief period.

The new attempts to reassert authority—denouncing writers, speakers, theologians, banning some from Catholic Church property, threatening to withhold the Eucharist from politicians, sparring with college presidents over curriculum and extracurricular activities ranging from support groups for gay students to plays advocating women's issues to an invitation to the president of the United States—generated a great deal of attention and press. Beyond hardening positions already at odds, what such measures accomplished remains a question.

Eugene Kennedy, an astute and long-time church watcher, and his wife, Dr. Sara Charles, a psychiatrist, were ahead of most in anticipating the sense of directionless drift that can occur in individuals and communities when authentic authority dissipates. The space age and information age, said Kennedy and Charles in their book, *Authority: The Most Misunderstood Idea in America,* graphically showed us an earth that was neither up nor down, but amid a vastness that was, itself, one among innumerable galaxies upon galaxies.[1] The images, as much as the information, turned the old natural order on its head. The ruse behind the curtain was revealed: There really was no up or down, no "natural order" upon which hierarchies of the past were based.

The authors note that just a few years after the "image of Earthrise" was "transmitted from the surface of the moon" several young engineers in California "invented the microprocessor and changed the world." It was a second blow to centuries-old assumptions about power and how it is maintained and controlled.

"In the Golden Age of hierarchy, information was perceived as power and was reserved to very few at the highest levels. It was sacred, an expression and source of power, reserved like the Holy of Holies, with access for the elect alone. Technological advances democratize information so that it is now instantly available to everyone within a country or an organization. It cannot be kept or controlled at the top. The top is no longer separate from the bottom."[2]

Vatican II was an ecclesiastical event in tune with, even anticipating, as Tickle pointed out, the new discoveries in the world of science and technology. It is surely no coincidence that Pope Paul VI, unfortunately known best by that last encyclical he issued, was thoroughly fascinated with space exploration. Vatican II opened the door to a more collegial expression of church, a move that was simultaneously exhilarating and terrifying. Those with the most to lose in that turn of events were the ones who were also in a position to stifle such initiatives. "Pope John Paul II began to reverse the collegial structure almost immediately after his election in 1978,"[3] and the project has been ongoing since. The reaction is understandable. As Kennedy and Charles point out in their work, the post-hierarchical time is a period during which occurs widespread experimentation with authority forms. Such experiments bear mixed results and are received with ambivalence; if the church's experience is instructive, they are sometimes met with anger and fierce resistance.

If the church itself foresaw the questions of the twenty-first century, it didn't do well in preparing the answers it gave, say Kennedy and Charles. "In large part we have stumbled into this ill-defined interlude because the great institutions that identify their authority with their hierarchical structure are, in effect, raising an empty monstrance and demanding that people accept the receptacle as if it were the sacrament. They thereby de-authorize themselves. When such de-authorization occurs, people lose faith in and turn away from institutions. . . . They begin to experiment, as people are now obviously doing, with extra–institutional, trial-and-error efforts to reestablish guidelines for living."[4] We are a community in search of itself, and an overriding question we confront has to do with authority.

Kennedy notes that the root of the word *authority,* shared with *author* and *augment,* is the Latin *augere,* meaning "to make, to enlarge, to make able to grow." Authority at its best is generative. It "frees the possibilities of other persons."

It is quite different from authoritarianism, "authority's ghostly doppelganger," which seeks to control, to effect conformity, and to maintain the status quo. Authoritarian behavior is the expression of power that we've seen increasingly from leadership in the church that perceives threats and a breakdown of institutional order in every direction. Yet the attempts to impose a new discipline, to somehow re-create the deference and unquestioning (at least publicly) acquiescence to hierarchical mandates increasingly show themselves ineffective.

As a bill to allow same-sex marriage was making its way through the Maryland state legislature in early 2011, the *Washington Post* took note of the fact that regardless of the outcome, the process itself was evidence of the waning influence of the Catholic Church not only in the public realm but among its own members. Maryland's rich Catholic heritage was reflected in its public leadership at the time the bill was being debated.[5] The governor, Martin O'Malley, is a weekly mass attendant, grew up in a Catholic family, and his education included a Jesuit high school and the Catholic University of America. He sent his four children to

Catholic schools. And when he speaks about how his Catholic faith has influenced his public service in this "blue" state known for its liberal leanings and socially conscious politics, he can sound like a poster boy for Catholic social justice teachings: he opposes the death penalty, is pro-environment, has worked hard to keep down the cost of college tuition, and supports the right of workers to organize. What's missing from that list, of course, are what some derisively refer to as the "pelvic issues" such as abortion and homosexuality. On the latter, O'Malley made it clear that he would sign the same-sex marriage bill if it got to his desk. "I'd be willing to sign any law that reaches me as long as it protects rights equally. I'm not going to get hung up on the words used to describe equal protection under the law," he told a *Post* reporter.

He wasn't, by any means, alone. Maryland's house speaker at the time, Michael E. Busch, used to teach and coach at a Catholic high school and the Senate president, Thomas V. Mike Miller, "grew up serving as an altar boy" in a church that his family helped to build. Busch said he wasn't swayed by the arguments against the bill advanced by Catholic leadership. Miller took a different view, saying he had "a hard time associating family values with people of the same sex being married" and voicing concern over expanding the definition of marriage. But Miller had departed in the past from church positions when he advocated placing protection for women into Maryland law in the event that Roe *v.* Wade, the Supreme court decision allowing abortion, were ever overturned.

The political positions of Catholic politicians in Maryland (where Catholics make up 17.8 percent of the population) highlight a worrisome matter for church authorities nationally. For instance, three other states with higher percentages of Catholics in the population—Massachusetts (42 percent), Connecticut (36.6 percent), and New Hampshire (24.3 percent)—have approved laws allowing gay marriage.[6]

Perhaps, as some church leaders contend, Catholics are being deeply affected by a pervasive secularism and relativism that dilute religious convictions and provide believers with loopholes through which to escape the most difficult conclusions of their beliefs. Certainly most parents—regardless of religious conviction or no religion, regardless of political preference—would agree that the culture each year ups the ante against efforts to sustain childhood and allow kids a certain innocence beyond toddlerhood.

It is easy, then, to affirm the validity of the church's concerns about the corrosive effects of some aspects of contemporary culture. But does that necessarily mean there is some evil "ism" behind every disagreement with hierarchical thinking or decrees? Does every question that is labeled dissent necessarily spring from a conscience malformed by a distorting culture?

The only thing that seems certain at the moment is that with every hierarchical assertion of absolute certainty, declarations meant to shore up authority, the opposite occurs.

The result is a commensurate diminishment of authority.

When Phoenix Bishop Thomas Olmsted issued his decree in late 2010 that St. Joseph's Hospital and Medical Center in that city "no longer qualifies as a Catholic entity," the intent was to establish what he felt the hospital had previously refused to accept: that he was the diocese's sole arbiter of both the truth about a clinical procedure and about an institution's Catholic identity. Referring to himself in the third person in his initial letter to the hospital, he concluded with the statement: "Bishop Olmsted, by virtue of his office, is the authoritative voice on faith and morals in the Diocese of Phoenix. This includes every official Catholic institution of the Diocese."

Olmsted revoked the hospital's Catholic status because its administrators, acting in consultation with ethicists, determined that in order to save the life of a woman who was both severely ill with pulmonary hypertension and eleven weeks pregnant, an abortion would have to be performed. "The chart notes that she had been informed that her risk of mortality was close to 100 percent if she continued the pregnancy," said a hospital statement in the wake of the controversy. "The medical team contacted the Ethics Consult team for a review. The consultation team talked to several physicians and nurses as well as reviewed the patient's record. The patient and her family, her doctors, and the Ethics Consult team, agreed that the pregnancy could be terminated, and that it was appropriate since the goal was not to end the pregnancy but save the mother's life."

Though medical personnel and ethicists said that the baby was, in effect, dying as a result of the mother's illness and would not have survived any of the possible eventualities, Olmsted was unmoved. It was a direct abortion, he said, intolerable in a Catholic hospital. He excommunicated a nun who had been involved in the decision as a member of the hospital's Ethics Consult team. Mercy Sr. Margaret McBride, as a result of the dispute, resigned as vice president of Mission Services and became vice president, instead, of Organizational Outreach.

It is notable that while the nation's bishops as a group released a statement affirming that it was within Olmsted's purview to issue such a decree, no individual bishop came to his defense. No bishop in his region took up his cause or affirmed the action, nor did the Metropolitan of the region, Archbishop Michael J. Sheehan of Santa Fe, New Mexico, go public with his position on the matter.

Sr. McBride, despite the bishop's excommunication decree, remained a member in good standing of the Mercy order. Daughter of Charity Sr. Carol Keehan, president and CEO of the Catholic Health Association, said, "St. Joseph's Hospital and Medical Center in Phoenix has many programs that reach out to protect life. They had been confronted with a heartbreaking situation. They carefully evaluated the patient's situation and correctly applied the 'Ethical and Religious Directives for Catholic Healthcare Services' to it, saving the only life that was possible to save."

It was the second time in a matter of months that Keehan had been involved in a disagreement with the hierarchy. During the healthcare-reform debate in early 2010, Keehan sent a letter to President Obama and congressional leaders strongly supportive of the Obama healthcare-reform measure, angering bishops who opposed the bill because, they said, it would lead to federal funding of abortion. Keehan and other groups of Catholic sisters, including the Leadership Council of Women Religious and Network, a Catholic social action agency, disagreed with the bishops' assessment of the bill, saying that it contained protections against use of federal money for abortion. In the end, in addition to protections contained in the bill, Obama signed a presidential order prohibiting such funding.

Both the Phoenix hospital incident and the flap over healthcare demonstrated another of those shifts in the Catholic landscape that has occurred subtly but certainly during recent decades. Religious women, once the "in the trenches" troops of Catholic education and healthcare, the teachers and nurses that staffed the institutions, now run them. They are on an education par or better with bishops and priests, and they are recognized as experts in their own fields of endeavors—in running schools, universities, hospitals, and enormously complex and demanding hospital systems. They are not antagonistic toward hierarchy—and Keehan went to some lengths to mend fences with the bishops after the two events—but sisters no longer feel it necessary to check in with male authority, priest or bishop, when making decisions in their own specialties.

The politics of the church has changed. The presumptions of the old up-and-down world are yielding to a flatter, more horizontal arrangement. Authority assumed by virtue of a "higher" position is easy to miss when the rest of the world is looking around at a different level for collaborators and partners.

The same sort of language used by Olmsted was employed, though in not so measured tones, in 2008 by Bishop Joseph Martino of Scranton. Martino interrupted a panel discussion on political issues that referenced "Faithful Citizenship," a document published by the U.S. Conference of Catholic Bishops. A form of this document is released every presidential election cycle. While speaking of abortion as a prime issue for Catholics, it allowed some room for voting for a pro-choice candidate if other criteria are considered. "No USCCB document is relevant in this diocese. The USCCB doesn't speak for me," Martino said angrily. "The only relevant document . . . is my letter. There is one teacher in this diocese, and these points are not debatable." In his letter he said no other issue or consideration outweighed a politician's approach to abortion. Martino at one point described Democrats as "the party of death."

Other bishops have made headlines for excommunicating individuals and whole congregations; more than a few have set up extremely stringent rules about who can be invited into the diocese to speak; at least one has devised a kind of "loyalty oath" for eucharistic ministers; and one drew headlines when he backed up a pastor who refused to admit the children of a lesbian couple to the parish school.

Under canon law and the church's structure, bishops have the right to impose such views and regulations, no matter how divisive or unreasonable.

But such aggressive tactics have the effect of pushing to the surface a host of questions that bubble constantly just below the surface of the debate about who determines what is Catholic and how a bishop's authority is exercised.

On the pragmatic level the heavy-handed approach has little effect. Obama won overwhelmingly in Catholic Scranton and environs. St. Joseph Hospital responded politely to the bishop, agreeing that the Blessed Sacrament would no longer be reserved in the hospital chapel and that mass would no longer be celebrated there. However Catholic priests and others would continue to minister there, and the hospital would continue to function as it had in the past.

The sisters and other lay Catholic groups who supported healthcare reform were credited by many inside Congress and the White House for pushing the measure over the top.

Some cheer the new episcopal assertiveness. George Weigel, for instance, wrote that Olmsted "has become an important leader" in holding the line against the further erosion of Catholic identity—those elements that clearly demonstrate an institution's adherence to Catholic teaching—in the wider culture. The debate about Catholic identity and, perforce, the authority of bishops, is often cast as a struggle between the forces of orthodoxy holding out against a hostile and increasingly secularized culture.

But as is clear in the above, the most bitter battles of late have been among Catholics, even Catholic leaders, espousing different views in the public arena. Some might see it as a healthy sign that hierarchical disagreements are now out in the open. But the most immediate result is the impression that the church is riven with deep disagreement over some of the most explosive issues. In a surprisingly frank interview in 2009,[7] Archbishop Sheehan of Santa Fe showed his anger with some of his peers following a meeting in which the U.S. bishops discussed the tactic of withholding eucharist from politicians who did not share the bishops' strategy on abortion. Sheehan said the Catholic community risks isolating itself from the rest of the country and that refusing to talk to a politician or refusing communion because of a difference on a single issue was counterproductive. He described such actions as a "hysterical" reaction.

The archbishop was forceful in describing the manner in which church leaders should handle significant disagreements with elected officials. He said his approach—whether dealing with civic officials or church members—relied heavily on collaboration, a technique he said he learned from the late Cardinal Joseph Bernardin of Chicago.

"I believe in collaboration," he said. "I am very committed to the concept called shared responsibility. Sheehan said he told his fellow bishops, "I don't feel so badly about Obama going [to Notre Dame] because he's our president. I said we've gotten more done on the pro-life issue in New Mexico by talking to people that don't agree with us on everything. We got Governor Richardson to sign off on the abolition of the death penalty for New Mexico, which he was in favor of." Governor Bill Richardson, in explaining why he reversed his longstanding support for the death penalty, said he was persuaded in part by discussions with church activists and with Sheehan.

"We talked to him, and we got him on board and got the support in the legislature," Sheehan said. "But you know, he's pro-abortion. So? It doesn't mean we sit and wait, that we sit on the sides and not talk to him. We've done so much more by consultation and by building bridges in those areas. And then to make a big scene about Obama—I think a lot of the enemies of the church are delighted to see all that. And I said that I think we don't want to isolate ourselves from the rest of America by our strong views on abortion and the other things. We need to be building bridges, not burning them."

Asked if there were any other bishops who agreed with him, he said, "Of course, the majority."

He was asked why none of the bishops who disagreed with the protests that dominated the news for weeks had spoken up. "The bishops don't want to have a battle in public with one another, but I think the majority of bishops in the country didn't join in with that, would not be in agreement with that approach. It's well intentioned, but we don't lose our dignity by being strong in the belief that we have but also talking to others that don't have our belief. We don't lose our dignity by that," he said.

At the same time, he acknowledged the loudest voices were creating what appeared to be the Catholic position for the general public. "Of course, that's always been the case," he said. "That's news, you know."

He said that in speaking to the other bishops he wondered aloud what was so bad about inviting President Obama to Notre Dame and giving him a degree. He noted that the month before we spoke, Pope Benedict had made French President Nicolas Sarkozy an honorary canon of St. John Lateran's. "And he [President Nicolas Sarkozy] is pro-abortion, pro-gay marriage, married invalidly to an actress, and the pope did that. It doesn't seem that [the Vatican] had quite as big a concern about this matter of Obama and Notre Dame as some of us."

"You have to be very careful. The Vatican doesn't do these big sanctions; you're out of the church if you vote this way. They've tried it, it doesn't work, and I try to learn from what the Vatican has to teach and to use that myself," he said. "The primary responsibility for someone receiving communion is the person [and his or her] conscience, to come forward to receive. The priest shouldn't be like a watchdog, looking around and finding out who's unworthy."

No one would place Sheehan in the liberal camp. He's rarely outspoken on the national stage. But he was expressing the views of more than a few bishops who, in private, will admit everything from frustration to anger with some of the high-profile antics of their fellow bishops.

Ecclesiologist Richard Gaillardetz, who teaches at Boston College, said that to some extent he shares the bishops' concern that "both individual Catholics and Catholic institutions are losing their moorings in the Catholic tradition and failing in their responsibility to apply the Gospel to contemporary issues." In a January 2011 interview he said that Catholic individuals and institutions face unique challenges today "regarding how to best hand on our Catholic faith and how to live it with integrity in a postmodern world."[8]

But the bishops are targeting the wrong influences and employing the wrong strategy by believing "that they have to hold the line or that Catholicism will roll down the slippery slope of relativism. My larger difficulty with this is that I think it's a strategy that's doomed to failure."

Gaillardetz cited Canadian sociologist David Lyon's analysis in his book *Jesus in Disneyland: Religion in Postmodern Times*, in which he speaks of the "deregulation of religion," or, as Gaillardetz put it, "the "tendency we have in the postmodern world to be religious but on our own terms, to define for ourselves what matters and what does not matter in questions of religious belief and practice."

Lyon's point is similar, he said, to what Belgian theologian Lieven Boeve "refers to as 'de-traditionalization.' Again, not a lessening of the fervor of religious belief but questions about how much we have to align our belief with a larger religious tradition."

It is these "larger reconfigurations of religion in the postmodern world" that the bishops are reacting against, he believes, and some have chosen to respond by attempting to reassert their episcopal authority more forcefully. "They shout louder, as it were, hoping thereby to counteract those cultural currents and reestablish their authority." But shouting louder hasn't worked well.

Gaillardetz believes that any "authentic exercise of authority" by church leaders "has to recall our longstanding tradition in the Catholic Church of distinguishing between a compelling and doctrinally binding moral vision and the difficult issues of concrete application. At the level of concrete application, we're often talking about prudential judgments about which Catholics likely disagree. I think authority is most effective when it's willing to be real clear about those distinctions."

In trying to counteract social currents they see as a challenge to faith, Gaillardetz said, too often the bishops "have chosen to reassert their authority on matters of great moral complexity and specificity. Whatever one thinks of the decision of Sr. McBride and St. Joseph Hospital, these people were facing a tragic moral situation and one that's haunted Catholic casuists for decades. And the same thing to some extent is true of the healthcare legislation issue." The legislation, he said, was "extraordinarily complex" and the bishops fashioned their position on the advice of a "very small group of legal consultants."

In the end, he said, the tragedy is that such questions and issues don't have to become confrontations and power struggles. "This is not a question of authority or no authority. This is a question of how you appropriately exercise authority and exercise it effectively in a postmodern world." Aspects of the deregulation or "de-traditionalization" of religion are troubling, he said, "and bishops should rightly be addressing the issues, but not by simply shouting louder or drawing arbitrary lines in the sand." What's needed, he said, is "a different vision for exercising episcopal leadership in the church today, and we're not seeing that being played out."

What does it mean, then, when a bishop (or bishops) draws a line in the sand, only to have it washed away beneath a tide of Catholic expert analysis or the consciences of faithful Catholics or other recognized Catholic leaders who come to different conclusions?

"Once upon a time nuns, no matter what they thought of their bishops, would probably be willing to go along" with pronouncements even if they disagreed with them, said Margaret Steinfels, co-director of the Fordham Center on Religion and Culture at Fordham University in New York. At least, she said, "they would not go public on these matters. And now, they're willing to." She said that Keehan, on the healthcare debate "is absolutely right, and I suspect she has a vast number of Catholics agreeing with her."[9]

That debate and the one surrounding the hospital controversy in Phoenix demonstrate "the fact that there are many different kinds of authority or credibility," she said. "If the bishop is merely asserting a juridical authority here, claiming that church teaching has been violated, Sr. McBride has all sorts of other kinds of authority" validating her view, Steinfels said, referring to the sister who was excommunicated by Olmsted.

The pregnant mother of four who was dying also brought an authority to the situation, she said. "A lot of people," said Steinfels, "think that bishops haven't the foggiest idea of what it means to be pregnant, or to be pregnant and sick, or to be pregnant and dying. I'm not opposed to juridical authority. After all, we depend on it in many ways, either in the state or in the church." But, she said, people today weigh against juridical authority "many other types of authority or ideas about what should have happened, and the bishop's authority has been found wanting."

Such open debates and disagreements, she said, might signal a crisis of authority, "but I think what we're seeing is the evolution of an adult church."

"I think there is an evolution of how the Catholic Church sees itself, how Catholics who are faithful members of this community see their relationship to it and their obligations to it, and, obviously, this is evolving in fits and starts.

"I suppose all evolutions have a certain number of dead ends," she said, "and I guess I'm kind of hoping that the current episcopal turn is going to be a dead end because I don't think it's going to work. I think we need bishops who are prepared to listen to people and to consult with them, and not necessarily to agree with them, but to deploy a certain power of persuasion rather than marching orders. I just don't think the marching-order model is going to work anymore."

Chapter 9

AMID THE TENSIONS

More than once during the year and a half I spent traveling to different corners of the U.S. Catholic Church I wondered when I would come upon *the* thing, or even the combination of things, that would unlock the answer to where the church was heading. I struggled with coming up with a neat list—the ten action items or the five-year plan—a version of "news you can use" for the Catholic who wants a clear idea of what works, or for the one who's dangling by the fingertips and wants hard data on why he or she should stay. Of course, no single thing is the answer. From Theology on Tap (a program that serves up beer and civil discussion to the younger set) to the local peace and justice organization, the church is awash in programs and opportunities for faith formation and for service.

The positive note is easy to strike: Remove the Catholic Church and the work of its people from our midst, and life in this country would be dramatically different and far worse than it is. Pick a city and begin removing the ministries and work of Catholic parishes and of independent Catholics acting out of their understanding of the gospel and of church social teaching. Take away, for instance, the center started decades ago by a couple of sisters that cares for children of poor, working, often single mothers; or eliminate the agency in that same city that works against the greatest odds to tend to the increasing numbers of men and women being released from prison with nothing more than the clothes on their backs. There are sisters transforming whole blocks of urban blight by caring for the outcast, training people for jobs, rehabbing homes, and running residential addiction rehab centers. Priests, sisters and lay leaders advocate from the Texas and Arizona borders to the immigration detention center in Newark on behalf of refugees seeking a new home and a new life. In some of the most desperate circumstances in this country an entirely "new evangelization" goes on, not with words and dogma but with the power of presence and transformative love. Kids are being rescued from unimaginable settings and taught to reimagine their futures; art and literature, urban farming and new forms of community become part of the resurrection story in hellish inner cities. Pick any city and start eliminating the soup kitchens and the clothing and food banks, the Catholic Charities–funded organizations that help people with everything from housing to counseling.

For all of the programs aimed at trying to bridge gaps among factions of the Catholic community, perhaps none finds a greater spread of common ground than JustFaith, the movement begun by Jack Jezreel. This is not a cheap-grace program. Participants commit to months of meetings with a small group, a large volume of reading in the area of social justice, and a determination to confront some of the world's more troubling problems from a Christian and Catholic perspective. The course includes ventures into seldom-seen portions of local communities, those parts where the broken and marginalized dwell and are given support. Tens of thousands of Catholics across the country have tussled over months with the complexities of determining what is just and what might bring peace to situations ranging from the scene outside their front doors to mega problems of war, poverty, refugees, and global environmental degradation. Many have found themselves changed forever in the process, made aware of things that they've not before pondered, from a point of view anchored deep in the Christian gospels, and in the end empowered to act as they may never have imagined.

Multiply these few observations hundreds and hundreds of times across the country. Strip out all of that human-to-human activity and the prayer upon which it is built and that accompanies it. Life for many would become exceedingly bleak and hopeless.

The Catholic presence in the culture is significant. From the parish to the statehouse, from Congress to the Supreme Court, from the academy to Wall Street, there probably has never been a time in our country's history when Catholic life has so robustly projected itself into American life.

And yet the feeling that all is not well is pervasive. There is an unsettled sense about what it means to be Catholic and what being Catholic means in the public realm. Catholic politicians are at odds with their bishops over public policy matters, particularly when it comes to political strategies involving abortion. Members of the hierarchy are at odds with each other, with Catholic institutions, and with vowed religious. Having Catholic business leaders doesn't guarantee a different kind of marketplace. Catholics by the thousands are involved in wars that successive popes have condemned. And with each new revelation of priest sexual abuse of children and teens and of official cover-up more credibility is drained from the hierarchical level. The divisions within the Catholic community are expressed in the most extreme ways in the blogosphere, which has opened a huge venue for irresponsible, undocumented, irrational, and unaccountable opinion and rumor-mongering. The attacks can be vicious and unrelenting, particularly from that element that John Allen has labeled "Taliban Catholics," self-appointed guardians of self-concocted measures of orthodoxy. The Big Tent of the Catholic Church strains today to contain it all.

Granted, most Catholics are not taking up with the extremes, and if such rigorist views remained on line they would play to a small and relatively silent audience. Catholic debates, however, have gone public in recent years, and some of the bishops are leading the way. As Santa Fe's Archbishop Sheehan said, most of the bishops may object to the tactics and positions of the loudest, but they also don't want to engage in nasty fights in public. So a tiny but vociferous group who publicly threatens to use the Eucharist as a political weapon, who engage in broad public excommunications, who unilaterally make absolute declarations of certainty over complex moral or legal issues, gets to fashion the Catholic narrative and Catholic positions for the wider public.

There are indications that such tactics may be on the wane. One reason may be the lack of success of the approach that draws lines in the sand and attempts to separate people and groups into neatly divided, opposing camps. The either/or stance works for a small segment of church and society, but most people don't live their lives in such stark black and white.

Dulling the take-it-or-leave-it approach to public discourse has been a change in Catholic involvement in the political arena in recent years. Prior to the 2004 presidential election between incumbent George W. Bush and Senator John Kerry of Massachusetts, there was little coherent political discourse from religious progressives. Conservative Protestants, predominantly from the Protestant evangelical tradition, together with conservative Catholics, were virtually unchallenged in crafting the "religious" view of political issues. Most of their energy was spent on sexual issues such as abortion and homosexuality. More often than not those views meshed nicely with the views of the local bishop and the Republican Party platform. That changed in 2004 as the groups Catholics United, Catholic Democrats, Catholics in Alliance for the Common Good, Faith in Public Life, and others began to work together to bolster the efforts of organizations like Network, a Catholic social justice lobby, to articulate a much broader view of religious concerns. Their interests often aligned with those of a progressive Protestant movement organized by Jim Wallis of Sojourners, who has long added an authoritative religious voice to national political discussions. Poverty, war, economic disparities between rich and poor, healthcare, environmental concerns, and access to quality education were finally articulated from a religious, and particularly Catholic, perspective. The groups became skilled at fashioning quick responses and in calling on experts from the Catholic academy. The political conversation became more thickly textured, more complex, and Catholics had more to consider than a few "hot button" issues when measuring candidates. High-profile pro-life figures and academics such as attorneys Nicholas Cafardi, dean emeritus of the Duquesne University Law School, and Douglas Kmiec, a noted constitutional law expert from Pepperdine University and former ambassador to Malta, refuted the view promulgated widely, even by some bishops, that Catholics could not vote for Barack Obama because the political strategy he espoused to deal with abortion differed from the outright ban favored by religious conservatives. Cafardi and Kmiec each held impeccable credentials as observant Catholics, and their considerable writing and speaking about their reasons for supporting Obama provided a significant window into the diversity of thought and opinion in the Catholic world. As the final vote showed, Catholics are not a one-issue constituency.

Another indication that the use of hot, confrontational tactics may be on the wane can be seen in the gradual change in the nature of the U.S. episcopacy. Just as John Paul II was able to fashion a national conference to his liking over twenty-five years, Benedict now has the opportunity to stamp his character on the hierarchy, and by all appearances he values prudence and competence over ideological fervor and blind loyalty.

Major sees have gone to moderates like Archbishop Timothy Dolan of New York and Cardinal Donald Wuerl of Washington. The first cardinal to be named in the southwest is Daniel DiNardo, who also has a reputation for moderate views and a pastoral approach. Two of the most divisive figures, who created national headlines, Cardinal Raymond Burke, formerly archbishop of St. Louis, and Bishop Joseph Martino of Scranton, were removed. True, in the *bella figura* ethos of Rome, Burke was named a cardinal and made head of the Signatura or Vatican Court, and Martino, claiming illness, was allowed to move offstage to teach at a seminary, just as Cardinal Law was permitted to take up a rather comfortable spot as archpriest of the Basilica of St. Mary Major in Rome and retain his membership on six influential Vatican committees. Except in extreme cases, members of the hierarchy don't get docked, they get shuffled. It is the culture at its protective and posturing best. In the cases of Law, Martino, and Burke, the downside of a sideways promotion was that they lost their base of operations and bully pulpits and they lost their votes in the national conference. Change within the clerical culture occurs at a glacial pace.

However that larger story of episcopal politics plays out, on the ground my hunch was reinforced that the walk of faith among Catholics continues in some remarkable ways despite the adversity. Throughout the country there are outstanding parishes that everyone talks about—you know them—the ones that have capable leaders with a knack for bringing people and vision together, that seem to have confidence in their mission, about what it means to be a community and how to project the community's faith into the wider world. My experience sitting at the editor's desk at *NCR*, however, immediately balances that optimistic side of things. I know the phone calls, more frequent in the years toward the end of my tenure in 2008, that catalogued a running tale of parish life upended by the arrival of a new priest or a new bishop. Without exaggeration, they were far too numerous to keep track of; we would have needed an editorial staff of dozens to begin to cover the woe.

So what's going on? Will the real Catholic Church please stand up?

It should not be surprising that so much good exists alongside and within the turmoil, divisions, and uncertainty. We are living in an in-between time, a time of tension, between the promise and openness of the documents promulgated by the world's bishops gathered nearly half a century ago at the Second Vatican Council and the real fears of what those documents mean and their implications for the institution. Fifty years may seem an eternity in the digital age, but it is a mere blip in an institution that measures time in millennia.

Just as it is impossible to write much about twentieth-century America without referencing the civil rights era or the feminist movement, one can't write much about contemporary Catholicism without acknowledging Vatican II for the touchstone it is and for the ensuing disputes about its meaning that continue to play out even today. They are debates "with implications for Judaism, Islam, science and secular politics as well as other Christians."[1]

The council was a jolt to the system. Some today, in an attempt to lessen the shock, speak of a "hermeneutic of continuity" as opposed to a "hermeneutic of discontinuity or rupture." The terms, once the stuff of academic discussions, have been reduced to campaign talking points. Continuity is the bullet point for those who insist that nothing radically new occurred at the council and that its intent was merely to dress up eternal verities in new language. Dividing people into "hermeneutic camps" has become a favorite tactic of some commentators and bishops. The categories provide an easily understood division between those who view the council as a moment of significant change and those who hold that it was merely a restating of ancient truths and a call for renewal of faith. "Hermeneutics" now echoes around the Catholic landscape; the term is used in the packaging of initiatives ranging from the investigation of religious orders to alterations in the liturgy.

During a 2009 meeting at Stonehill College in Easton, Massachusetts, a gathering said to have been influential in the decision of Cardinal Franc Rode to open an investigation of women religious in the United States, Bishop Robert C. Morlino of Madison, Wisconsin, used the term to refute the idea that Vatican II represented a break from the past: "The language that many people have learned . . . is the language of the discontinuity hermeneutic, the language of the rupture, between pre–Vatican II and post–Vatican II," he said. "Many if not most of our people have learned the language of the discontinuity hermeneutic. And in order to learn the language that Pope John Paul the Great and Pope Benedict are trying to teach us they have to unlearn the language that they learned."[2]

In another context Sioux City, Iowa, Bishop R. Walker Nickless, outlining his plan for the future of his diocese, remarked: "The so-called 'spirit' of the council has no authoritative interpretation. It is a ghost or demon that must be exorcised if we are to proceed with the Lord's work."

The politics of such statements are transparent in their wish to scrub from the record the questions and new insights that were the very cause of the four-year endeavor. They are an expression both of fear of what the council unlocked and the wish to return to an era of certainty, that time when young priests had all the answers; the locked-in knowledge of the GPS device that can drive right by the truth of the matter, no questions asked, because it knows that the truth is really seven miles down the road.

The current use of the terms *hermeneutic* and *discontinuity* takes to an extreme an analysis that Pope Benedict advanced in a 2005 speech to the Roman curia in which he described "two contrary hermeneutics" that came "face to face with each other and quarreled." Benedict's alternative is the "hermeneutic of reform," which he also describes as the "hermeneutic of renewal in the continuity of the one subject—church—which the Lord has given to us. She is a subject which increases in time and develops, yet always remaining the same, the one subject of the journeying people of God."

The tricky part comes, of course, in translating the words into real-life situations. What precisely does it mean to develop and increase while remaining the same? What is renewal, if it doesn't involve some change? How does one measure the sentiments of Benedict today with those he penned as a peritus (expert) at Vatican II, when he extolled the possibilities of decentralization of church government, saw the emergence of a "horizontal Catholicity," and claimed that a pope has "a moral obligation to hear the voice of the church universal."[3]

Scholars are yet parsing the change in tone and point of view of the cardinal become pope, and even whether there was one, though it seems fairly obvious. The point is that the effort to persuade us that no radical changes occurred seems to be fueled by the very data on the ground showing that something significant indeed *has* occurred. The dispute itself is a sign that the church has admitted into the old certainties a new set of understandings and questions, and that they continue to roil the waters even today.

The antagonism of some toward the council is understandable. It has been amply documented in the past half century that the odd thing about the council is that its implementation was left in the hands of members of the curia, or church's central administration in Rome, who fought any talk of renewal and change from the moment Pope John XXIII let it be known he intended to convene the gathering. As council documents go, those promulgated by the participants at Vatican II have a decidedly different tone from those of any councils before it.

The matter of language is not insignificant, as Jesuit historian Fr. John W. O'Malley draws out at some length in his essay in *Vatican II: Did Anything Happen?* O'Malley argues, first, that it would hardly be exceptional for a council to be "discontinuous" or distinctive from past councils. Perhaps the only thing common to councils prior to Vatican II, he says, is that they were all assemblies of bishops "that have made authoritative decisions binding on the whole church. Other than that they differ considerably among themselves" and were "to a greater or lesser degree discontinuous with one another."

What made Vatican II especially different from all councils that preceded it, writes O'Malley, is the language used, a language so distinctive that it requires "a new hermeneutic . . . that takes serious account of the discontinuity, thus putting the council's continuity in perspective." For lack of a sound-bite phrase, one might just call O'Malley's version the third hermeneutic.

Further, he says, the "characteristic style of discourse" of prior councils comprised "two basic elements"—the canon, or law, formulated to impose a punishment, and the vocabulary appropriate to that genre. The discourse of prior councils employed "power words," or "words of threat and intimidation, words of surveillance and punishment, words of a superior speaking to inferiors or . . . to an enemy." The language is used to define and limit, to make clear who is included and who excluded.

In contrast, Vatican II used "empowerment words," words of reciprocity and persuasion as different from commands and anathemas. "There is scarcely a page in the council documents on which 'dialogue' or its equivalent does not occur. 'Dialogue' manifests a radical shift from the prophetic I-say-unto-you style that earlier prevailed and indicates something other than unilateral decision-making." Such language, writes O'Malley, did not make it into the documents "without a fierce battle."[4] Things, indeed, were different about Vatican II at a fundamental level. Whether that difference is expressed in a hermeneutic of discontinuity or of renewal is a battle that still rages, along with, in some circles, the original fight over the language itself.

O'Malley's view, of course, is that of one person. But it is widely seen, if the reviews are to be believed, as an updated and valuable articulation of the segment of the church that believes that the council represented significant change from previous ways of doing church business.

O'Malley's analysis was important enough in the eyes of those advocating the hermeneutic of continuity to draw considerable attention from conservatives, not least of which was the late Fr. Richard John Neuhaus in the October 2008 issue of his magazine, *First Things*. He disapprovingly termed O'Malley's longer treatment of the subject in his 2008 book, *What Happened at Vatican II*, "a 372–page brief for the party of novelty and discontinuity." He declared at review's end that the 2008 book *Vatican II: Renewal within Tradition*, edited by Matthew L. Lamb and Matthew Levering, and offering an opposing view to O'Malley's, makes "it evident that the hermeneutics of continuity is prevailing, if it has not already definitively prevailed."

Figuring out how the scorecard ultimately nets out is probably more complex than the scoring system for Olympic figure skating.

Longtime Catholic church observer and former *New York Times* columnist Peter Steinfels, reviewing O'Malley's 2008 book, notes that the world's bishops fifty years ago could have simply "rubberstamped a series of routine texts prepared under Vatican oversight and gone home."[5]

"How the bishops took charge of the agenda and radically re-shaped the outcome is a story of bold confrontations, clashing personalities and behind-the-scenes maneuvers," he writes. Acknowledging that some, claiming that elusive and probably over-used "spirit of the council," have staked claim to changes well beyond any imagined by the council's participants, Steinfels none-theless argues that "any effort to shuffle the cards of continuity and discontinuity so as to minimize the profound reorientation wrought by the council borders on the ludicrous."

If, indeed, a "profound reorientation" occurred because of the council, what does that mean today? And does the talk of a need to relearn language signal an attempt to return to, for lack of a more nuanced phrase, a pre–Vatican II reality? Morlino's com-ments would certainly suggest such a course as would the later words of Rodé, who said in an interview with *NCR* that Vatican II precipitated "the greatest crisis in church history."[6]

If there is little love in the Vatican these days for the council, experts in liturgy and history still exist who understand how pro-foundly some things have changed. Benedictine Sr. Mary Collins, a liturgy expert and former prioress, recalled in an interview that it wasn't long before the council that Pope Pius XII, in his encyc-lical on liturgy, declared "quite matter-of-factly that the role of the priest is essential and the role of the laity is not essential in the mass, that it is the priest who effects the sacrifice of the Eucharist."

In contrast, she noted, the *Constitution on the Sacred Liturgy* and *The Dogmatic Constitution on the Church* that came out of Vatican II articulated a far different ecclesiology, one in which "it is the right and privilege and responsibility of the baptized, who are fully involved in the liturgy of the Eucharist." The point, she said, was not to downplay the role of clergy, but rather to explain the more integral role of laity in the Eucharist.

"Twenty years from now," she said, "I hope we're not still ar-guing about Vatican II. I think the way this gets played out and resolved will make a massive difference in the shape the church takes fifty years from now. This is not a matter of irrelevance to the future of the church, but I would not presume to predict how it sorts itself out."

The struggle for the meaning of Vatican II is encapsulated in the story of the struggle for control of liturgical translation. Indeed, while the council set up a process for doing translations of sacred texts and prayers for worship, a widely consultative process that went on under the guidance of English-speaking bishops from around the world and liturgical and scriptural experts for more than thirty years, the "reform of the reform" began in earnest in a secret Vatican meeting in 1997. That year, eleven men met in secret in the Vatican "to overhaul the American lectionary, the collection of scripture readings authorized for use in the mass. Short-circuiting a six-year debate over 'inclusive language' by retaining many of the most controversial uses of masculine vocabulary, and revamping texts approved by the U.S. bishops, this group decided how the Bible will sound in the American church. . . . Powers in Rome handpicked a small group of men who in two weeks undid work that had taken dozens of years," reported John Allen.[7]

In ensuing years the International Commission on English in the Liturgy (ICEL), which was created at the Second Vatican Council as a joint project of eleven English-speaking bishops' conferences and not under control of the Vatican, has essentially been supplanted by a Vatican-controlled agency, the Vox Clara Committee, with a mandate to advise the Congregation for Divine Worship and the Discipline of the Sacraments on English translations.

ICEL, meanwhile, under great pressure from the Vatican, has revised its statutes and overhauled personnel to be more in line with Vatican wishes and a 2001 Vatican document, Liturgiam Authenticam.

In early 2010 Vox Clara released a statement saying its work on a new English translation of the *Roman Missal,* the book of prayers used at mass, was nearly complete. When it goes into use, expected in Advent 2011, a major battle in the liturgy wars will have been won. Under John Paul II, the process for determining liturgical translations, a process that grew directly from the council, was hijacked. Can the factions that fought, sometimes bitterly, come together in the future in the kind of unity the liturgy begs? Liturgist Collins, professor emeritus at Catholic University, said, "I do think there needs to be a change of heart running through the whole ecclesial body." A reality in the church today, she said, "is that we are still in the winners-and-losers game. I think unless the church can get beyond that, we can't tell ourselves we're responding to the call of the Holy Spirit."

The liturgy, controlling as it does how we pray as a community, and thus our communal understanding of God, is at the cutting edge of the debate over the direction of the council. While in the English-speaking world the "continuity hermeneutic" seems to have won the day with new prayer versions that attempt to be one-to-one translations from the Latin, the arguments seem far from resolved.

Fr. Michael Ryan, pastor of St. James Cathedral in Seattle for more than two decades, in December 2010 began a campaign to slow down implementation of the new translations of the *Roman Missal*. "For some time I've followed the bishops' debates, read many of the new texts, discussed them with brother priests, and visited about them with Catholics in the pews, and I've become aware of how difficult it's going to be to 'sell' ordinary, faithful, good Catholics on the new, Latinized translations of the Missal," Ryan said in an *NCR* interview. He and others have criticized the new texts for being awkward in their phrasing, confusing, and even "not very English."

By early 2011 his efforts had garnered more than twenty thousand supporters in an online campaign at whatifwejustsaidwait.org. At the same time, Ryan conceded, in an announcement to his parish in February of that year, that the campaign had failed to stop the implementation of the new liturgical prayers and that the parish "would make the best of it" when the new missal was introduced.

Ryan, however, retained his reservations about the translations, and he has some highly placed fellow critics. Benedictine Fr. Anscar J. Chupungco, director of the Paul VI Institute of Liturgy in the Philippines and former president of the Pontifical Liturgical Institute at Sant'Anselmo in Rome, gave a stinging critique of the "reform of the reform" in January 2010, a phrase used weeks earlier by none other than the papal master of ceremonies, Msgr. Guido Marini.[8]

In a talk at Australia's University of Newcastle's program of liturgical studies, Chupungco responded to Marini's claim that the Vatican II liturgical reform has "not always in its practical implementation found a timely and happy fulfillment."

"What are the possible implications of a reform of the post-conciliar reform?" Chupungco asked. "What remedy does it offer for a reform that according to some Catholics has gone bad? What agenda does it put forward so that liturgical worship could be more reverent and prayerful?"

The liturgy envisioned by the council, he stated, "was marked by noble simplicity and clarity. It wanted a liturgy that the people could easily follow. In sharp contrast is the attempt to revive, at the expense of active participation, the medieval usage that was espoused by the Tridentine [or pre–Vatican II] rite and to retrieve eagerly the liturgical paraphernalia that had been deposited in museums as historical artifacts."

Comparing the reforms of Vatican II to a springtime renewal, Chupungco lamented that after more than four decades "the church is now experiencing the cold chill of winter brought about by contrasting ideas of what the liturgy is and how it should be celebrated." Such tension, he said, "could be a healthy sign that the interest in the liturgy has not abated." But he cautioned that after the council, "we are not free to propound views" apart from principles established by the council. "There are surely instances of postconciliar implementation that are debatable, but we should be careful to distinguish them from the conciliar principles, especially the full, active participation of all God's people in the liturgy."

Undoubtedly the debates will go on. These are the tensions we live in and through in the Catholic Church of the West in the beginning of the twenty-first century. But that significant change occurred as a result of the council, in some cases clearly discontinuous with past thought and practice, is indisputable. O'Malley points out that the changes had to do with far more than language: "What happened at Vatican II? That question is usually answered by indicating how certain elements in the key decrees were discontinuous with previous teaching or practice. *Unitatis redintegratio,* the decree on ecumenism, was discontinuous not only with the polemics of the Counter-Reformation but more pointedly with the encyclicals *Mortalium animos* of Pius XI (1928) condemning the ecumenical movement and *Humani generis* of Pius XII (1950) condemning 'eirenicism.' It was discontinuous with the mind-set that as late as 1963 forbade a nun in a Catholic hospital to summon a Protestant minister for a dying person. *Dei Verbum,* the *Constitution on the Word of God,* was discontinuous with the tradition that since the 16th century had made the Bible practically a forbidden book for Catholics. *Dignitatis humanae,* the declaration on religious liberty, discontinuous not only with the long 'Constantinian era' but particularly with the condemnations of separation of church and states by the popes of the 19th and 20th centuries."[9] He notes, at the end of that passage, that the Jesuit theologian John Courtney Murray, whose thinking largely accounted for the council's acceptance of separation of church and state, was, on the eve of the council "in difficulties with the Holy Office for questioning that the Catholic confessional state was the ideal to be striven for."

Change happens, as Jesuit theologian Mark Massa points out. Whatever issues remain unsettled out of Vatican II, the one settled question (save for the opinion of a tiny minority who dismiss the council altogether) is that the "very vibrancy and size of Catholicism made dealing with historical consciousness necessary." Less than a half a century after Pope Pius X attempted to reassert the "Tridentine brand of Catholicism [which] posited the church as a perfect society founded by Jesus and entrusted to St. Peter during Christ's earthly ministry," the force of history itself drained the notion of any credibility.[10] The church, alas, is not immutable and above the fray. It is, like all human institutions, constantly shaped and formed in part by the winds and abrasions of history and, as Massa puts it, the law of unintended consequences.

Chapter 10

WHERE FROM HERE?

The way ahead is through uncharted territory. Any one of the crises with which the American church is dealing—sex abuse, authority, money, demographics, priest shortage, or the massive exodus out of the church—would challenge the integrity of an institution. In combination and coupled with the rapid change that is occurring in other spheres of human activity—the information age, the constantly expanding boundaries of science and technology, growth in religious tolerance, and an increase in religious pluralism—the challenges threaten to overwhelm the best intentions. The project of moving ahead becomes enormously complicated.

Yet it is also understood, to paraphrase of bit of common wisdom, that all religion is local. Proof enough exists that people will do what they have to do to sustain themselves in a religious community, even if it means, unfortunately, finding one outside the Catholic community.

It would have been nice to wrap up my work on the emerging church by gathering in all the disparate strands and fashioning a happy ending. The truth of the matter, however, is that the story remains open ended. While the church remains an unparalleled source for good in the world, it also is going through a time of wrenching crisis and deep change, much of which remains hidden and off the agenda of our leaders' national meetings. What I've tried to outline, without becoming rigidly categorical, is a community subjected to a range of forces attempting to shape its future. Those who want to reinstate certitude and doctrinal rigor coexist, often uneasily, with those whose questions and expansive views at times seem to know no limit. Redemption is the province

174

of no single faction, and no one can claim the only program that works. There was a reason why the sense of motion implicit in such phrases as *pilgrim people, people of God, pilgrim church,* and *earthly pilgrimage* has become a staple image of the church. A static image in an era of great change simply wouldn't make sense.

In lieu of a five-point program or a ten-year plan, it is appropriate at least to make some observations that may be helpful when considering the future. The first of those looks at a condition that is normally outlined in whispers and intimations but rarely if ever in full voice in a public forum. But enough time has passed since John Paul's passing that one can respectfully if soberly come to grips with what he has meant to the church, especially in the United States.

Effect of the John Paul Papacy

Vatican II didn't occur in a flash out of nothing. It was formed of the stuff that was being assembled for decades by theologians and liturgists who were looking ahead and anticipating the questions of the new millennium through the lens of the church's traditional teachings and practices. They were responding to new circumstances and a new understanding of old verities. The council was not a product of the status quo.

Likewise, the future of the church, as we look from the beginning of the twenty-first century, does not reside with those who believe that our salvation lies in a return to that era when we believed we had all the answers. It is being imagined, instead, by those willing to keep the questions, even if it means at times unsettling the community. As an institution the church may experience (putting no limits here on the Holy Spirit) bursts of insight—another council, perhaps—but if past is prologue, institutional change comes incrementally. And along the way, at the hierarchical level, the community can expect pushback against change. It's the nature of the office.

We saw that in abundance during the papacy of John Paul II. While he fully understood the mechanics of the information age and a shrinking globe and exploited them well to his and the church's own ends, his preference clearly was for a model of church that had about it the aura of Vatican I reenactors. On the global stage he understood how to take advantage of the moment when the world's hierarchies and old constructs were crumbling, but he wasn't able to reimagine the parallel, what the flattened hierarchies that nature was projecting into our lives in graphic form, meant inside the church.

If we are to proceed, then, we must come to grips with the fact that we are living through the consequences of that shadow side of John Paul's papacy.

Throughout the quarter century of his reign he advanced a model of church exemplified by the new movements and orders. Most of the movements are fairly benign displays of Catholic thought and action, often with a particular focus, say, on the poor or evangelization or building bridges to other religious groups. Two of them, however, Opus Dei and the Legionaries of Christ, were particular favorites that he promoted as ideals of church life.

Opus Dei came in for special treatment—the equivalent of its own worldwide diocese—and he made certain that Opus Dei founder, Josemaría Escrivá, was placed on the express track to sainthood. In 2002, John Paul canonized Escrivá, who died in 1975. The paranoid-laced, if riveting, fiction of Dan Brown's *Da Vinci Code* aside, and granting that Opus Dei has modified in recent decades its most severe expressions, the organization still remains an esoteric manifestation of Catholicism. Even in moderated form it is unlikely to ever constitute more than a tiny fraction of the entire community.

Most revealing, however, of John Paul's model of governance and vision for the church was his long, uncritical support for the Legion of Christ and its founder, Fr. Marcial Maciel Degollado. John Paul consistently held up the Legion as an ideal, promoting, praising, and rewarding it. Maciel was one of his personal favorites, and he occasionally accompanied John Paul on papal trips. He received special recognition from the pope as an exemplar of religious life and, in that now infamous and distressing accolade, an "efficacious guide to youth."

Improbable as it might be to imagine that John Paul was completely shielded by his handlers from all of the bad news about Maciel, if that indeed was the case, that fact alone would be a telling commentary on his leadership style and judgment. That he could for years ignore the charges and pleas of those abused by Maciel is a clear indication of how incurious he was about the greatest scandal the church has faced in modern times. He did little to confront the crisis during his long reign as pope.

More significant is that John Paul considered the Legion a model of religious life and its lay arm, Regnum Christi, a corresponding ideal of lay involvement. The organization as a whole was from its inception an extreme personality cult. The central figure, Maciel, was protected from scrutiny by the imposition of bizarre vows that prohibited anyone in the order from saying anything critical of Nuestro Padre (our father). The arrogance of it all, in retrospect, is breathtaking.

But this was the ideal, in John Paul's estimation, of "intense, generous, and fruitful priestly ministry."

Secretive, manipulative, dripping with piety and clerical correctness, its young recruits represented a clean-cut, obedient, docile vanguard in John Paul's campaign for a "heroic priesthood."

Yet it was fraudulent at its core. Maciel was a world-class abuser of young boys who also maintained at least two female lovers on the side. He knew how to display the wheedling deference that played well in John Paul's Vatican, and he was expert in his knowledge of the clerical culture and how to manipulate it to his own ends.

He wined and dined important people, lavishly spread money and gifts around the Vatican, and always made sure that his order took care of the clerical culture's leading figures.

This was the church and the style that those who carried ambitions to higher office understood as the protocol of the realm during John Paul's tenure. Obedience, deference, working the system, loyalty above all else, and the minutiae of rubric, garb, and personal pieties properly displayed.

It doesn't take an expert in organizational dynamics to understand how the clerical culture works. For those who want to get ahead in the institution, mimicking those at the top of the pyramid is essential. One joke has it that if a pope were to become vegetarian, all the butcher shops in Rome would go out of business within a week.

Of course there are those who will retain their individuality, think outside the box at times, and even push back. But they are likely to come to a moment of decision, realizing that beyond a certain point acting on conscience can threaten a career.

Being a theologian of any note during the John Paul II years became a dangerous occupation. A steady stream of them, some the intellects behind the council documents, were investigated and made to endure lengthy inquisitions by the Congregation for the Doctrine of the Faith. Some saw their books condemned and their reputations smeared.

The effects of the John Paul II papacy can also be seen today in the ranks of young priests who identify themselves by his name—they are John Paul II priests—and they're not shy about rendering judgments of their peers, including a bishop here and there, whom they might not consider sufficiently "orthodox." It can be seen, too, in the bishops who refer to him as "the great" and who, through John Paul, perceive tacit approval to denigrate the Second Vatican Council. Though John Paul's case was placed on the express track to beatification, his legacy is hardly a settled matter.

In retrospect, the cardinal electors may have had insights that much of the rest of the world didn't when they chose Joseph Ratzinger as the next pope in 2005. He came to the office with a reputation as "The Enforcer," one well earned as head of the Congregation for the Doctrine of the Faith. But as Benedict XVI he has displayed other characteristics that markedly change the style and tone of the John Paul II era. For starters, he has dialed down the volume and dimmed the spotlight on the papacy. One senses he has neither the disposition nor the desire to be constantly on the big stage. He is a quiet German intellectual and musician, apparently introspective by nature. If his papacy has anything heroic about it, it is the heroism of suffering the humiliation of the sex abuse crisis, which, despite his own missteps, he probably understands better than any other bishop on earth. As a cardinal and prefect of the Congregation for the Doctrine of the Faith, he weekly studied the abuse files from the United States, and in so doing was transformed from one skeptical of the claims of the victims and their advocates to the highest level church leader to be convinced of the evil of the scandal.

In his final months as a cardinal he reopened the investigation of Maciel, and early in his papacy, with significant evidence of

Maciel's depravity in hand, he disciplined John Paul's model priest, removing him from the public stage. He later ordered an investigation of the Legion. What will survive of the order is still in question.

Forces over which he has little control have undoubtedly fashioned Benedict's papacy in a way he never anticipated. His plans to reevangelize Europe and to take on the twin influences of secularism and relativism were largely derailed by this internal curse. It is difficult to strike a triumphal pose while admitting the devastating humiliation of such shocking sin within the church.

For those on the ground, it is essential to know that the church fashioned by John Paul's appointments is not an unchanging version of things. The model of church that he advanced through the Legion is already a failed project. In another observer's metaphor, we are waiting in the lobby between acts, not quite knowing what's next.

The Crisis and the Culture

The sex abuse crisis and clergy/hierarchical culture are inseparable. In order to deal with and get beyond the crisis, it will be essential to deal with the clerical/hierarchical culture. The rules and programs for protecting children are a welcome acknowledgment that a problem existed and needed to be addressed. But the new mechanics address only part of the trouble.

When the scandal surged to wide public attention in 2002 in Boston, I began receiving calls at *NCR* from high-profile Catholics in the archdiocese who were active in the academy, in the law, and in business. They were people who spent their lives solving problems and deciding which requests to join boards, committees, and commissions they would honor. When the sex abuse crisis hit the papers, they went to the archdiocese to offer their help and were stunned to be turned away.

The problem involved a clash of cultures. Those from the secular realm worked in arenas with stringent accountability procedures. In times of crisis, when malfeasance, incompetence, or both threatened an institution, there was no returning to business as usual. When it was clear that things had to change, things changed.

Not so in the church. The solutions being proposed, those on the inside knew, would require a degree of transparency and accountability they were not ready to exercise

At one point following the disclosures in Boston, Cardinal Law gathered a well-known child psychologist, her physician husband, and two psychiatrists—all Jewish—for a working lunch with himself and two priests, his "point men" in trying to get control of the sex abuse problem.[1]

Carolyn Newberger, the psychologist, told *Boston Globe* reporters: "The scene struck me as something out of the Middle Ages. You had all these priests in clerical garb on one side, all these secular Jewish experts on the other, and all these nuns serving us." The Jewish doctors, who respected the cardinal for his outreach to Jews, had been sought out for their expertise in the area of sexual abuse of children. The four guests were frank in their assessment that the archdiocese had badly mishandled the crisis and further endangered children. They emphasized the importance of reporting cases to civil authorities. They also concluded they were having little effect on the clerics' thinking. They weren't saying what the priests and Cardinal Law wanted to hear.

One recalls that at the end of the lunch, having offered to help the cardinal "shape a new approach" to dealing with the scandal, Law "smiled at them and looked deeply into their eyes as he shook their hands, thanking them. But he never contacted any of them again."[2]

In February 2002, Law called together a group of high-profile and wealthy Catholics, some of whom had been with him in Rome when he became a cardinal in 1985. He was expecting support from them. What he received was a sober assessment. At one point in his defensive presentation Law "acknowledged that his handling of the crisis had been 'flawed,'" at which point William Bulger, president of the University of Massachusetts, interrupted and said the cardinal was using the incorrect word and proceeded to pronounce his handling of the matter "disastrous."

The interruption, wrote *Globe* reporters, "was a rebuke of enormous symbolic significance, suggesting that the deference Boston's archbishops had enjoyed for more than a century was under attack not just from the outside, as the laity rebelled and prosecutors convened grand juries, but from the inside, by the church insiders convened around a huge table in the cardinal's residence."

That symbol has echoed down the years, manifested in different ways and in various circumstances as the scandal has continued to unravel. There have been many of these kinds of encounters, and each of them has further worn away the presumptions of good will and moral rectitude that members of the Catholic clergy once enjoyed.

Equally striking to those who left such meetings was the realization that they were powerless to effect change. None of the mechanisms usually available to address a serious breach of ethics was available. There appeared to be no levers within the clerical culture available to anyone outside it, no means for addressing clear wrongs committed by the leaders of the community. Their impunity was implicit once they made their pledges of obedience to superiors who oversee a realm they believe is a degree or two removed from the rest of human experience. If there were to be retribution, it would be meted out according to a kind of well understood but unwritten palace code.

The erosion of those distinctions and boundaries is occurring slowly but surely and often in unseen ways, like limestone structures hidden in geological complexities dissolving against the flow of unseen aquifers. The admission of something gone terribly wrong has occurred in too many places to think that the culture remains unaffected. The momentum is moving toward full disclosure and unqualified apologies. Archbishop Diarmuid Martin of Dublin, during a dramatic service in early 2011, one designed by victims of abuse, washed the feet of several victims and declared: "For covering up crimes of abuse, and by so doing actually causing the sexual abuse of more children . . . we ask God's forgiveness. The archdiocese of Dublin will never be the same again. It will always bear this wound within it."

Not long after the U.S. bishops' historic meeting in Dallas in 2002, one of the leaders of the conference announced, apparently with more optimism than data, that the scandal was "history."

Martin, the more realistic of the two, spoke for the entire church. None of us will ever be the same again. We all bear, to one degree or another, the scars of this ugly period. Time, which once appeared to be on the side of those who would simply wait out another scandal, has now become a relentless adversary. The problem won't go away. Watch out for recurring sinkholes in the ecclesiastical landscape.

Ecclesiologist Richard Gaillardetz, a theologian at Boston College, believes a fundamental problem "in our understanding of vocation in the church" contributes to the problems of the clerical culture.[3] He believes that "office should follow upon charism, that we should be identifying people who display charisms and then call them to office. We don't do that."

Instead, he realized during ten years of teaching at a seminary, the seminary system "is constructed to discern impediments, not charisms. And that's a huge systemic problem. Our whole system is based on a flawed theology of vocation that says, 'Your vocation's your own and we need to take it on faith that if you say you've got one, you've got one, and our job is to look for counter-indications, signs you don't have one.' I just think that's theologically flawed. The vocations are ultimately manifested for the building up of the church, at least these ecclesial vocations, vocations concerned with office. And the church has to be involved with discerning the requisite charisms that are going to bear fruit in somebody who holds office. So until we start thinking about how we call people to office in terms of not impediments but recognizing genuine charisms, a predilection for pastoral leadership and all that implies, we're going to struggle with this."

A consequence of the system as it exists is that leaders may emerge but "in spite of not because of our system."

He believes the same kinds of systemic flaws "are present in the way we call forth people to the episcopate." During John Paul's papacy, he said, pastoral leadership—"with notable exceptions"—has not been a preeminent charism required for selection as bishop. "We've made other concerns preeminent, and we're reaping the fruit of that kind of policy."

The Catholic Diaspora

The sting of what Jesuit political scientist Thomas Reese has termed the "quiet exodus" of millions of Catholics has been made less painful by the constant influx of immigrants, many of them from Mexico and Central America. The church has championed their cause, as it should, seeking humane fixes to immigration laws that would allow a rational track toward full citizenship and shielding from deportation those who came here as children and have become fully inculturated.

The numbers—and their implications—are indeed daunting and justify the hierarchy's increased attention. About one-third of the 65.6 million Catholics in the United States are now Latinos, according to a 2007 study done by the Pew Hispanic Center and the Pew Forum on Religion and Public Life. And that percentage continues to grow, not only because of immigration but also because of the new generations of those who have been U.S. citizens for a long time. The study concluded, "Hispanics are transforming the nation's religious landscape, especially the Catholic church, not only because of their growing numbers but also because they are practicing a distinctive form of Christianity."

Numbers alone, however, don't guarantee a lasting effect on Catholicism. As University of Notre Dame theology professor Timothy Matovina points out in an essay, "Latinos in U.S. Catholicism," thousands of U.S. Hispanics defect each year from Catholicism, and younger Latinos do not demonstrate the same fervor as their parents. "According to Carmen Cervantes, cofounder and executive director of the Latino youth ministry organization Instituto Fe y Vida," he writes, "Latino/a teens will soon be more than half of all adolescent Catholics in the U.S., and as a group they are even more religiously inarticulate and disengaged than other Catholic teens."

That is similar to conclusions reached by William V. D'Antonio and others in studies of Catholic attitudes. They surveyed Hispanic Catholics who had been in the United States for some time and found that on nearly all measures—commitment to the church, attitudes about church teaching, church attendance, and so on— Hispanic Catholics varied little from non-Hispanic Catholics.[4]

It would be a shame if church leaders, in a kind of religious capitalism, directed considerable energy and resources to capturing this "new market" before studying in detail the diminishment occurring in older and more experienced segments of the community. It has become apparent, in the pain of closings and mergers, that the church created an unsustainable model in the flush decades of the '50s and '60s. Having been through it once, why not spend time thinking through creative models for the Catholic community of the future? Doing a deliberate and thorough study of what worked, what went wrong, and what can be sustained in conjunction with looking at personnel needs and who's available to keep parish communities going would necessitate a good, hard look at the clerical culture and how it functions. What is the role of priest in the future? Who else can minister? In what ways?

It would also necessitate a thorough study of what I consider the Catholic Diaspora, the 28 million or so former Catholics who've found homes elsewhere. Let's drop the presumption, just for the moment, that they've somehow lost their way and presume, instead, that they might have something to offer, even if they don't intend to return. Could it be that they might be recoiling from the church for very understandable motives, reasoning that an organization that has tolerated and hidden the abuse of tens of thousands of young people might have issues of its own that need to be dealt with before it resumes coaxing back those who have left? Fr. William J. Byron advances a compelling suggestion when he recommends doing exit interviews with those who are leaving or have left the church. "The church in America must face the fact that it has failed to communicate the Good News cheerfully and effectively to a population adrift on a sea of materialism and under constant attack from the forces of secularism, not to mention the diabolical powers that are at work in our world," he wrote in *America* in January 2011. It is an observation that bears consideration, but to which I might attach the question: Is the church capable, given the corruption that has been evident in its clerical ranks, of preaching the Good News cheerfully and effectively? Are we again asking the wrong questions, presuming that the culture and structure in place simply need an infusion of new skills? Or is something deeper the matter?

Byron's aim, one I agree with, at least in part, is to find "ways of welcoming back those who have left" and to help "leaders find ways to strengthen the current worshipping community."

Certainly the information gleaned from exit interviews—and he provides some samples that he's collected by email—would be valuable. But his samples include more than a few that cite reasons that have a great deal to do with structure, clericalism, and certain church teachings. Exit interviews, the chance to listen without preaching to those who've left, could provide valuable, candid insights into why so many are abandoning the church.

But who would listen? And what would anyone do with the information? What can change?

Theologian Thomas Beaudoin of Fordham University talks of "Catholicisms" that exist in the United States today. He cites the numerous studies of religious adherence and practice in the Catholic world and beyond and suggests that one of the obligations of the pastoral worker today is to look around and realize that maybe "80 percent of the Catholics within a 10 mile radius of his parish probably don't attend his church."[5]

Beaudoin continues, "Maybe the vision that we have for what Christian life is like is not interesting or compelling," or perhaps we're too small in our thinking, or maybe "there's something we need to learn about this. The question would become, then, what's going to be an action that's going to have a chance of fostering more life in a situation where basically 80 percent of the family is estranged? That means they may show up to some Catholic reunions at Christmas or Easter or they may not. They have other friends and networks now; they no longer answer their emails."

And the question may deliver an answer, he said, that the "governors" of the institution don't want to hear. "What does more life mean in this situation?" More life, in his understanding, "does not necessarily mean, I think, getting everybody back going to [the parish] all the time. I think it means finding out spiritually where people went and asking how pastoral workers can be of service helping all those who went elsewhere to take their next step in spiritual maturity, whatever that is. Pastoral work becomes less about aggregating the quantity in the institution and more about supporting the quality of the integrity of people's spiritual lives wherever that is leading them."

Beaudoin, who has written about young Catholics, understands what's going on in the far reaches of what, for lack of a better term, could be called "borderless Catholicism." There's a great deal of that, especially among the young and the older disenchanted. But many "formers" carry a great deal of their Catholic

DNA to those other circumstances. Some of the deepest instincts of the Catholic tradition are moving along with the exodus and helping to shape that "second largest denomination." Finding the future on the margins can take on a lot of meanings.

The development of Catholicisms, Beaudoin believes, "while not determinative for the rest of the world," will continue to spread and will occur "in all secularizing cultures," including Africa, which he believes will secularize because of capitalism, education, and other forces common to Western cultures.

"A normative Catholicism of the governors [his term for Catholic leadership], which tries to specify what a Catholic life must be in order to count in the institution—and that is the discourse of normative Catholicism—is in the ascendant right now among the bishops." At the same time a force is going in the opposite direction, away from "normative Catholicism," in what he estimates is a majority of American Catholics, based on the Pew data. He and others call that movement away "deconversion."

Many, if not a majority of, American Catholics "are choosing at some level to define their spiritual life in ways that are different from normative Catholicism, and so you have a range of differences" when it comes to acceptance of church teachings. "And we know those ranges are solid in terms of support for women's ordination, support for GLBT [gay, lesbian, bisexual, and transgendered] life and ministry in the Catholic Church. Those numbers are steady and increasing," he said. The change in attitudes include those who believe one doesn't have to be in a marriage to be in a sexual relationship or go to mass regularly to be a Catholic. "That's Catholicism in the United States," he said. "That's what Catholicism is becoming and I see almost no theological interest by leadership in how Catholics themselves are changing. What we don't have is a rich sense for the data about what has happened to the non-normative Catholics which, again, are the majority. This is the Catholic Church."

Beaudoin believes that part of the reality he perceives—the almost total disinterest among younger Catholics in ecclesiastical debates and the opinions of hierarchy—can be traced to their distrust of church leaders whose "authority has been completely eviscerated by the sex abuse crisis." He says, "What the young people know of Catholic governance makes them skeptical and cautious.

But that is surrounded by a larger chasm of awareness—they simply, for the most part, are not living in the same Catholic world as the bishops."

Beaudoin believes that "we need people to say the church is corrupt in a deep way and what happened in the sex abuse crisis is not just something on the surface of the church's operation. This is something that actually exposes something about the heart of Catholicism. . . . We have a whole generation of Vatican II folks who mourn the church that hasn't happened, but now we have another kind of mourning which we are not really able to acknowledge yet." The new mourning is over the realization that "Catholicism itself is a tradition with a constitutively destructive dimension. That destruction is part of the tradition." He compared the realization to what occurs in families where abuse occurs and people have to acknowledge that there are both beautiful and ugly parts to the family story. "And admitting that this tradition is thoroughly ambiguous all the way down is perhaps impossible for the governors of normative Catholicism, but it is necessary for the church in the United States and for the therapy that is necessary for the clerical culture." It is also necessary, he believes, if the relationship between the church and the majority of Catholics—the "moderate and marginal disaffiliated who think by and large that the institutional church can't tell the truth about itself"—is ever to change.

Staying

Fr. Donald Cozzens, writer in residence at John Carroll University in Cleveland, isn't terribly sanguine about the emerging church, thinking instead "that before I see the church emerging into new forms, it actually is going to do some submerging. A good percentage of the church is grieving right now. We're closing parishes. We're consolidating parishes. Fewer people are going to mass on Sunday." The notion of new things emerging may be "pregnant with possibility, but how it's going to emerge, I don't know," he said during an interview in his office.[6]

What he does know is that emergence of any sort will be affected by the attitude of bishops toward laity, toward vowed religious, and toward priests. "If what I've written earlier is more or less on target, we're witnessing the last era of the feudal church, especially in the West. . . . If we are witnessing the last decades or generation of the feudal church, what is going to happen?"

Cozzens, as a well-traveled speaker, sees the church in the larger picture, but as a priest of the Diocese of Cleveland, he has an especially visceral connection with the pain that diocese has been experiencing in one of the country's more wrenching and contentious episodes of closures and mergers. He also knows that for many informed and engaged Catholics the tensions of the moment are made worse because they "can't understand why women are treated the way they are. They can't understand why the church insists on mandatory celibacy. They can't understand why some pastors won't let their daughters serve mass. They're not leaving. They're just heart sick, I think. I think many of them feel sad. I used the word *grieving* earlier. I think we are grieving, and so what goes on during this period of being submerged?"

What goes on, for his part, is arguably one of the most candid examinations of the contemporary Catholic priesthood and the hierarchical culture in the United States. Cozzens has published a series of four books on the subject since 2000, and he speaks with authority as an insider, one who has stayed as a gentle critic from within. Whatever emerges, however the church gradually changes, it will have been with the benefit of an abundance of "true truths" as only one of its own could deliver.

Sr. Christine Schenk may have her own reasons to be gloomy about the prospects of emergence, but long ago she found a way to push aside pessimism. She does what a trained community organizer does. "It's not good to sit on your anger," she said in an interview in Cleveland. "You've got to organize."[7]

She started in 1990 and formed FutureChurch soon after the bishops promulgated a ritual to be used for Sunday worship in the absence of a priest for parishes that wouldn't otherwise have access to mass on Sunday.

The group was ahead of its time in understanding the fundamental problem and took advantage of Richard Schoenherr's and Lawrence Young's groundbreaking work on the coming priest shortage. She has a reputation as a reformer who is under no illusions about what might change or how soon. In the meantime, she keeps assembling the data and wondering what will come of it all.

She said she used Schoenherr's data "diocese by diocese when we went out with our work to let Catholic people know what was going to happen. Over about three years I probably spoke to about sixty or seventy dioceses." The bishops may have disliked the data, but they couldn't refute it.

The organizer had a strategy. She coordinated often with chapters of Call to Action and other local reform groups who would notify the religion writer at the local paper. "We would go in with the statistics from Schoenherr-Young. The news media would go to the diocese and say, 'Is this true?' The dioceses would say, 'Yes, it's true,' and then the whole story would come out. Very often it was the first public acknowledgment by the diocese that, yes, the priest shortage was real and it was happening."

On one level the mission was advocating for ordination of married men and of women, but at quite another it was, and remains, equally about preserving Catholic communities. When the pope said no one could talk any more about women's ordination, FutureChurch had to adjust. The group developed a second project inspired by a study done by the Leadership Conference of Women Religious that named fifteen things that could be done to advance women's roles in the church.

Schenk knows all about the demographic shifts under way and the effects of the clergy shortage. She doesn't believe all parishes should be saved, but she does believe that instead of simply mandating downsizing to better match the number of parishes with the number of priests, dioceses should look into alternatives—from greater use of lay parish coordinators to encouraging greater economic sharing among rich and poor parishes. And, somewhere down the road, even ordaining people who now are excluded from that level of leadership.

Her motivation at times is personal. She took her master's degree in theology at St. Mary's Seminary and Graduate School of Theology in Cleveland. Her thoughts initially didn't run to ordination. "I was just so glad to have the opportunity, but when I was finishing and my classmates were being ordained and I wasn't, I got it at a whole other level how wrong this was." Her teachers loved to hear her preach and wished they could hear more of her, but there came a time when the pulpit became off limits to her as her male classmates moved on.

"It was at a much deeper level that I recognized what a violation this was of the call of the Spirit in a person. I went through a pretty big grief time, but I have always been blessed with wonderful spiritual directors and I still am."

Since then, she said, she's "come to the realization that my deepest call is more about reform than ministry. I have to say [being prohibited from ordination] was extraordinarily painful because I loved all the theology. I was growing by leaps and bounds inside, and then to see that that was cut off by something as arbitrary as gender. If anything, that fuels my passion for the work I'm doing now."

Her consolation now is the understanding that "Jesus struggled his whole life with his religious tradition. He was about helping it come to a fuller awareness of the breadth and depth of the love of God and stretching their own boundaries. I feel like I'm following a good path there."

She says she regularly checks her motivation. "I ask myself, 'Where is this coming from? Is this coming because you're mad or because it's a passion about being about that big and wide reign of God like Jesus was?'" If it's done out of some sense of political correctness, she said, it won't last. "The other thing is far deeper. I console myself that Jesus was rejected by his own tradition, and so was Paul. He was thrown out of all the best synagogues in the Mediterranean world, so when I get upset that one diocese or the other won't let me speak on church property, I just remind myself that it's all part of it. . . . The end result is going to be so worth it."

What is the end?

"The end result is that we can come to a bigger knowledge of how wide the love of God is."

Chapter 11

FINAL THOUGHTS

I once heard a poet say, "We live at the intersection of mysterious freedoms, God's and our own." The thought is as good a guide as any for the situation we face. *Mystery* is the old Catholic elementary school euphemism for "we don't know" or "you wouldn't understand." But the mysterious freedoms are more than a state of bafflement, they are an understanding of, and in the best circumstances, an experience of, the transcendence we all seek, acknowledgement, perhaps, of "a Presence from beyond us and yet in our midst."[1]

We stand at that intersection, that paradox, understanding that in the end it is God's church yet simultaneously our community in which to act; that it is our business to both trust in Providence yet take responsibility for how we live and how we treat others. Playwright Robert Bolt gives Thomas More wonderful words on the matter: "God made the angels to show him splendor—and he made animals for innocence and plants for their simplicity. But Man he made to serve him wittily, in the tangle of his mind!"

Tangled, indeed, it can become. It is both the wonderful and awful fate of humans to be so made.

In overseeing for so many years coverage of some of the uglier episodes of contemporary Catholicism, I've been asked more than a few times how I could, as a lifelong member of the church, continue to be involved with stories that painted the church in such a bad light. Wasn't I concerned with damaging the reputation of the church? In a phrase, the answer was always "yes and no."

Yes, I was concerned about what stories dealing with sex abuse, cover-up, financial malfeasance, and such would do to the public image of the church. But I had a deeper conviction overriding my reservations, a conviction that the kind of evil that affects the community as deeply as, say, the sex abuse crisis, is best dealt with in the light. Secrecy, as we've seen, is no solution. It merely allows the evil to metastasize.

I am also quick to note that if one were to read the entire record—that is, in *NCR*'s case, the entire content of the paper and in recent years, the website—one would quickly conclude that on balance there was far more "positive" material written about the life of the church and its members than about scandal. News and human nature being what it is, it's the coverage that shows institutions, civil or otherwise, out of alignment that gets the most attention.

My mentor in things journalistic, the late John Strohmeyer, a Pulitzer-prize winning editorial writer and Neiman Fellow, would regularly give his young charges during the 1970s what amounted to a sermon at the monthly meetings he held in a dingy newsroom in Bethlehem, Pennsylvania. "You stand in the stead of those who don't have access to power and who can't ask the questions!" he would bellow. He termed the arrangement a "sacred trust" and warned us not to betray it.

I became a believer. Asking questions in the name of others who can't because they have neither access nor platform for doing so is one of journalism's sacred duties. I also think that the mission, to hold power accountable, however badly that might be executed at times, is a fundamental obligation of journalism and fits well with the ethos of a healthy Christian community. If such a relationship is sometimes awkward for those whose actions are being scrutinized, for the journalist it often means a conscious effort to forego the temptation to "chumminess" and insider status that is forever present when one has privileged access to power.

I also confess to taking consolation in a strain of Christian history that for me legitimizes both our faith and a community as genuinely as any expression of apostolic succession. I am referring to the trait that traces through our history to the earliest days of the earliest followers and that demonstrates—our experience of peace and joy notwithstanding—that we have been a rather contentious lot all along. From the start we've gotten certain things right: we were to take care of the widows and the weak, take special care of the children, make sure those who didn't have enough to eat or a place to live were looked after, never forget those in prison. There wasn't much debate about the teaching that told us the least and the outcast are our brothers and sisters. But about other things there were big disagreements. I have always been grateful that the writers of Acts weren't subjected to some first-century public information specialists. We never would have gotten the good stuff. There were big fights over who was in and who was out of the community and what the community could eat. Who in the Christian community today isn't happy that the resolution to those arguments was "everyone" and "everything."

Who doesn't feel sympathetic to a leader, the Rock, who was all over the place, one minute professing unyielding devotion and the next denying he even knew Jesus? Peter, the metaphor for all of us in our weakest and our grandest moments. It is difficult to dislike a pope who gets it wrong, publicly, more than once and, more than once, admits it. And then life goes on and, in that moment *in extremis*, where there is no longer any distraction, where one is called to complete clarity, hung upside down, there's no more waffling.

In the rest of that speech to his daughter and son-in-law, More says: "If [God] suffers us to fall to such a case that there is no escaping, then we may stand to our tackle as best we can, and yes, Will, then we may clamor like champions . . . if we have the spittle for it. And no doubt it delights God to see splendor where He only looked for complexity. But it's God's part, not our own, to bring ourselves to that extremity! Our natural business lies in escaping."

There are wannabe champions clamoring all over the Catholic lot these days. Those who want to nail things down, square the boundaries, reestablish a muscular, well-defined, doctrinally impervious Catholic identity.

Our history attests to a Catholic culture of another sort that has coexisted all along. It is captured in James Joyce's overused but perfectly apt expression: "Here comes everybody."

The poet within us recognizes the layers of life and meaning the phrase contains. John Updike, whose religiously laced secularism could yield a yearning as only he might describe, has one of his characters in the short story "Sunday Teasing" explaining the difference between Catholics and Protestants: "The reason why in

Catholic countries everybody kisses each other is that it's a huge family—God is a family of three, the church is a family of millions, even heretics are kind of black sheep of the family, whereas the Protestant lives all by himself, inside of himself. *Sola fide.* Man should be lonely."

Perhaps it's because of our Mediterranean roots, but in our best moments we really believe that no one should be lonely. Isolation is to be overcome, not sought after. Undifferentiated crowds and families are not as canonically precise as some might like in a metaphor for the Catholic Church. They're dynamic, always changing, harboring flashpoints for pettiness as well as seedbeds of great grace. Families, especially, can be unpredictable and messy, with love and hate, comfort and irritation, running together, mixing, confusing us so that at times we don't know which is which. Families understand gatherings where everyone clamors and there's little room for champions, no need for them, really. Families hug, if for no other reason, simply because we're there. Updike's character yearns for what Catholics intuit.

Perhaps our future vision of heroic priests ought to take its cue from someone like Sr. Thea Bowman, a humble hero who holds a mirror up to our complexity. Sometimes we'll do things her way, sometimes ours. Thea, great granddaughter of a slave, who understands better than most the messy reality of sin and redemption, of being both out and in, who knows how porous religious borders can be, who can, even when dressing us down with a smile, convince us to cross arms and find a common song.

The church, she said, "is a family of families, and the family got to stay together." And in that family, let no one feel like a motherless child.

Notes

Introduction

1. Originally named the *Religious News Service,* the organization was re-named *Religion News Service* when sold to *Newhouse News Service* in 1994. It is now an independent news outlet.

1. True Truths

1. Sr. Thea's speech was taped, and I received a copy from Sr. Charlene Smith, FSPA, a contemporary and biographer with John Feister. The text of her speech was also printed in *Origins* 19, no. 8 (July 6, 1989).

2. Charlene Smith, FSPA, and John Feister, *Thea's Song: The Life of Thea Bowman* (Maryknoll, NY: Orbis Books, 2009), 181.

3. Ibid., 182.

4. "He was a magnificent pope who presided over a controversial pontifi-cate," *National Catholic Reporter,* April 2, 2005. Bias in favor of a colleague's work aside, I think of all the accounts of John Paul's pontificate in the imme-diate aftermath, John Allen's obituary/analysis is the most thorough, balanced, and sober of any I've read. When so many others were caught up in a breath-less, uncritical assessment, he took account of John Paul's soaring international and interfaith triumphs without losing sight of the glaring flaws and deficien-cies apparent in his handling of church administration and personnel.

5. Ibid.

6. Ibid.

7. Ibid

8. Ibid

9. Peter Hebblethwaite, *Pope John Paul II and the Church* (Kansas City, MO: Sheed and Ward, 1995), 57.

10. Peter Hebblethwaite, *The Year of Three Popes* (London: Collins, 1978), 97.

11. J. N. D. Kelly, *The Oxford Dictionary of Popes* (New York: Oxford Uni-versity Press, 1986), 325.

12. Bishop Albino Luciani, quoted in Hebblethwaite, *The Year of Three Popes,* 97.

13. Ibid., 97.

14. Mark S. Massa, SJ, *The American Catholic Revolution: How the '60s Changed the Church Forever* (New York: Oxford University Press, 2010), 101.

15. Ibid., xvi.

2. The Shrinking, Expanding, Changing Church

1. The material on Cleveland and some of the statistics in this chapter are contained in the In Search of the Emerging Church series, which is available in its entirety on the *NCR* website.

2. Patricia Lefevere, *National Catholic Reporter*, June 13, 2008.

3. The data on the number of priests available for ministry is from the talk by Marti Jewell at the 2008 national ministry summit in Orlando, Florida. Much of the rest of the data was gleaned from the website and publications of the Center for Applied Research in the Apostolate (CARA) at Georgetown University, as well as through numerous conversations with CARA researchers.

4. Dean Hoge, talk to Australian Catholic Bishops Conference, October 2006.

5. Mark Gray, *Our Sunday Visitor*, June 27, 2010.

6. Archbishop Timothy Dolan, quoted in *Catholic News Agency*, August 13, 2009.

7. The Rev. Eileen W. Lindner, quoted in Tom Roberts, *National Catholic Reporter*, "The 'Had It' Catholics," November 11, 2010.

8. Reported material from Newark contained in the In Search of the Emerging Church series.

3. The Sex Abuse Crisis Begins

1. Cardinal Francis George, *The Difference God Makes: A Catholic Vision of Faith, Communion, and Culture* (New York: Crossroad, 2009), 189.

2. Notes to the author about the incident from Arthur Jones; also detailed in conversations with Thomas C. Fox, who was editor at the time.

3. This and following are from a series of interviews and conversations with Fox.

4. Dana Kennedy, *AOL News*, "Priest's Dream to Help Others Became a Nightmare," April 2, 2010.

5. Tom Roberts, "Bishops Were Warned of Abusive Priests," *National Catholic Reporter*, April 3, 2009. The story also ran on the *NCR* website. The entire cache of documents used for this story is available at www.bishopaccountability.org, which has become the principal repository for the extensive documentation of the scandal that now exists.

6. Jason Berry, *Vows of Silence* (New York: Free Press, 2004).

7. Thomas Doyle, "Online Column," *National Catholic Reporter*, December 21, 2010.

8. Arthur Jones, "Priests Say Dismissal Lacked Due Process," *National Catholic Reporter*, August 13, 2004.

4. Into the Depths of the Crisis

1. Philip Jenkins, quoted in Joe Feuerherd, "Special Report: Leaked Numbers Provoke Dispute," *National Catholic Reporter*, February 27, 2004.

2. Gary Schoener, quoted in ibid.

3. *The Boston Globe, Betrayal: The Crisis in the Catholic Church* (Boston: Little, Brown and Co., 2002), 5.

4. Ibid., 5-6

5. Ibid., 8.

6. Philadelphia was one of six dioceses in which either a grand jury or attorney general gathered data on the abuse crisis. The documentation of those investigations and all of the grand jury reports can be found on www.bishopaccountability.org.

7. The *National Catholic Reporter* did extensive coverage of the 2005 Philadelphia grand jury report. The first story, by freelancer Ralph Cipriano, was an extensive report on the grand jury findings and appeared in the October 7, 2005 issue.

8. Ibid.

5. A Problem of Clerical Culture

1. Editorial, *National Catholic Reporter*, April 30, 2010.

2. Cardinal Law, quoted in Michael Papesh, *Clerical Culture: Contradiction and Transformation* (Collegeville, MN: Liturgical Press, 2004), 17.

3. *The Boston Globe, Betrayal: The Crisis in the Catholic Church* (Boston: Little, Brown and Co., 2002), 7.

4. Cardinal Mahony, quoted in Tom Roberts, *National Catholic Reporter*, March 30, 2009 (quoted from a *Los Angeles Times* story).

5. Cardinal Francis George, *The Difference God Makes* (New York: Crossroad, 2009), 189.

6. Ibid., 189

7. An audio recording of Bishop Serratelli's talk is available on the website of the National Leadership Roundtable on Church Management. The author worked from a transcript made from the recording.

8. John Allen, "Cardinal George's Plan to Evangelize America," *National Catholic Reporter*, October 7, 2009.

9. Most of the material presented here on Maciel and the Legion is drawn either from the abundant public record that had already been established in the *National Catholic Reporter* prior to 2010, most of it reported by Jason Berry and the late Gerry Renner; or from a two-part series Berry wrote in April 2010: "Money Paved Way for Maciel's Influence in the Vatican" (posted online on April 6), and "How Fr. Maciel Built His Empire" (posted online April 10). Two more related analyses by Berry were posted December 30, 2010: "Gambling with History: Benedict and the Legion of Christ" and "George Weigel: Whitewashing History."

10. Mary Ann Glendon, letter of support for Fr. Maciel, published on the website of *First Things*, May 23, 2002.

11. George Weigel, *The End and the Beginning: Pope John Paul II—The Victory of Freedom, the Last Years, the Legacy* (New York: Doubleday, 2010).

12. Tom Roberts, "Critical Question Leads Priest to Question Lax Abuse Policies," *NCR* website, July 2010.

13. The following discussion was first presented in Tom Roberts, "Some Bishops Questioning Clerical Culture," *NCR* website, August 2010.

14. While most of the names in the list have been identified elsewhere in the text, a few have not. For identification purposes they are DAVID GIBSON, award-winning journalist and author of *The Coming Catholic Church: How the Faithful Are Shaping a New American Catholicism* (HarperSanFrancisco, 2003); SCOTT APPLEBY, director of the Kroc Institute for International Peace Studies at the University of Notre Dame and one of the lay people invited to address the bishops at their 2002 meeting in Dallas, at which they approved the Charter for the Protection of Children and Young People; MARY GAIL FRAWLEY-O'DEA, a clinical psychologist who works with victims of sexual abuse and was another lay person invited to speak to the bishops gathered in Dallas in 2002. She is the author of *Perversion of Power: Sexual Abuse in the Catholic Church* (Vanderbilt University Press, 2007); RUSSELL SHAW, long-time Catholic author and former spokesman for the U.S. bishops. He is author of *Nothing to Hide: Secrecy, Communication, and Communion in the Catholic Church* (Ignatius Press, 2008), a strong critique of clericalism and secrecy in the Catholic hierarchy; and ROD DREHER, a writer and editor with a conservative bent who has written critically of the hierarchy's handling of the sex abuse crisis and of his disaffection from Roman Catholicism as a result of covering the scandal.

6. Travels on the Margins

1. The stories in this chapter are published here, with few changes, as they appeared in the *National Catholic Reporter* as part of the series In Search of the Emerging Church. They are available at www.ncronline.org/emergingchurch.

7. Of Rummage Sales and the New Cosmology

1. Large portions of this chapter were previously published in *National Catholic Reporter* as part of the In Search of the Emerging Church series, available at www.ncronline.org/emergingchurch.

2. Phyllis Tickle, *The Great Emergence: How Christianity Is Changing and Why* (Grand Rapids, MI: Baker Books, 2008).

3. Richard Rohr, online interview with John Allen, *National Catholic Reporter*, May 25, 2010, available at www.ncronline.org.

4. From a 1996 article for *Lutheran Woman Today* distributed electronically by Benetvision.

5. Ibid.

6. Joan Chittister, "The God They Never Told Me About: A Convergence of Opposites," speech, Kansas City, Missouri, November 7, 2009.

7. Ronald Rolheiser, *The Holy Longing* (New York: Doubleday, 1999), 21.

8. Ibid.

9. Andrew Greeley, "New Encyclical Out of Step with Tradition," *National Catholic Reporter,* October 15, 1993.

10. Ibid.

11. Charles Curran, *Loyal Dissent: Memoir of a Catholic Theologian* (Washington DC: Georgetown University Press, 2006).

12. Thomas C. Fox, *Catholicism and Sexuality* (New York: George Braziller, 1999), 78.

13. Ibid.

14. Mark S. Massa, SJ, *The American Catholic Revolution: How the '60s Changed the Church Forever* (New York: Oxford University Press, 2010), 37.

15. Ibid., 41.

16. Ibid., 44.

17. Fox, *Catholicism and Sexuality*, 81.

8. In Search of Authentic Authority

1. Eugene Kennedy and Sara C. Charles, MD, *Authority: The Most Misunderstood Idea in America* (New York: The Free Press, 1997).

2. Ibid., 11.

3. Ibid., 14.

4. Ibid., 28.

5. John Wagner, "Md.'s Top Leaders Cross Catholic Hierarchy on Gay Marriage," *Washington Post*, February 24, 2011.

6. Figures as of 2008. Website of the United States Conference of Catholic Bishops.

7. Tom Roberts, interview with Archbishop Michael Sheehan, 2009.

8. Tom Roberts, interview with Richard Gaillardetz, January 6, 2011.

9. Tom Roberts, interview with Margaret Steinfels, January 4, 2011.

9. Amid the Tensions

1. Peter S. Steinfels, "New Book Reaffirms Depth of Change Wrought by Vatican II" [book review of John W. O'Malley's *What Happened at Vatican II*], *The New York Times*, Decmeber 19, 2008.

2. For fuller treatment of the themes, see Tom Roberts, "Battle Lines in the Liturgy Wars" and "New Spin on Vatican II," March 1 and March 2, 2010, *NCR* website.

3. Cardinal Ratzinger, quoted in John Allen, *Cardinal Ratzinger: The Vatican's Enforcer of the Faith* (New York: Continuum, 2000), 59.

4. John W. O'Malley, "Introduction" and "Vatican II: Did Anything Happen?" in John W. O'Malley, Stephen Schloesser, Joseph Komonchak, Neil

J. Ormerod, *Vatican II: Did Anything Happen?* ed. David G. Schultenover (New York: Continuum, 2007).

5. Steinfels, "New Book Reaffirms Depth of Change Wrought by Vatican II."

6. John Allen, "The Man at the Center of the Storms," *National Catholic Reporter*, October 28, 2009.

7. John Allen, "Cover Story: On the Lectionary, 11 Men Made the Ceal," *National Catholic Reporter*, September 25, 1998.

8. Tom Roberts, "New Spin on Vatican II," *National Catholic Reporter*, March 2, 2010.

9. O'Malley, "Vatican II: Did Anything Happen?" 67.

10. Mark S. Massa, SJ, *The American Catholic Revolution: How the '60s Changed the Church Forever* (New York: Oxford University Press, 2010), 150.

10. Where from Here?

1. Carolyn Newberger, quoted in *The Boston Globe, Betrayal: The Crisis in the Catholic Church* (Boston: Little, Brown and Co., 2002), 152.

2. Ibid., 153.

3. Richard Gaillardetz, interview with author, January 2011.

4. William V. D'Antonio, James D. Davidson, Dean R. Hoge, Mary L. Gautier, *American Catholics Today: New Realities of Their Faith and Their Church* (Lanham, MD: Rowman and Littlefield, 2007), 165-71.

5. Tom Roberts, interview with Thomas Beaudoin, January 24, 2011.

6. Tom Roberts, interview with Donald Cozzens. The article that resulted, part of the In Search of the Emerging Church series, was published as "The Church Will Submerge before Any Emergence," *National Catholic Reporter*, May 15, 2009.

7. Tom Roberts, interview with Sr. Christine Schenk. The article that resulted, part of the In Search of the Emerging Church series, was published as "A Map to the Future Church," *National Catholic Reporter*, July 16, 2009.

11. Final Thoughts

1. Thomas H. Groome, *What Makes Us Catholic: Eight Gifts for Life* (New York: HarperCollins Publisher, 2002), 7.

Index